Albert Dresden Vandam

Undercurrents of the Second Empire

Notes and recollections

Albert Dresden Vandam

Undercurrents of the Second Empire
Notes and recollections

ISBN/EAN: 9783337310264

Printed in Europe, USA, Canada, Australia, Japan

Cover: Foto ©ninafisch / pixelio.de

More available books at **www.hansebooks.com**

UNDERCURRENTS OF THE SECOND EMPIRE

Notes and Recollections

BY

ALBERT D. VANDAM

AUTHOR OF
"AN ENGLISHMAN IN PARIS," "MY PARIS NOTE-BOOK," Etc.

LONDON
WILLIAM HEINEMANN
1897

CONTENTS

CHAPTER I

How the Empire was restored.—The influence of the Napoleonic legend during the Restoration and the Monarchy of Louis Philippe. — The Bourbons and Cambronne. — The Duc d'Angoulême and Drouot.—The Duchesse d'Angoulême at Avignon.—Her attempt to convert a veteran of Napoleon.—Charles X. and another veteran of la Grande Armée.—Louvel on his trial for the murder of the Duc de Berri.—The propaganda of the Napoleonic legend by the poets.—Talleyrand's journey to Vienna in 1830 in quest of the Duc de Reichstadt. —Louis Philippe's attitude.—Thiers' part in the removal of Napoleon's remains from St. Helena.—Prince Louis Napoleon's knowledge of all this.—The Bonaparte family.—Jérôme, ex-King of Westphalia, and his son.—Jérôme at Hesse-Cassel.— Louis Napoleon's one ally among the Bonaparte family.— Mathilde Bonaparte, Comtesse Demidoff.—The rest of Louis Napoleon's relations, legitimate and illegitimate.—A story of Louis Napoleon's impecuniosity.—Mathilde and her cousin.— Mathilde and Nicolas I.—Nicolas I. and Prince Louis Napoleon. —Mathilde keeps her cousin posted up.—Why Louis Napoleon's attempt at Strasburg was not more severely punished . *Page* 1

CHAPTER II

How the Empire was restored (*continued*).— A game of political bluff.—The players.—Lamartine, practically the only honest man among them. — Cavaignac, Thiers, Victor Hugo, and Changarnier.—Prince Louis Napoleon's opinion of them.—An estimate of his opponents, proving that Louis Napoleon was one of the most brilliant talkers of his time.—The game of bluff

CONTENTS

... ... The tactics of the players. Louis Napoleon's luck ... ... Thiers and Changarnier keep in till the end of the game. The Prince-President keeps shuffling the cards and cheats them. The on-lookers at the game and the backers of the players. The Prince-President gets "fours" . . . *Page* 28

CHAPTER III

How the Empire was restored *continued*.—Some silhouettes.—Dupin aîné, President of the Chamber during part of the Second Republic.—His share in the restoration of the Empire (?).—Morny. Persigny. Prince Jérôme Bonaparte, otherwise Plon-Plon. Fleury.—Why Fleury rallied to the cause of the Prince-President.—His share in the Coup d'Etat.—The state of the Prince-President's exchequer on the eve of the Coup d'Etat.—The evidence of Baron James de Rothschild.—The supposed bribing of the army.—Did the army want bribing?—Why Fleury was sent to Algeria to find a Minister for War, and why Persigny was not sent. Dr. Louis Véron, the proprietor of the *Constitutionnel*.—Thiers and Véron.—Thiers, the irrepressible Thiers.—A glimpse of the minor collaborateurs, Maupas, Carlier, Magnan. . . . . *Page* 58

CHAPTER IV

The beginnings of the Empire.—The new Emperor's real friends.—Their number according to the Emperor.—Mocquard, the Emperor's private secretary.—An absolutely unknown scene at the Elysée a few days after the Coup d'Etat.—Plon-Plon's and his father's attitude towards the new Emperor.—A dastardly insinuation on their part to prevent the Emperor marrying.—The result.—Fleury's suggestion for a comedy.—The Emperor determines to make the suggested comedy a reality.—A hasty marriage. Louis Napoleon's ante-nuptial love affairs.—Mdlle. de Montijo's ante-nuptial flirtations.— Louis Napoleon's search for a wife. A consultation between Queen Victoria, Prince Albert, Prince Hohenlohe, and Lord Palmerston. — Louis Napoleon's original intention with regard to Mdlle. de Montijo. The announcement of his forthcoming union and the effect it produced in Paris and in France.— Dupin *aîné* gives his views. The Faubourg St. Germain and the Orleanists' salons.—The Faubourg St. Honoré, the Chaussée d'Antin and the Faubourg St. Antoine. . . . . . . *Page* 90

CHAPTER V

The beginnings of the Empire (*continued*).—The Tuileries in the early part of '53.—A conversation between Vély Pasha, the then Turkish Ambassador and an English nobleman.—An attempt to poison the Queen's mind against Louis Napoleon.—Palmerston supported by the Duke of Wellington takes the Emperor's part.— France's naval resources at the beginning of the Empire.—The only question which the Emperor could take up in a hostile spirit then.—The problem proposed by the Turkish Ambassador and worked out by the author of these pages.—The real reason of the French support of England during the Crimean War.—The household of the new Imperial couple.—Adventurers and worse. —A sponsor wanted for the new Empress.—The Bonapartes in clover.—A suitor for the hand of Princess Mary of Cambridge (the present Duchess of Teck).—Palmerston nips the contemplated proposal in the bud.—The immediate *entourage* of the new Imperial couple.—The Emperor as a scapegoat.—The period immediately before and immediately after the outbreak of the Crimean War.—The news of the first victories arouses little or no enthusiasm.—The Imperial couple's disappointment at the failure of their combination.—Sudden and almost unexpected success by means of a cleverly enacted scene before Lord Cowley.—The invitation to visit England.—The visit itself.—The comedy enacted an hour after the arrival in London of the august visitors.—London applauds and England follows suit.—A reception at the French Embassy in London.—An American diplomatist and his awkward remarks.—The Queen's return visit to Paris.—Comments in the streets.--A few lines of criticism by a French officer . . . . *Page* 126

CHAPTER VI

The transformation of Paris.—The attempts in that direction of Napoleon III.'s predecessors.—Louis XIV. and Mansart.—The origin of the idea.—The opposition to its realisation.—Not a single honest objection.—The objections being overruled, the erstwhile objectors fatten and batten on the scheme.—A chapter of dishonesty, jobbery, corruption and greed.—The story of the Quartier Marbœuf.—An unknown episode in the life of Balzac. —An unpublished page from the " Mémoires " of Alexandre Dumas, the elder.—The probable origin of a chapter of Dickens's *Great Expectations*—Birds of Prey in the Law Courts.—The late Jules Ferry's beginnings.--A historical pamphlet.--The

... ... opinion of it and its author. Jules Ferry's likeness ... ... "Zampa's heir in custody of a gendarme."— ... ..., fictitious leases, sham balance-sheets and stock... ... He Emperor's discouragement. He proposes to take ... ... ly M. Haussmann, in imitation of Napoleon I.'s strolls with ... ... *Page* 156

CHAPTER VII

His prologue to the Franco-Austrian War.—The attempt of 14th January, 1858. The police at fault. The Emperor's estimate of the police. The miraculous escape of the Emperor and Empress. Undercurrents of the police system.—The Emperor's connection with the *Carbonaria*.—Previous attempts on Louis Napoleon's life.—The Emperor's want of circumspection with regard to women. A pseudo-fairy tale published by the Belgian papers.—The Emperor's secret wish that the authors of the attempt should go scot-free.—The reason why.—The prospect of a united Italy and the Catholic priesthood.—The respite granted by the *Carbonaria* to the Emperor.—The Emperor's visit to Chêne. Orsini's political testament.—The police once more. Plon-Plon's marriage with the daughter of Victor Emmanuel.—The hand of Cavour.—Why he considered the marriage necessary. A comparison between Cavour and Bismarck.—The betrothal of Plon-Plon and Princesse Clotilde.—A letter from Prince Albert to Leopold I.—The Franco-Austrian Campaign.—At the very outset of it the Emperor becomes aware of the rotten condition of the army.—Some instances of ... rottenness.—The disaster of Sedan foreshadowed in the victory of Magenta.—A remark of the Empress on the prince of Nice.—A narrow escape of the Emperor.—A narrow escape of MacMahon.—The battle of Magenta won ... . *Page* 183

CHAPTER VIII

The heyday of the Second Empire.—The prosperity.—Henri IV.'s "fowl in the pot."—The savings of the peasantry and the *petite bourgeoisie*. The big-wig of the Third Republic and the ... of the Second Empire.—The Emperor as a *bon-vivant*. Marsan's definition of a *bon-vivant*.—The Emperor's attitude towards the Republicans in general and Thiers in particular.— A scene between the Emperor and Morny.—Life at the

Tuileries.—Every one master except the master himself.—The twenty-three new deputies of the Opposition.—Buffooning at Court.—The Clergy.—The Abbé Bauer and Crémieux.—Monseigneur Dupanloup.—Warriors.—Count Tascher de la Pagerie.—General de Cotte's remarks at the outbreak of the Franco-Austrian War.—" As yet, however, the cloud is not bigger than a hand."—Théresa's " Rien n'est sacré pour un sapeur," and the lesson it conveyed.—Vivier, the Emperor's double.—Vivier at Mme. de Païva's.—The jester in ordinary to the Court and the jester who performs "by command."—The corps de ballet.—The Païva's, the Skittles, and the Cora Pearls.—Over-zealous officials. —Païva, Skittles and Cora Pearl delighted.—" Les femmes comme il faut et les femmes comme il en faut."—Horseflesh and pigskin.—An afternoon in the Champs Elysées.—The Emperor, the Empress, the Prince Imperial, the Court beauties.—The beauties that were bred in alleys.—English Ambassadors.—Lord Cowley and afterwards Lord Lyons.—An important footnote about the Prince Imperial . . . . *Page* 212

CHAPTER IX

How Joshua, the Son of Nun, went to work.—The author adopts his method for the nonce.—The Rahabs of the Second Empire.—Alex. Dumas' preface to "Le Demi-Monde" quoted. —The Emperor largely responsible for the corrupted state of society.—Glimpses of Skittles and Cora Pearl.—The Vicomtesse de Païva.—A bit of biography.—Her spitefulness.—Smart attachés make all this the subject of their correspondence.—The result of this correspondence and that of the documents and communications emanating from the Quai d'Orsay.—A glance at Compiègne.—Warriors bold.—A prologue to the Mexican Campaign . . . . *Page* 245

CHAPTER X

Undercurrents of the war in Mexico.—Jecker and his claim against the Mexican Government.—Did Napoleon III. engage in that war for the sake of a prospective share in the claim?—"Distinctly not."—A suspected interview between Napoleon and Jecker.—Morny and Jecker.—The prologue to the war invented after the war itself had been decided on.—The deep-seated religious dissatisfaction in France at the probable sequel to the Franco-Austrian War as far as Rome was concerned.—

CONTENTS

... Rome ... glance into the past. The Concordat. ... Napoleon ... the professed heir to his uncle's universal ... committed to the latter's policy of con... ... the Papacy. This policy of conciliation not ... feeling on the part of Napoleon III.; but ... Napoleon III. and the Archbishop of ... "eldest daughter" of the Church openly accused ... Victor Emmanuel, and Garibaldi in en... the Papal States from the Papacy.—In ... the feeling the Emperor allows his officials ... real. The dress rehearsals of Gounod's ... known letter from Napoleon III. to Pius IX. It produces no effect in Rome. What Napoleon I. would have done under the circumstances.—The spirit of ... his nephew. Weak-kneed Cæsarism and ... opinion of it. The French the spectators of ... ment. The necessity for constant novelty at ... House.—"Sire, you must do grandiose things." Napoleon III. endeavours to act upon the advice.—Notes of ... nesses.—Jealousy of the growing influence of the United States. Antagonism of some of her public men ... Empire. President Buchanan and reference to a ... d.—Abraham Lincoln and Juarez.—"The Log... showing their usual and admirable common sense."—The House of Commons and the Jecker claim.—The Jews ... and Morny's dealing with them.—Mexico ... rupt. Lord John Russell and the Comte de Flahault. Napoleon III.'s knowledge of the iniquity of Jecker's law. Very many undercurrents in one.—The Jecker claim ... better than a pretext.—The offer of the crown of Mexico to Maximilian practically a comedy.—Appendix . . *Page* 275

CHAPTER XI

Influence of the Battle of Sadowa.—The Emperor, Metternich Beyer, and Randon.—A sentence of the Emperor.—A sentence of Beyer. A sentence of Randon.—The three combined show Metternich the military nakedness of the Empire.—Four years later he will remember it and will secretly advise his sovereign not to contract an alliance with France.—The dearth of French diplomats. Competent and incompetent French generals.— Jealousy of each other.—Some stories in support.—The Emperor does not know his best men.—He confers promotion in a hap-hazard way.—Cleanliness and discipline.—The Cent

Gardes take a bath before going on duty.—The other troops do not.—Pedantism.—The scheme for the thorough reorganisation of the French army. The Exhibition of 1867 prevents, or at any rate delays, its realisation.—I take a walk to see the preparations for the Exhibition.—France once more sacrificed to the interests of Paris.—The scenery for the third act of "Sardanapalus."—Arbaces and Belesis.—Rejoicings in the Republican camp at the battle of Sadowa.—Opposition to the army scheme.—"That damnable Exhibition."—The invitations to the feast.—Joshua would have been equally glad to get such an invitation from the kings of the land of Canaan.—A parterre of kings at the Rue Le Peletier.—King Wilhelm, Bismarck, and Moltke in Paris.—King Wilhelm's recollections of a former visit long ago.—An excursion to Montmartre.—Bismarck at the review at Longchamps.—A quotation from "Macbeth" . . . *Page* 315

CHAPTER XII

The outbreak of the war.—Diplomacy.—Moral opinion of Europe.—Is Prussia afraid?—An interesting footnote.—The remodelling of Europe on the basis previous to 1814.—A glance at the Quai d'Orsay.—Drouyn de Lhuys.—Duplicity of the Emperor.—The Emperor too certain of the support of Austria.—Story of the bandmasters.—Duc Agénor de Gramont.—A heaven-born diplomatist.—Lord Granville on pseudo-heaven-born diplomatists.—The Hohenzollern embroglio.—The diplomatic path of France clearly mapped out.—Benedetti and the Prussian Minister for Foreign Affairs (Herr von Thile).—Gramont, Benedetti and Valette.—Desprets, the Permanent Secretary at the Quai d'Orsay.—The Emperor very ill.—Benedetti's claims to the title of a high-class diplomatist.—A story of Gouvion St. Cyr.—The moral of the story.—The Luxemburg Affair.—Lack of discipline at the Quai d'Orsay.—The Emperor's foreign policy.—An anecdote in a footnote.—Adolphe Thiers and my promised indictment against him . . . . *Page* 341

CONCLUSION

Paris on the night of the 16th July, 1870.—My opinion about France's ability to hold her own in the forthcoming struggle undergoes a considerable change before bedtime.—My recollections of '59 in Paris and of '66 in Berlin.—A comparison forced upon me.—Germany on the eve of the war, from a French eye-

CONTENTS

The Café de la Paix and a group of Imperialists.—Joseph Ferrari. A bit of spy-mania.—There is, in my opinion, no need for employing spies.—France's state of siege. Ferrari explains the situation.—Victor Emmanuel could not help if he were willing.—Francis-Joseph of Austria's need. A glance at the past in order to judge the present. Gramont's overweening confidence. Napoleon III.'s peaceful proclivities illustrated practically. My reception at the Louvre. My friend Korner and his troubles.—I tell how he strikes the balance of goodwill between Austria and France. The truth about the Emperor's illness.—His virtual detention by the Empress and her party.—Supposed ignorance of his critical state of health.—His departure.—Louis and Lebrun at Saarbruck. Lebœuf after Forbach and Wœrth. Pietri's telegram. The Empress's reply.—Fleury the only man who could have saved the situation.—The Empress and Émile Ollivier. The Empress's belief in tokens.—M. Benedetti at Metz. His return to Paris.—The Emperor's second attempt to return to Paris.—The possible effect of his presence there. The Empire might have been saved by one resolute man. M. Estancelin in the Chamber.—Henpecked heroes.—Henri IV., Peter the Great.—Victor Emmanuel.—Mme. de Maintenon and the Revocation of the Edict of Nantes.—Napoleon's exit a theatrical one. . . . . *Page* 373

UNDERCURRENTS

OF

THE SECOND EMPIRE

CHAPTER I

EVEN before the fall of the Second Empire, historians of high attainments like Lanfrey and Taxile Delord were "whittling" the gigantic figure of Napoleon I. They were probably prompted by a desire similar to that which caused Jacob to pill white strakes in the rods of green poplar and hazel and chestnut tree in Laban's field. With this difference, though, that Lanfrey and Taine after him did not set the whittled Titan before the mentally strongest progenitors of the coming generations, but before the mentally weakest. Lanfrey and Taine have had a kind of reward, notably among French Republicans, who have brought forth a generation which keeps yelling that the Napoleonic gods are dead. They, the French Republicans, remind one of the early Christians who constantly cried out that the Pagan gods were dead, when, in fact, these gods were not dead at all, but simply made the

…y eater of the new faith quake with fear. I too … do not believe that the Napoleonic … are dead; they are wrapt in a deep sleep; whether we shall see the man with the power to awaken them is another question.

Thus much concerning the present, let us look at the past, at the period between Waterloo and the overthrow of the dynasty of Louis Philippe, during which period the Napoleonic legend was to France in particular, but to Europe in general, what the stories of the Civil War and the Franco-German Campaign are still, first to Americans and Germans respectively, then to the whole of the civilized world; namely, a living, breathing, romantic and heroic drama upon which the curtain had only fallen a short time since; a drama most of the actors of which still walked the earth, while its chief hero, like Abraham Lincoln, was already numbered among the immortals of history, by reason of his martyrdom; a drama from the influence of which even those who had most cause to dread and dispel that influence could not escape. I am quoting from memory, but the reader may rest his mind on that point; my memory rarely attempts to deceive me without arousing my suspicions to that effect. We have lived for many years on the footing of a jealous husband and wife; the slightest sign of such deception on its part breeds a corresponding watchfulness on mine, and in this instance I feel absolutely convinced of its faithfulness. Both Generals Cambronne and Drouot had followed Napoleon during the Hundred Days; the first is credited with having flung a more forcible than elegant monosyllable at his assailants at Waterloo in reply to their summons to surrender; the second has had his name bestowed on one of the principal streets in Paris. On their return, the Bourbons after harassing Cambronne to no purpose, conferred a title on him, and finally, I believe, gave him the command of the Lille division; a frontier post of trust if ever there was one. Drouot retired to his native city, Nancy. Some time afterwards when the elder son of Charles X. that was to be—the Duc d'Angoulême who in 1830 abdicated with his father in favour of his nephew the Duc de Bordeaux, subsequently the Comte de Chambord—passed through the capital of Lorraine, he immediately inquired for the residence of Napoleon's favourite general, and called upon him. "Monsieur le Général," said the Prince, "I have come to beg a favour—that of exchanging my sword for yours." Drouot acquiesced, and the son of the House of France carried away the sword as a relic, as a talisman, as a badge of honour.

A few years later, the Duc's wife and cousin, the daughter of Louis XVI. and Marie Antoinette, the erstwhile prisoner of the Temple, spent a couple of days at Avignon, where at that time there was a branch establishment of the Hôtel des Invalides of Paris. She stayed at the Préfecture and on the Sunday, as a matter of course, went to Saint Agricol in semi-state. Scarcely had her foot touched the first step leading to the church when the air resounded with the stentorian cry of "Vive l'Empereur!" Under the circumstances the cry was considered as nothing less than an outrage; the offender was apprehended there and then, and would probably have been rent to death on the spot, for the masses are tigers when they are not apes, and frequently both in one. The offender would have been torn to pieces; the men who seven years before had inaugurated a series of foul murders with that of Maréchal Brune, would not have scrupled to crown the series with another but for the interference of the Duchesse herself and the Prefect. The offender turned out to be a former sergeant in the Imperial Guard named Jean Boucard. An interview took place the same afternoon between the veteran of la Grande Armée and the presumptive Queen of France at which no one was present but the Prefect, who afterwards told the story to many of his friends among whom were some of my relatives.[1] This story is, however, too long to be given in full here. For

---

[1] For an account of those relatives and their influence upon me as a writer, I must refer my readers to *My Paris Notebook*. London: Wm. Heinemann; Philadelphia: J. B. Lippincott Co.

the first time in her life perhaps the daughter of the Bourbons found herself face to face with an eye-witness of that marvellous Napoleonic era and no considerations of courtly etiquette could prevent him from limning it in all its brilliant, glowing colours as well as in all its sombre and tragic incidents, for Jean Boucard had been rendered childless by the god he adored; his eldest son had been killed at Leipzig, his younger at Waterloo. "Ah, you see, M. Boucard," said the Princess when the veteran came to that part of his story; "we cause the death of no one." "Pardon me, Madame," interrupted Boucard, "you had some one killed who was dearer to me than both my sons; you killed my general, my marshal, you killed Michel Ney." In spite of this rough reminder of the crime of her uncle (Louis XVIII.), the Princess endeavoured to convert Jean Boucard to the existing *régime*, nay, fancied she had converted him, for he accepted a generous bounty for himself and his widowed sister. But Boucard was not converted, though he also construed his acceptance of the Princess's subsidy in that spirit, and felt remorse gnawing at his heart in consequence. He no longer held up his head, shunned his fellow veterans, and from an occasional tippler became a confirmed drunkard. During these drunken fits he was silently arrogant, staring his former comrades in the face, evidently bent on provoking them. On one occasion he told the Prefect that he would like to earn the money that had been given to him by killing one of them. "The gold bears the bloodmarks of the murdered Michel Ney," he said; "I have tried to wash it clean in wine; only more blood will do it." Time went on and the birthday of Louis XVIII. came round. On that morning Boucard was more helplessly drunk and more defiant than usual. He loudly announced his intention of drinking the King's health at the dinner given on that occasion. He tried to be as good as his word, but the "Vive le Roi" stuck in his throat. Then with a supreme effort he gasped "Vive l'Empereur," and dropped to the floor. When they picked him up he was dead.

I might fill a book with stories of the unalterable devotion of these veterans to the memory of the leader for whom they had shed their blood. A few more must suffice. After his coronation, Charles X. was about to enter the archbishop's palace at Rheims when he noticed an old man, minus one arm, who stood quietly smoking his pipe, profoundly indifferent to the ceremony which had just concluded, and not bestowing as much as a glance on the newly-crowned king. Though the man wore no uniform, the martial air was unmistakable; it was moreover emphasized by the absence of the limb. The sovereign stopped on the threshold of the palace and sent an aide-de-camp for the apathetic veteran who came immediately, with his pipe still alight in his hand. "That pipe seems a great comfort to you, friend," said the King, breaking the ice at once. "It is a comfort," replied the old soldier pointedly; "it compensates for many things." "Which means," retorted the King, "that you are not too well-pleased to-day?" "I am aware, Sire," was the instantaneous rejoinder, "that in Rheims to-day every one is well pleased; I, unfortunately, am unable to take any share in the rejoicings." "And why?" queried the King. "Because I remember too well another coronation, in which I took my humble part." Charles X. was not easily disconcerted; he had a ready wit. "That's right," he said; "we should never forget those who led us to victory. But why are you not at the Invalides?" "Because I prefer to eat my crust at home in my own country. I am satisfied to live on the pension my cross [of the Legion of Honour] brings me." "The Invalides is your home by right, it is not a question of charity," remarked the King, still bent on conciliating the old soldier, and bowing to him. The veteran stood at the salute until Charles X. had disappeared, then went back quietly to his sunny spot to resume his smoking, mumbling to himself as he went, "He is a good sort after all." An hour later, an aide-de-camp dispatched by the King found him there. "His Majesty has sent me to tell you that he has granted got a pension of 300 francs from his privy purse," said the officer. Jean Latapie (for that was his name) stood at the salute once more.

"Very well," he remarked, with a somewhat sardonic smile. "Please to thank His Majesty for me, and to tell him that his kindness will enable me to buy two new ribbons instead of one ribbon per year for the cross given to me by the Emperor."

Thousands of these veterans were scattered through the French provinces, for Jean Latapie was not singular in his preference for a crust at home to two good meals daily at the Invalides. They propagated the Napoleonic faith and embellished the Napoleonic legend, in spite of their being, some of them, at any rate, republicans at heart. "I weep," said one, "because Napoleon has taken the Republic from us to smother it in his imperial bed; I weep because he who comforted us for the loss of the Republic, is chained to an English rock." They despised the dynasty that had been imposed upon France by the aid of alien bayonets. When Louvel stood arraigned for the murder of the Duc de Berri, the Procurator-General flung the word "coward" repeatedly into his face. "Coward, coward," cried Louvel at last; "you do not know, Monsieur, how much courage it implies to kill a man who has never done you any harm." And when asked to state the motives that had made him commit the deed, he exclaimed : "*Since the 18th June, 1815, I have never ceased to hear the cannon of Waterloo.*"

I made a mistake just now when I said that these veterans embellished the Napoleonic legend; they did not embellish it, there was no need to do so : they had but to tell the unvarnished truth about that giant who in a few years transformed the whole of the political geography of the European continent ; who made a King of Sweden out of a lawyer's son like himself ; a King of Naples out of an innkeeper's son ; a score of dukes and marshals out of as many stable-lads, millers' boys, coopers' apprentices, and Heaven alone knows out of what else. The rise of David and that of Joseph, as told in the Bible, are as nothing to that sudden leap into fortune of that lank-haired, sallow-faced Corsican lieutenant of artillery who, four years before the whole of the world rang with his name, was almost unknown to his brother officers. And when some sergeant, like Boucard or Latapie, told these marvellous tales and at their conclusion asked, in imitation of Sergeant Goguelat of Balzac's *Médecin de Campagne*, " Do you think that all this was natural ? " the simple listeners sitting in the ingle-nook could but reply, " No, it was not natural." And the hero of the tales, " Le Petit Caporal," became a god in the imagination of those humble folks to whom for nearly two decades he had proved a scourge by taken from them their husbands, fathers, brothers, and sons, of those humble folks who suffered most from the two invasions, for let us bear in mind that the Napoleonic cult was ever much stronger in the rural than in the urban districts. The recollection of that fact will stand us in good stead by and by, when we shall have to watch the nephew of the giant "spiking" the ground for his rivals in the Presidential elections, when we shall see him fight the Ulm of his electoral Austerlitz.

Nor must it be thought that the propagation of the Napoleonic cult was confined only to those who had founded the cult by the power of their swords—the surviving legionaries of the Grande Armée. Shortly after the sword had been sheathed the pen began its work, and before long, nay, even before the "martyr of St. Helena" had breathed his last, the glory of the victors of Waterloo had paled before that of the vanquished, for those who wielded the pen were poets, to whom a Cromwell, a Frederick the Great, or a Bonaparte is either God or Satan, sometimes both in one, poets who attempted, if they did not always accomplish a "Paradise Lost," when they became inspired with the deeds of an immortal " clothed with mortal flesh." They were poets, not literary Cuviers and Owens, whose system admits not of heroes or criminals, but simply of vertebrate or invertebrate animals. Considerable though the space at my disposal may be, I cannot dwell at greater length on this apotheosis of Napoleon by Byron, Goethe, Heine, Hugo, Mickiewicz, and their satellites; one ought to have heard a Dumas—whose father suffered at the hands of Napoleon—and a Béranger speak of the modern Cæsar, as I have heard them speak at my uncles' home, to be able to judge of the effect of their words, especially upon the younger generation of that period. Hence, as early as 1830, during the Revolution that cost the elder Bourbons their throne, there was already an attempt to restore the Empire. I can give chapter and verse for what I state. Talleyrand went to Vienna in secret, and but for the opposition there, would have brought the Duc de Reichstadt (the King of Rome) to Paris. Louis Philippe owed Talleyrand nothing with regard to the crown which for eighteen years "rested" so uneasily on his head, and he was well aware of the absence of all obligation. Nay, it is extremely doubtful whether Louis Philippe, who was one of the cleverest men on record, was not perfectly cognisant of his inability to struggle against the ever growing influence of the Napoleonic legend, especially after the death of his eldest son and notwithstanding the fact that this legend was frequently sung to the tunes of the "Marseillaise" and "Le Chant du Départ" rather than to that of "Partant pour la Syrie." He knew that Napoleon during the Hundred Days had allowed his soldiers to intone the revolutionary hymn attributed to Rouget de l'Isle, just as Napoleon's nephew made the military bands play it "by order" during the month of July 1870. He knew, moreover, that the most formidable successor of Talleyrand—I am alluding to Thiers—would not scruple to use the lever of Imperialism to attain his own ends; he knew that he himself had contributed to the spread of the Napoleonic faith by the removal of the remains of Napoleon from St. Helena to Paris. Some one who knew it even better than he was Prince Louis Napoleon.

I repeat, Louis Napoleon knew all this even better than Louis Philippe. Of the various members of the Bonaparte family, he alone had followed step by step the evolution of the Napoleonic legend, not only in its effects on France herself, but on England and Russia, whence, in the beginning, he foresaw the greatest opposition to his action when he should deem the time for action ripe. He alone had acted on two distinct occasions, while his relatives had looked on indifferently; some of these, notably Jérôme, the ex-King of Westphalia, and his son, who will be known to posterity as Plon-Plon, applauding most probably in their hearts of hearts at his failures; others, like Joseph, constantly advising him, especially after Strasburg, to abstain from all further attempts. I have chapter and verse for everything I state here and throughout this volume, and this time I am not at all inclined to submit tamely to criticism from so-called eminent personages who know no more of the secret history of the heirs to the Napoleonic legend than the man in the moon. Jérôme and his son were probably inclined to regret that these failures had not led to a more fatal issue so far as Louis Napoleon himself was concerned, albeit that his success then would have given them the material prosperity and exalted position which they so undeservedly and greedily enjoyed during the Second Empire, for which they clamoured incessantly, and for which they began to clamour before Louis Napoleon was fairly seated in the Presidential chair. "You have nothing of your uncle about you," said ex-King Jérôme one day, huffed at his nephew's refusal of his constant demands for money. "Yes, I have," was the Prince-President's answer, "I have my uncle's family." But Louis Napoleon was not the man to refuse money to any one, provided he had it or could borrow it; yet, notwithstanding his generosity to them as well as to others, the two Jérômes (father and son), would have almost rejoiced at the frustration of his hopes, for their dislike of him—let us say their jealousy—was even stronger than their greed. There could be no doubt with regard to Louis Napoleon's right to the succession of his uncle's

(?) ne after the death of the Duc de Reichstadt and Louis Napoleon's two elder brothers. Napoleon's distinct wishes on the subject, embodied in the Constitution of the Empire, left not the smallest loophole for misconstruction; nevertheless in virtue of Napoleon's former dispositions, which were afterwards revoked and with very good cause, apart from the claims of primogeniture, Jérôme never ceased to consider himself as wronged, as having been despoiled of the Imperial inheritance, and to a great extent imbued his son with the same ideas. As we proceed we shall see the effect produced by these ideas in Plon-Plon's attitude towards his cousin during the latter's occupancy of the Imperial throne.

Of all the brothers of Napoleon, the younger was doubtlessly the least worthy; there is equally no doubt that in spite of Napoleon's knowledge of that worthlessness, his affection for him was stronger than that for any other member of his family, except, perhaps, for his sister Pauline. On this theory alone can one account for Napoleon's error in making Jérôme King of Westphalia. For he who knew the working of men's hearts almost as well as Shakespeare, though he lacked the poetry wherewith to describe these workings, could not for one moment have flattered himself that the contact of this utterly feather-brained scapegrace, devoid of the slightest idea of moral responsibility, with the sober-minded, honest, though heavy Brunswickers, Hanoverians, and Hessians could be productive of the slightest good. And, as a matter of course, Jérôme impaired the prestige of his brother, and proved a thorn in his side during the whole of his (Napoleon's) reign, just as Jérôme's son impaired the prestige of his cousin and proved a thorn in his side during the whole of the Second Empire. With this difference, however, that the son was even more guilty than the father; for the latter had not an ounce of his offspring's brain, while on the other hand the son had not a grain of his sire's courage, which was that of the lion.

But even in the days of Napoleon, courage, though counting for much, did not make up for everything, especially with the ruler of populations already exhausted by war. I hold no brief either for the memory of Napoleon I. or for that of Napoleon III. I am fully aware that the war contributions levied by the former were often very terrible; at the same time the very poor were not systematically ground down. Edgar Quinet, who assuredly is not suspected of a leaning towards Cæsarism, tells us that in the humbler dwellings in Spain, crude representations of the Emperor and of the principal events in his life hung side by side with the presentment of the Cid. In Russia the Napoleonic songs of Béranger were translated and became popular with the masses. The Count Lepic, travelling in Egypt, came at every step on "grateful recollections" of the "great Kebir," "who only ...vied taxes once," whom the people called "the ...st, the most magnificent title the Arab can bestow. After the fall of the Empire, the gondoliers of Venice refused to carry Marmont, and pointed the finger of scorn at him. "Do you see this man?" they cried to one another. "Well, he was the friend of the great Napoleon, and betrayed him." I fancy one might go from one end to the other of the former kingdom of Westphalia without finding the faintest trace of such goodwill to the memory of Napoleon's brother, and I am not speaking of the present time, but of more than thirty years ago. On the day of the ex-King of Westphalia's funeral, I happened to sprain my ankle and was taken home by an old German gentleman who was a native of Cassel, and by his grandson who was a Parisian by birth. The elder Körner's stories about the Court of King Jérôme caused my granduncles to take a great fancy to him, and he and his grandson became frequent guests at our home. Those who have read *My Paris Note-Book* are aware by this time of my relatives' mania for "taking notes," a mania which I have inherited. It is from their papers that I cull the following stories, only a few among nearly two hundred.

Among the various individuals who followed and accompanied Jérôme to Cassel—some clever, others hopelessly incapable, but all tainted with the same greed—there was a former captain of engineers by name Morio, who had been one of Jérôme's aide-de-camps during his successful campaign in Silesia (1807). Morio was not devoid of courage or knowledge, but he was a " muddler," and a pretentious one at that, with a hankering for reforming things, and a " money-grabber " besides. Jérôme made him his War Minister, and Morio, who saw his subordinates grow fat on the moneys extorted from the Westphalians under the then prevailing system of " substituting " for " military service," began to rack his brain for a reform that would likewise fill his purse. He issued an order that henceforth all officers should pay for their horses' fodder, intending of course to charge the War Chest—empty enough in all conscience—with the cost of said fodder and pocketing the proceeds. Most of the officers complied with the new regulations; a few proved absolutely refractory; among the latter General Allix, an able and meritorious officer whom Napoleon had sent to look after his brother's artillery. Shortly after this there was a grand field-day in presence of the young sovereign, who, to his intense astonishment, beheld General Allix trudging on foot behind his batteries. " Why are you not on horseback, general ? " shouts Jérôme. " Because I cannot afford to pay for my cattles' fodder, and the State, it appears, cannot afford it either," shouts the other in reply, panting for breath and trying to keep up with his men. This was long before Hervé had written his *Petit Faust*, in which Valentine recommends his *foot-soldiers* " not to forget that they are on *horseback*." Jérôme, therefore, simply lent the general a mount there and then, and rescinded Morio's orders. General Allix's victory in this instance had apparently no effect on his outspokenness. A couple of days later Jérôme paid a visit of inspection to the Cassel arsenal. Catching sight of several obsolete pieces of ordnance in an angle, the King remarked, " General Allix, your guns are rather rusty." " Parbleu, Sire," was the immediate answer ; " they are not intended for court carriages."

It was an indirect reminder to Jérôme that " show " in military matters, and especially in sober matters of war, was out of place, and Jérôme needed such a reminder, for notwithstanding his undoubted courage and by no means inconsiderable tactical skill, he was too much addicted to the theatrical display with which the Bourbons previously to the Napoleonic era conducted their campaigns. The campaign in Silesia, which I mentioned just now incidentally, had been an instance of it, and he was not a crowned sovereign then. In the one undertaken after his coronation, by order of his brother, who was already preparing the ground for Wagram, he might have been a veritable

Louis XIV. or Louis XV., accompanied as he was by his ministers, the foreign ambassadors, his mistresses, a company of play actors, scullions and so forth. To the Blanche Carnegas and her fellow concubines, as well as to their husbands, he distributed titles, distinctions, money, and estates with lavish hand. In this respect he differed from his son in after years, for liberality, no matter in what form, was not one of Plon-Plon's pet sins.

Both father and son had been residing in France for over a twelvemonth by favour of Louis Philippe when the Revolution of 1848 broke out. In after years when the would-be historians hinted that Louis Napoleon had played his cards well by selecting his uncle and cousin to watch events for him, he invariably smiled with that sphinx-like smile which might be construed into anything the interlocutor chose. Well might the Emperor smile at the idea of having derived help from these two. Bismarck said once that too much stress had been laid upon Napoleon III.'s intellectual capacities and not sufficient stress upon his generous and lovable disposition. The erstwhile chancellor was not far wrong, but Napoleon III., though not an eagle, was not an imbecile, and to have expected the two Jérômes to help him would have shown him to be a hopeless one.

After his escape from Ham and until the

beginning of '48, the greater part of which time
Louis Napoleon spent in England, he had but
one ally—or, to speak by the card, a faithful
watcher of his fortunes—among the members of
his family whether legitimate or illegitimate; and
that friend was a woman, his cousin Mathilde
the daughter of ex-King Jérôme. Prince Louis
had forfeited the countenance of the rest, in consequence of his social mistakes, as well as political
blunders. Morny never saw his half-brother
until the latter had weathered the storm of
the Presidential elections. There is no trustworthy evidence that they ever as much as
corresponded before then. Morny was an
Orleanist, and if the truth were known, had no
exalted idea of Prince Louis's capacities; Colonna
Walewski, the illegitimate son of Napoleon I.,
was to a certain extent affiliated to Thiers, and
Thiers's views with regard to the game he meant
the exiled Prince to play in the immediate
future, if the opportunity should occur, were, I
feel perfectly certain, never communicated to
Walewski. I can but faintly touch here on the
latter and Morny; they will appear again, and
the reader may rest assured that then I will
not skimp their portraits. Prince Louis's
cousins on the father's side, the family of
Lucien, were too occupied with their own affairs
to bestow much thought on him; his cousins
on the mother's side, the posterity of Eugène de

Beauharnais, were allied by marriage to some of the reigning Houses of Germany and to Czar Nicholas himself, whom the rumblings of the revolutionary storm which was to break all over the continent of Europe filled with rage, while they filled the others with fear ; and it must not be forgotten that Prince Louis had the reputation then of being an ardent republican, a reputation perfectly justified. Besides, all these, in common with Morny, were not far short of considering him a hare-brained dreamer and—his private life did not meet with their approval. That private life cannot be sketched here ; we shall get glimpses of it as we proceed, when, though seated on the throne, he paid the penalty for some of its errors, and paid right nobly. Worse than all from their point of view, Prince Louis was poor, and, to aggravate matters, not always careful to husband his poverty. He was prone to dissipation, addicted to gambling, and not always punctual in the payment of his debts. " Je vous revaudrai ça un jour," said Gambetta, in acknowledgment of any favour in the days of his impecuniosity. I am not certain that he kept his word when prosperity came. Louis Napoleon, who had a similar way of giving his friends liens on the future, never broke his, except in one instance, and that instance is sufficiently amusing to be recounted here, especially as it will afford the reader at least one glimpse of that private life to which I alluded just now.

It was in the summer of '60 or '61 that I went for the first time to Baden-Baden in company with my two grand-uncles, among whose acquaintances were all sorts and conditions of men. My relatives were talking to a M. Martin, a superannuated *croupier* of Frascati in Paris, who had been appointed inspector of the gaming tables under the late François Blanc, of Monte Carlo fame. We were standing on the steps of the Kursaal—I, a lad of seventeen, but a precocious one, keeping my eyes and ears wide open for everything that was said and done. It is well known that the late Wilhelm I. of Prussia, before he succeeded to his brother's throne, had several interviews with Napoleon III. at the fashionable resort, mainly through the instrumentality of Bismarck. On that day the Emperor was at Baden-Baden, and Prince Wilhelm and he were to meet in the Lichtenthall Allée. As a matter of course, the majority of the visitors were flocking thither. "Aren't you going to the Lichthenthall Allée, Martin?" asked my uncle. The old croupier shrugged his shoulders. "The sight of Prince Guillaume is no novelty to us. He comes pretty well every year." "True; but what about Emperor Napoleon?" "Emperor Napoleon," quoth Martin, pondering as it were, "I saw the first one when I was a lad. This one is the third son of Queen Hortense, the one who used to travel about a good deal. If I am not mistaken . . . ."—"You are not mistaken, Martin," came a voice from behind us. "He still owes twenty-five *louis* to the Bank." I looked round and saw a thin, shrivelled, old man, below rather than above the middle height; it was the famous François Blanc.

If one of the Emperor's relatives had been near at the time, he or she would have smiled at the recollection of such a shady passage in the life of the man who at that very moment was virtually the arbiter of the destinies of Europe, and have offered to pay the money there and then; but thirteen or fourteen years before that moment Blanc's sally would have roused his or her virtuous indignation. Princesse Mathilde Bonaparte, Comtesse Demidoff, was no such time-server. To begin with, her own chequered existence had bred a large-minded tolerance for the foibles of men; no one had suffered more from such foibles then she, for her husband, Comte Anatole Demidoff, had the most marvellous and complete collection of them, and was little short of a madman besides. She knew, moreover, that her cousin Louis was not half nor a quarter as mad as her husband and the male members of his family, and that he had all the generous impulses of the Demidoffs. Thirdly, if Louis Napoleon had been the veriest raving maniac, she would have still clung to his fortunes, and furthered them to the utmost of her abilities and resources, for she acknowledged but one god, her uncle, the great Napoleon, and she could then conceive of no other prophet than her cousin, the third son of Louis, ex-King of Holland and Hortense de Beauharnais. "Call a dog Bonaparte, and I will love him"; she might have said, paraphrasing Johnson. In that respect she was the daughter of her mother, that heroic Catherine of Wurtemberg, of whom Napoleon spoke with such admiration till the day of his death; she loved the name of Napoleon for the sake of the halo with which it was surrounded, not for the material gain it might bring. It was that fervent, disinterested love for Napoleon I. that won her the heart of Nicholas I., who, in spite of his real or fancied grievance against him, worshipped him as fervently as she did, and virtually freed her from the marriage bonds she had contracted with one of his nobles, as much for the sake of Napoleon's memory as from respect for her. This grievance was not due to Moscow or to Napoleon's European policy, but to Napoleon's somewhat offensive rejection of Nicholas's sister, Anna Paulowna, who became the wife of William II. of Holland. In principle Napoleon, who divorced Josephine because he wanted an heir, and as a matter of course, a physically and mentally sound heir, was right at the moment of that rejection, apart from the proposed bride's youth. Subsequent events do not absolutely prove that Napoleon was wrong in his rejection, for though William III. of Holland and his brothers and sisters were as physically and mentally sound as any one, the same could not be said for the descendants of William III. ; I mean for those who are dead. However, the goodwill of Nicholas, as we shall see presently, only extended to one member of the Bonaparte family; on personal as well as political grounds he objected *in toto* to "that lank-haired adventurer, the son of the devil knows whom, and the devil's firebrand-envoy." It was another illustration of the pot calling the kettle black, for Nicholas himself was the grandson of "the devil knows whom"; it is very certain that his grandmother, the great Catherine, could not have told him with certainty who was the responsible author of his (Nicholas's) father's being.

To Mathilde Bonaparte all these contemptuous epithets, flung at her cousin's head, were as nothing, especially after Prince Louis's attempt at Strasburg, more especially after his attempt at Boulogne, and still more especially after his escape from Ham. Princesse Mathilde is a septuagenarian, and, as far as I know, a hale and hearty one. The time to write her full biography is, let us trust, far distant; when that time comes the historians will have to add her name to those of the Duchesse de Berri (the Comte de Chambord's mother), Princesse Adelaide (Louis Philippe's sister), and Queen Hortense of Holland, as one of the four women who have shaped to a certain extent the history of France during the nineteenth century. For the present I must confine myself to a preliminary statement. It was she who kept her cousin informed of the progress of the Napoleonic legend after Strasburg and after Boulogne; it was she who inspired him with courage by giving him the real reasons why those attempts had not been more rigorously visited on the participators in it, especially on the officers of the 46th of the line and the artillery troops of Colonel Vaudrey. It was she who repeated to him the answer " Il y aurait eu trop à punir," of the Duc d'Orléans (the father of the late Comte de Paris) to Colonel Taillandier, who had stemmed the tide of the insurrection at Strasburg, and who asked the Duc the question. It was she who bade her cousin humour or blindfold Lamartine when the latter in March '48 asked the former to return to London. It was she who supplied part of the sinews of war for the Presidential elections when her cousin did return; it was she who coached him in that game of political bluff with Victor Hugo, and Changarnier and Thiers after he, Prince Louis, had been elected President; it was she who kept Dupin Aîné in good humour, so that he might signal to the future Emperor the cards held by his adversaries, only one of whom, Thiers, was formidable. The description of that game must be left for my next chapter.

CHAPTER II

In the previous chapter I spoke of Princesse Mathilde as the prompter of Louis Napoleon before and after his election as President of the Second Republic. At the first blush this admission may appear a contradiction of my equally former statement to the effect that the future Emperor was thoroughly aware of the magic potentiality contained in the name of Napoleon. But no actor, whether great or small, and however letter-perfect and certain of his audience can afford to dispense with a prompter, for, known or unknown to the player, there may slip in among that audience a section hostile to him and bent upon "queering his pitch." The expression is not elegant, but it is the appropriate one, as theatrical authorities well know. That section, numerous or the reverse, may work jointly or separately. It may post its members singly in different parts of the house or gather them into a serried phalanx as was done during the "Tamburini Rows" at Her Majesty's Theatre more than fifty years ago.[1] It may express its hostility openly by hisses and catcalls, or by pretended and exaggerated marks of approval and sympathy. The latter device is popularly called "guying." Nay, more; it may enlist in its cause a fellow-actor of the comedian to hamper him on the very stage.

To continue the theatrical metaphor for another moment. The members of that "omnibus-box," or to use the French term "*loge infernale*" who had determined to "queer Louis Napoleon's pitch" either in furtherance of their own and strictly personal aggrandisement or for the purpose of showing what an inferior "mummer" he, Louis Napoleon, was in comparison with the great classical actors they had selected for the part of rulers of the French, these members all adopted the tactics enumerated just now. Among them, Lamartine is the only one entitled to a certain amount—a very small amount—of respect. He, at any rate, fought Louis Napoleon with uplifted visor, and would fain have avoided fighting altogether. The consciousness that his motive for fighting was not a lofty one may have

[1] A word to the wise. The "Tamburini Rows" have been immortalised by Barham in the *Ingoldsby Legends*. But I cannot explain every allusion I may have occasion to use in the course of these pages. Many years ago I wrote in a preface to one of my books, "The writer who has time to explain everything has not much to write. The reader who is too indolent or indifferent to look up references ought not to read." I hold that opinion still.

I red this reluctance, for the poet-historian of *Les Girondins* had not the invincible conviction of his infallibility in all things of the poet-pamphleteer of *L'Histoire d'un Crime*, nor the facility for blinking unsavoury facts connected with his own ambition of the historian of *The Consulate and the Empire*. Lamartine was more honest and more honourable than either Victor Hugo, or Adolphe Thiers, though that is not saying much. Joseph Méry, the friend of the elder Dumas and Balzac, the genial, amusing, and almost matchless humourist, who is scarcely known to English and American readers, but who ought to be known to every one, Méry, who rarely said an unkind word of any one, openly averred that Lamartine proclaimed the Second Republic on the 24th February, 1848, as a means to stave off his most pressing creditors. Lamartine's subsequent explanation of his action on that day virtually substantiated Méry's indictment, for the poet admitted that at noon on that historical Thursday "the establishment of a republic was farthest from his thoughts." But if he forsook his royalist faith, he was in no way pledged by any of his previous utterances either to Bonapartism in its ostentatiously republican form as advocated by the "nephew of his uncle," or to republicanism in its Cæsaric form as interpreted by the "uncle of the nephew." Unlike Goethe, Heine, Byron, Hugo, and the rest, Lamartine had never worshipped at the shrine of the deified Corsican lieutenant of artillery; he had endeavoured, though unsuccessfully, to drag down the idol and impose silence on its high priests by that one scathing line—

> Rien d'humain ne battait sous son épaisse armure;

he had opposed the removal of Napoleon's remains from St. Helena and their triumphal reception in Paris, and when defeated, his cry of surrender had been, as it were, prophetic. 'Very well," he exclaimed, " bring back his remains, considering that nothing less will satisfy you. Let the pedestal to his statue be the column;[1] after all, the work is his, the monument created by him, but at any rate, do this: write on the socle, 'To NAPOLEON ALONE.'

Thus, nearly a score of years before the *coup d'état*, Lamartine saw and felt whence and whither the wind blew. At that very moment the son of the great Napoleon was dying at Schoenbrunn; the second son of the great Napoleon's brother and Hortense de Beauharnais had died a twelvemonth before without issue. The least dangerous enemies to the welfare of France —from Lamartine's point of view—and also the least enterprising were gone; the most daring—

---

[1] The Austerlitz column, better, though wrongly, known as the Vendôme column, whence the statue had been removed in 1814 after the entry of the Allied Troops in Paris. Lamartine's speech dates from 1832, when it was proposed to reinstate the statue.

the mother and the third son remained, and the poet-statesman guessed, if he did not absolutely know, their temper. Louis Napoleon's attempt at Strasburg four years later (1836), his second attempt at Boulogne-sur-Mer four years after that (1840) and his writings during his subsequent confinement at Ham could have left no doubt in Lamartine's mind with regard to Louis Napoleon's further plans; and Lamartine's first thought and care when the hour for the execution of these plans had obviously struck, was their frustration. On the 2nd March, 1848, Louis Napoleon and Lamartine met in secret; and the poet prevailed on the prince to return to England. Few of the real particulars of that interview, and of the arguments employed by Lamartine to induce Louis Napoleon to this step have ever leaked out; I may honestly claim to possess some slight information on the subject denied to others. Truly, that information is open to the charge of being one-sided, considering that it was gathered from the lips of the Emperor himself a couple of years after his accession, at which time a national subscription was set on foot to relieve Lamartine of his debts, to which fund the Emperor contributed a handsome sum. "If he were the merest rhymester instead of being one of the greatest poets of contemporary France, I should still owe him that much," remarked Napoleon III. during one of those

occasional conversations with my relatives to
which I have alluded elsewhere.[1] "I owe him
that much for his treatment of me in March
1848. Neither Thiers nor Changarnier and least
of all Cavaignac would have acted like that had
they been in Lamartine's position. I feel certain
they would not have counselled me to return to
England, but opposed that return with all their
might when once they had me in their power,
for I was virtually setting at defiance the
decree of banishment against our family which
had only been specially relaxed in favour of my
uncle Jérôme and his children—a proof by the
bye that Louis Philippe was not afraid of them
and that he was afraid of me, so I could not have
been the utter nonentity people said I was. I
should not like to say for certain what Thiers
or Changarnier would have done with me, though
I have a pretty correct idea; as for Cavaignac,
he would have had me shot as, I am sorry to
say, my uncle had the Duc d'Enghien shot; that
is, without the formality of a trial. Republican
though he professed to be, he had all the making
of an irresponsible tyrant in him; republican
though he was, he would not have scrupled
to pose as a kind of avenger of the son of the
Duc de Condé, and what is more, the people would
have let him do it, even if he had condescended to
apprise them of his intention; they would probably

[1] My *Paris Note-Book*.

have applauded if they had only been told of the accomplished fact; mainly, because the masses are prone to applaud accomplished facts, or at any rate to acquiesce in them, provided they are accomplished boldly and promptly. If Louis XVI. had had the Tennis Court at Versailles surrounded and shelled instead of letting the proceedings take their course, there would have been no Revolution. Again, Cavaignac, if he had deigned to give a reason at all for thus disposing of me so unceremoniously could have given an apparently valid one. He could have represented me as having come to overthrow the new-born Republic, not of having come with the intention of serving it as a French citizen. He might have been correct or not in his assertion, that is not the question. The people would have acquiesced, for it is a lie to say that the people side with the weaker; they side with the stronger, and during the first days of March 1848, it was not only the people but the populace that had the upper hand, not the *bourgeoisie* as in 1830, although the people in 1848 allowed themselves to be hoodwinked by a set of the meanest and most contemptible *bourgeois* that ever lived. To this wholesale statement there are only two exceptions, Lamartine and Emile de Girardin, both of whom thoroughly despised the *bourgeois*. Lamartine's impecuniosity notwithstanding, there was not an ounce of greed in his composition;

Girardin in despite of his affluence, was not quite so indifferent to money, but his support of the Second Republic was due to other than money causes. There was, to begin with, a personal as well as a political feud between him and M. Guizot; apart from the resentment he felt against the whole of the aristocracy on account of the wrongs he had suffered at the hands of his father. "*I take it,*" added the Emperor in a most significant tone, "*I take it to be more noble to father a child which one knows not to be one's own than to deny the flesh of one's flesh, the blood of one's blood, because it happens not to be born in holy wedlock.*"[1] Girardin had, moreover, a grudge against Cavaignac for having given him a terrible fright, of which I will tell you one of these days.

"As for Changarnier," the Emperor went on, after a few moments, "he would have done with me what the Bourbons did with Ney; that is, given me a public trial; a kind of spectacular melodrama in some specially constituted court, in which drama he would have endeavoured to run me very hard as the hero, for he was conceited and idiotic enough for anything, and provided he succeeded in drawing public attention

---

[1] The first part of the sentence in italics is unquestionably an allusion to the frequent doubts cast upon Louis Napoleon's own legitimacy; the second, a condemnation of the conduct of General Alexis de Girardin with regard to his natural son. General de Girardin did not behave well to his "love-child" even after he had "legitimized" it.

to himself, he would not have minded drawing public attention to me. What Victor Hugo would have done in Lamartine's stead, it is impossible for me to say. He might have treated me as he treated his imaginary opponents in the Chamber; viz., credited me with sentiments and projects altogether foreign to my heart and mind, in order to 'place' an eloquent speech. He might have had me tried and sentenced to death for the sake of writing another immortal *Dernier Jour d'un Condamné;* I might have become at his pen *le plus grand des Napoléon* instead of *Napoléon le Petit,* but my posthumous greatness would have been less useful to me and to France than my actual littleness. All nonsense apart," the Emperor interrupted himself with a smile, "I am not at all sorry that I incurred the enmity of Victor Hugo, though I yield to no man in my admiration of him as a poet. But I did not want a constant repetition of Boileau's line to Louis XIV.—'Cessez de vaincre, sire, ou je cesse d'écrire;' and I should have inevitably had that line over and over again if I had retained his friendship. The age of le Roi-Soleil is passed, probably never to return in connection with the fulsome and non-critical worship of a ruler. Better so. The poet has had to make room for the historian and leader-writer especially with regard to living sovereigns. The poet who would endeavour to drown critical appreciation with indiscriminate panegyrics of the sovereign thus criticised, would most probably harm that sovereign instead of serving him; he would, at any rate, make him look ridiculous; and in France ridicule maims when it does not kill, especially if it be levelled at a civilian; and according to a great many, I was only a civilian and a sorry one at that.

"What Thiers would have done with me had he been in Lamartine's place, I repeat, it is equally impossible for me to say," the Emperor went on. "I have often tried to think it out, but must frankly confess that I dared not pursue my thoughts to their logical conclusion. I am certainly not less prone than others to think evil of my fellow-men, but I fancy there is a tacit compact between my mind and my heart—say, between my understanding and my conscience— to find extenuating circumstances for an enemy, and that Thiers is my personal enemy, to an even greater extent than my political one, I have not the faintest doubt. I sometimes think that if Thiers had had the disposal of me at that time there would have been neither a summary execution as in the case of Cavaignac, nor a public trial as in the case of Changarnier or Hugo, but a kind of *escamotage*. I should have disappeared, whether temporarily or permanently would have depended on circumstances. There might have been a second mystery of the 'Iron Mask' in history, for Thiers is a mental and moral as well as a physical coward who would not have had the pluck to resort to secret assassination, and there was no Lady Macbeth by his side to screw his courage to the sticking point. Cavaignac is a brute, but has the courage of the brute; Changarnier has courage also; it is not the courage of Henri IV. of whom it was said, 'Son courage riait;' for Changarnier's courage grins rather than laughs. To be absolutely correct, it makes others grin; it being more or less theatrical, like that of the Prince de Condé, who opened the trenches at Lérida to the sound of a score of violins; it is the dandy courage of some of the captains under Louis XIV., but it is courage for all that. Nor is Victor Hugo a coward. 'Show me how a man sings and I will tell you how he will fight,' said Carlyle, whom you admire so much; and I fancy the axiom is generally though not invariably true. All these men, Lamartine included, have courage; Thiers, I repeat, has none. His courage spells craft. Lamartine had the courage to show me indirectly that he was afraid of me by advising me to return to England; I say indirectly, for he did not put it in that way; he alleged that there was danger to me, not to him; but his fear strengthened my courage; and that is why I owe him a good turn, which I have endeavoured to repay by heading the national subscription for the settlement of his debts with a handsomer sum than I would have given had he been simply the great poet he is."

This then was Louis Napoleon's opinion of the men with whom he had engaged in that game of political bluff which lasted for more than three years, though only two of his adversaries kept playing to the last. Lamartine threw up his hand almost directly after the first round, *i.e.* when he had objected to Louis Napoleon's joining the game at all—and discovered that Louis Napoleon meant to join it in spite of his objection; in other words, that neither intrigue nor threats would keep him out of France.[1] For, immediately after the disturbances in June,[2] during which Cavaignac had virtually given himself away to a great many of his intending backers by showing the kind of game he contemplated playing henceforward, Louis Napoleon slipped into Paris while the streets around the Northern Railway Station were still encumbered with the remains of the barricades. "I was compelled to leave my luggage in the cloak room and to make my way on foot to the house of my friend who had offered me his hospitality. I only carried a very small carpet bag," said the Emperor afterwards, when recounting the incidents of

[1] The order for Louis Napoleon's arrest, transmitted by telegraph to every prefect and sub-prefect in France on the 12th June, 1848, and posted up in every commune almost immediately afterwards.

[2] Not to be confounded with the revolt of June 1849, which was quelled by Changarnier.

his arrival. "I had scarcely gone a hundred yards when I was stopped by an old woman. 'I say, young man,' she cried, 'just put a paving stone or so in their places; help us a bit to get straight; we are all sixes and sevens, some one must put an end to the confusion.' 'That's exactly what I have come here for, madame;' I replied. The old woman did not know how absolutely true these words were; I myself have often pondered them since; and invariably been reminded in connection with them of that incident in Edmund Kean's life when he trudged to Drury Lane in the snow on the night of his first appearance on that stage which was to witness his greatest triumphs."

Cavaignac's first and practically last hand was, then, as I have said, a bad one from the outset; nevertheless he "came in" and drew cards, trusting first, to his own faculty for "bluffing;" secondly, to that same faculty as displayed by those who were still betting on his game; namely the whole of the staff of *Le National*, founded eighteen years previously by Thiers and Armand Carrel and edited at the period of which I treat by Armand Marrast. That staff ought to have been warned by the fate of one of the founders of the paper (Armand Carrel), of the danger of excessive "bluffing," nay, of the mortal penalty attached to such "bluffing." But a few months of phenomenal success in this respect had made them absolutely reckless. *Le National* literally governed France for a little while,[1] and its staff fancied they would be allowed to continue governing, if Cavaignac should succeed in his candidature for the Presidency. But neither their bluffing, nor that of Lamoricière and Dufaure, who were staking on Cavaignac's game with the moneys of the State, was of much avail; Cavaignac's game was lost before Louis Napoleon had said that he would "see him." "Your candidate does not stand the ghost of a chance;" wrote an electioneering canvasser from the provinces whither he had been sent by Lamoricière. "Even his name is against him. Cavaignac, Cavaignac," said an elector, "Cavaignac means nothing at all to Frenchmen. You say he has been in Africa; but I never heard of him. If his name were Geneviève de Brabant or that of one of the four sons of Aymon,[2] it might do; it would convey some kind of story, but I repeat, that of Cavaignac conveys nothing at all. I prefer that of Napoleon; there is a ring about it; it arouses echoes in one's mind and heart, the echoes of battle marches to which our fathers and grandfathers went to victory at Jena, at Austerlitz,

---

[1] See *An Englishman in Paris*, vol. ii., chap. i., where there is a list of the government appointments held by the members, literary and otherwise, of *Le National* in the beginning of 1848.

[2] The four knights of a Carlovingian legend who were mounted on *one* horse named Bayard.

at Marengo. To defeat also, as at Waterloo, as you say." This in answer to a timid remark of mine. "Well, yes, Waterloo was a defeat; a defeat more glorious perhaps than a victory; but your General Cavaignac won't retrieve it and a second Napoleon may. I am afraid," concluded the agent, "that eleven-twelfths of the electors hold a similar opinion." As will be seen from this, the Boucards and Latapies had done their work; the Napoleonic legend which they had sown broadcast was blossoming into fruit.

I have already remarked that only two of Louis Napoleon's adversaries continued to play after the first round, in which Cavaignac was so signally worsted as to fling common politeness to a successful rival to the winds with the rest, when the newly-elected President offered to shake hands with him. These two adversaries were respectively Adolphe Thiers and General Changarnier, for Victor Hugo also flung up his cards and began to yell that Hortense's son had been cheating, because the latter would not divide the stakes by giving him the portfolio for Foreign Affairs which he may have coveted, like two of the greatest statesmen-poets of his own time, Chateaubriand and Lamartine. Some say that Hugo aimed higher still and wanted to be President of the Second Republic himself. Judging by the material of which some of the Presidents of the Third Republic have been made, one feels inclined to think that such a wish on the part of a man of note would be a condescension, unless that man were a Louis Napoleon or a Changarnier—in other words, unless he intended to usurp the crown for himself or offer it to others.

Was Changarnier working for a restoration or for a dictatorship? Opinion is divided on the subject. We will endeavour to find out directly, though I doubt if we shall succeed; but in that first round it looked uncommonly as if he wished to emulate Monk, for he only completed his "ante" in order to draw four cards to a supposed king;[1] but they were not sufficiently good to admit of his betting, and before his turn for betting came, he flung them away, and determined to "sit tight" or a while and not to "come in" except on a good hand, when he would bluff on sure grounds.

Different from Changarnier's tactics were those of Thiers, who did not attempt to play in that first round, but sat watching the game or rather the principal gamester, Louis Napoleon, in order to get at his system.[2] He might as well have

---

[1] The Comte de Chambord. There is no doubt that the 4,687 votes polled by Changarnier at the Presidential elections were given by isolated Legitimists in batches of two, three, and four. They, the voters, saw in him a would-be Monk of another Bourbon Restoration.

[2] It is worthy of record that among the stray votes at the

watched Kaempffer's automatic chess-player for all the information he got. Though we shall meet with Thiers again, when the outlines of his portrait as given by the Emperor *will be filled in as it were*, it is time to look on our own account at Thiers, "the great Thiers" as some of the French journalists continue to call him; these same journalists denying the epithet of great to Bismarck "on account of his craft," although it is very doubtful whether the ex-Chancellor could have resorted to meaner shifts than those which crop up daily, nay, hourly, in the life of the French statesman of whom, moreover, it is difficult to record one private or political action sufficiently generous to throw a lasting ray of light in the otherwise sombre picture.

Of course, I am not going to write Thiers' biography. I cannot too often remind the reader that I lay no claim to the title of historian or to that of biographer. I would, moreover, state, once for all, that, notwithstanding the many assertions to the contrary of both friendly and unfriendly critics, I hold no brief for the late Emperor of the French, and that least of all have I been engaged as the Devil's

Presidential elections there were not a dozen for either Thiers or Hugo. Thiers, for reasons that will appear directly, had not even come forward as a candidate. Hugo never had a desire to become President of the Republic, but coveted the portfolio of Foreign Affairs.

Advocate against the memory of the first President of the Third Republic. The French Republicans may canonize him with Gambetta and Favre, for what I care, and if they want another trio of such saints as " understudies " I will give them a long list from which to choose. This much I do say : whenever and wherever historians put the memory of Napoleon III. on its trial for the calamities that resulted to France from the Franco-German War, the memory of Thiers ought to stand arraigned by the side of the other as *an accessory* before the fact. Lest this should appear an unfounded accusation on my part, I will at the outset of this book solemnly undertake to produce at the end chapter and verse for what I have just stated. At least two of the actors in that particular prologue to the War are alive. They will have the right of contradicting me.

At this early stage it will be sufficient for me to prove that at no time in his career was Louis Napoleon the dupe of Thiers, not even immediately before or during the miscarried attempt at Boulogne when the future Emperor issued a decree appointing his enemy—for he always knew Thiers to be such—chief of the Provisional Government. Thiers, in spite of everything that has been said about his marvellous intuition and the rest, was, at times, absolutely purblind to the effect of his duplicity and craft upon others. Out of that duplicity and craft he had woven around himself a fabric so thick as to be literally impenetrable from the inside, and he fondly imagined that those outside could not espy his actions. He was a bad sportsman, or he would have known that the experienced hunter watches the dense undergrowth that hides the wild brute and not the wild brute himself, whom in reality he cannot see, and whose movements are only revealed to him by signs imperceptible, by sounds inaudible to the inexperienced, but of the brute's presence in that undergrowth he is nevertheless practically certain, because he has "tracked" his quarry thither, guided by the devastation the latter has spread around in his course, by the blood of his victims. Thiers' track was positively reeking with the blood of his victims, the blood of the Republicans whom he had pitted against the Bourbons in 1830, against the d'Orléans in '48; it was bestrewn with the maimed remains of two dynasties, and yet he fancied that he would secure another victim in Louis Napoleon, whom he had already endeavoured to kill physically, if possible; politically, if failing in the other attempt, eight years before the latter's advent to the Presidency. I am referring once more to the affair at Boulogne, which every one was agreed in saying was a trap laid by the little man for the son of Queen Hortense. What every one did not and does not know is this. Prince Louis suspected it to be a trap, though he did not expect it to close upon him, as it did, for six years. I have by me several notes referring to private remarks on that subject by the Emperor, which preclude all doubts as to Prince Louis Napoleon's mental grasp of the whole situation. Their reproduction here, even in the most condensed form, is unfortunately out of the question. These notes show conclusively: 1. that Louis Napoleon fostered few illusions with regard to the success of the projected Boulogne attempt; 2. that had he considered it to be even more of a forlorn hope than he did consider it, he would still have attempted it, because he wished to draw attention to himself at any cost, and because his financial position was almost desperate. Of two things, one would assuredly happen: he would be tried in some superior court and his name would be on every Frenchman's lips; or if Louis Philippe was still frightened of untoward revelations with regard to the influence of the Napoleonic legend, as he had been in 1836, he would send Louis Napoleon out of the country once more with a decent sum of money. 3. The appointment of Thiers as chief of the Provisional Government meant nothing in the event of Louis Napoleon's success. That appointment could be rescinded at the first convenient opportunity; for even as early as 1840, Louis Napoleon had no intention of affording Thiers the smallest chance of reducing to practice in his (Louis Napoleon's) case, the formula Thiers had invented in order to lord it over Louis Philippe: "The king reigns, but does not govern." The notes of these conversations bear no particular dates, only the years in which they took place are mentioned. Those to which I am referring just now more especially are labelled 1853, hence a few months after Thiers' return from exile; at which time the Empire was settling down to its new position, and when, as some critics might remark, "the Emperor could afford to pretend to be wise after the event." That Napoleon III. pretended to no such wisdom, that he would not have intrusted Thiers with a portfolio at no matter what period of his presidential or imperial career will be sufficiently patent from the following fact. During the Odilon-Barrot Ministry, the opposition of Thiers became so utterly unbearable that the Premier had him and several members of his faction summoned to the Elysée, and at the end of the interview proposed that Thiers himself should form a Ministry. Thiers declined the offer and for very good reasons, for after he was gone, the Prince-President turned to Barrot. "Do you imagine, my dear Minister," he said, "that if M. Thiers had taken you at your word and consented to accept a portfolio, I would have consented to intrust him with one? If you entertained such an idea for a single moment, you must have been strangely mistaken in me."

No; a thousand times no; Louis Napoleon never for one single instant mistook Thiers' character or intentions. He knew the value of Thiers' agitation in favour of the removal of his uncle's remains from St. Helena to Paris, which agitation was coincident with the publication of the *History of the Consulate and the Empire;* consequently intended as an enormous self-advertisement for the author; he also knew the reasons that had prompted the laying of the trap at Boulogne. If in the face of all this he appointed Thiers the chief of the Provisional Government, it was to meet craft with craft. If the expedition had been successful, the appointment would have been rescinded; the expedition failing as it did, it simply discredited Thiers in the eyes of the adherents of Louis Philippe, for there were letters to prove that Thiers had not been thus appointed without his knowledge or against his will. Louis Napoleon made many mistakes in his life; he never made a mistake with regard to Thiers' potentiality or goodwill to him and his dynasty.

Thiers, on the other hand, made few mistakes from his own point of view, and fewer still in pursuit of the aim of his life which was, as M. Charles Merruau, who knew him better than any one, expressed it, "to found a Conservative Republic and to marry *her* in the capacity of President." But he made a terrible mistake in his estimate of Louis Napoleon's potentiality before and after his election to the Presidency. One single instance among a hundred will bear out my contention. Immediately after the insurrection of June '49, Thiers, frantic with apprehension, ran to his stockbroker, yelling to him, "Sell all my securities." "Leave them alone," said the other quietly; "Napoleon will save you all from spoliation and bankruptcy." "He," exclaimed Thiers, scornfully, "he is too great an imbecile."

This was the man with whom the Prince-President had to contend everywhere, but principally in the Chamber. Was the game an equal one? Yes, and it would have remained an equal one during the Empire if the Emperor had trusted to himself alone. But during '49—'51 the game was absolutely equal, although at the beginning of that period, Louis Napoleon had scarcely an ally in the Chamber. For when Dupin *ainé* and Morny joined the small group of his *apparently* faithful partisans, the game was more than half-won or they would not have joined. They as well as those who completed the victory; Persigny, Fleury, Maupas, Saint-Arnaud, and Dr. Véron shall have a chapter to themselves; for once more, I wish to remind the reader and above all the critics, that I have neither the skill, the energy, the perseverance, the courage, nor the inclination to incorporate all these into one group or *genre* picture. Fortunately for myself and for others, I am aware of my deficiencies in this respect; but I fancy that with the aid of my notes I may succeed now and then in producing a portrait or small scene, after the manner of some of the Dutch, with whom I claim affinity in origin. And it is because of this knowledge of my shortcomings on the one hand, and my confidence on the other, that I would fain avoid the error committed by one of those great Dutchmen whose best-known picture stands close to Rembrandt's masterpiece in the Museum in Amsterdam.

I am alluding to Bartholomew van der Helst, who in his "Civic Guard's Banquet" painted four and twenty distinct and separate masterpieces in the shape of as many portraits, and who to a very considerable extent spoilt the effect of each "severally and jointly," as the lawyers would say, by trying to amalgamate them into one whole. To accomplish such a task successfully, one must be able to ply one's brush like Rembrandt, or one's pen like Motley or Green. In default of such talent on my part, the reader will, perhaps, be content with the "single figure" of General Changarnier, the second of Louis Napoleon's two adversaries who kept playing to the end. It is sketched with the aid of hitherto unpublished notes left to me by eye-witnesses of the contest, at least two of whom were more than ordinarily interested, and unless these notes are utterly misleading, I should be tempted to assign to Changarnier the position of first adversary.

"The other day," says one of these memoranda which only bears the name of the month and the year, February, 1849, "Changarnier allowed the Prince-President the opportunity to make his first bow before the Paris garrison as a general officer of the National Guard. The Prince-President was, of course, too sensible not to take it, for he never shows to greater advantage than when in uniform and on horseback, and he was probably not sorry to show the army that he was something better than the despicable *pékin* Cavaignac's swashbucklers have tried to make him out. I am not in the Prince's confidence with regard to his personal or public policy, but it requires no very astute observer to foresee that within an appreciably short time we shall have a second performance of the 18th Brumaire, only slightly altered from the original, for in the coming version the army will be the "god from the machine," just as it was in the first. There will not be the slightest difficulty in casting the part of Lucien Bonaparte, which will go to Dupin *ainé* and not to Morny, but I am at a loss to guess who is to fill the *rôle* of Generals Bonaparte and Moreau in one. The Prince-President cannot undertake it himself; if he did, failure would be a foregone conclusion, for, though he is not the despicable *pékin* the

Cavaignac party proclaim him to be, the army would assuredly only follow one of their own, and what is more, one of their own with an acquired reputation, not to say a magnificent prestige. Lamoricière and Bedeau are as much out of the question as Cavaignac himself, for there is still the feeling among the Monarchists that the 24th February of last year would have finished differently than it did if Bedeau had wished to nip the revolution in the bud as he could have done. Rightly or wrongly construed, this means that the Monarchists suspect Bedeau of being sympathetic to republicanism, and the general who is to guard the deputies as Moreau guarded the Directory or the Directorate must be free from such suspicion. The Prince-President would be ill-advised indeed to confide his thoughts and intentions to a general about whom he was not perfectly sure. Bugeaud is unquestionably well-disposed and friendly to the Prince-President; it was he who made the sensible suggestion that he should adopt the uniform of a general officer of the National Guard as his official dress, instead of that of a general officer of the regular army which he had a thought of adopting and which would certainly have given umbrage to a great many officers; for the susceptibility of the French Army defies logical analysis. But it is a moot point whether Bugeaud would lend himself to any plot, even if he were fully convinced that

that plot would be beneficial to France. Hence, unless they are going to send to Africa for someone, there only remains Théodule Changarnier; and though the thought seems too ridiculous for words, they may have selected him to act when the time comes. After all, why not? An ass carried Christ into Jerusalem, why should not the warrior whom Bugeaud compared to the packhorse of the Marshal de Saxe carry the nephew to the Imperial throne of his uncle; for that the nephew is going to seat himself eventually on that throne, unless he be killed before or during the attempt, there is not the faintest doubt in my mind, and mine is only the reflex of several millions of minds. Yet, the thought that the Prince-President and above all Persigny could have taken Changarnier into his confidence seems pretty nigh impossible. They could not have been so utterly bereft of their senses; they might just as well have bawled their secret from the top of Notre-Dame, for Changarnier is absolutely incapable of holding his tongue even to save his own life. Some years ago Ingres called him Narcissus and Echo in one.[1] He has

[1] The *Charivari* dubbed him " Bergamotte and Pommadin."

" Changarnier, revenu de la rive africaine,
   A de plus doux exploits exerce son talent,
   Il voudrait voir finir l'ère républicaine,
   Pour briller à la cour en costume galant.
   Mais les eaux de senteur, poudres et bergamottes,
   Ne rendent point la vie à ses charmes défunts,
   Et le guerrier, malgré tous ses parfums,
   N'est pas en bonne odeur auprès des patriotes."

an incurable mania for speechifying and for striking attitudes and for making himself conspicuous which not all the courage in the world—and no one denies his courage—could redeem. He must put in his word; he will not or cannot obey orders silently, which unenviable idiosyncracy earned him the name of the Marshal de Saxe's packhorse. "I fancy I have followed the trade of war long enough to know how to set about it;" he interrupted Marshal Bugeaud one day when the latter was giving him his final instructions for an expedition against the Kabyles. Bugeaud might have ordered him under arrest; but he simply smiled. "That proves nothing, my dear general!" he said. "The Marshal de Saxe had a baggage mule which followed him in all his campaigns, but I never heard that the animal was supposed to understand aught of the Science of Warfare."

"The lesson was entirely lost upon Changarnier, and if the Prince-President has selected him for the part I suggested just now, he must be sorry for it already, in spite of the magnificent manner in which Changarnier managed the Prince's first entrance on the scene. For that first entrance was premature and uncalled for, it has let the cat out of the bag too early, unless events are to follow one another much quicker than I and a great many with me anticipated."

My uncle was mistaken, Louis Napoleon had

made no compact with Changarnier but was
simply allowing him to bluff to his heart's content,
without as much as attempting to see him until he
considered his own hand good enough, and in the
meanwhile not at all dismayed by the constant
boast of Changarnier that every one of his hands
contained a king or a pair of kings. The Prince-
President kept quietly shuffling and cutting the
pack for "fours," having at the same time marked
the "joker" in the shape of Dupin *ainé*. At last
the clever manipulator managed to get his
"fours" in a "rigollot," as the French card-
sharpers call it (anglicé, a plaster), and drew them.
Some historians say they were four knaves, others
compare them to the four sergeants of La
Rochelle, with a better lot in store for them than
Bories and his fellow plotters. I myself simply
call them Saint-Arnaud, Vieyra, Espinasse, and
de Maupas. The *rôles* of three of these have
often been commented on; Vieyra has not had his
meed of notice from the historians, although it
was practically he who prevented the National
Guard from repeating their swaggering of four
and a half years previously. He had been a
captain of that body for a good while. A couple of
days before the *coup d'état* he got his colonelcy-
in-chief on the grand staff vice General Foltz.
On the 2nd December he frustrated all their plans
of foregathering in numbers; had he not done so
there would have been a terrible shock between

them and the regulars, for the latter were neither disposed to fraternize with nor to be made the victims of the civic warriors, as they had been compelled to do by the lukewarmness of their chiefs on the 24th February, 1848. (See *An Englishman in Paris*, vol. i., ch. x.) Nevertheless, rumours of a rising of the National Guard reached the Elysée, and on the morning of the 3rd December Colonel Vieyra was sent for. "They are beating assembly," said Louis Napoleon. "Your Highness is mistaken," replied the Colonel; "they can't beat assembly for every one of their drums was cut early yesterday morning." That was how Vieyra nipped all attempts at swaggering in the bud. Not heroic, perhaps, but clever. "My dear colonel," said the Emperor a couple of years later, "had you failed, you would have had a collar of hemp; as it is, allow me to present you with a collar of silk." And he handed him the grand cross of the Legion of Honour. The last time I saw Colonel Vieyra was during the Exhibition of 1889. He was then eighty-five years old and almost as active as I am now. He died a few months later.

CHAPTER III

When my uncle opined that Dupin *aîné* and not Morny would be cast for Lucien Bonaparte's part in the expected revival of the 18th Brumaire, he did not imply a compliment to Louis Napoleon's half-brother by suspecting him of being less venal than the great lawyer, and therefore less susceptible of being tampered with. He was simply foreseeing, not a difficult thing to do, that in the next Chamber, Dupin would resume the place he had filled for many years with much *éclat*. Both Morny and Dupin were equally venal, and it was probably the only thing they had in common with each other. Morny had a great deal of physical courage—the kind of courage the teaching of which forms part of a French gentleman's education. Dupin was a coward, but with the courage to admit his cowardice. An anecdote of his early life will explain what I mean. His father had narrowly escaped death on the scaffold during the Reign of Terror. Though a staunch Republican, he hailed the advent of the Directory and the Consulate with intense relief, and sent his eldest son to Paris to study law under Tronchet, the same who with Malesherbes had solicited the dangerous honour of defending Louis XVI. at his trial. The stripling—for he was little more—remained absolutely impervious to the seductions and fascinations of the capital, and in six years obtained the highest distinctions his Faculty had to bestow. When complimented on his success, and the perseverance and pluck implied in the achievement, he answered, "I accept the compliment as to my perseverance. I cannot accept it as to my pluck, for it was not pluck but fear that made me accomplish these things. I trembled like an aspen leaf when I beheld the First Consul during the reviews in the Champ de Mars, and said to myself, " The brute will take us all as food for powder. I must escape such a death as that. That is why I studied so hard." Original, if pusillanimous, is it not? In fact, Dupin, as we shall see directly, was original from beginning to end—original even in his venality; Morny was not original at all. The half-brother of Louis Napoleon played his part in the *coup d'état*, the importance of which part has been much exaggerated, through the force of circumstances; Dupin performed his share in the preliminaries to the *coup d'état*, the importance of which share has not been sufficiently insisted on, unconscious, perhaps, of its importance, at any rate in the beginning, but from pure choice afterwards.

I will deal with Morny first; the accident of his birth befriended his necessities, and his necessities prompted the assumption of his *rôle*. Unlike Persigny, Morny had not even the faith that moves mountains, nor the generosity that hides such want of faith. But for his knowledge that he had gone too far either to serve the Republic or the Orleanist dynasty again, he would have retired from his position at the eleventh hour. As it was, he tried to induce Louis Napoleon to do so by informing him that he had secured a retreat for both before it was too late. "What if you should fail?" he is reported to have said, according to Persigny, who was present at the interview. "We shall not fail," replied the latter ; "but if we do, you need only concern yourself with the arrangements for our funerals, unless you would like to take your share of this." "This" was a small packet wrapt in white paper which he took from his pocket. "It's poison," said Persigny quietly, "and of the deadliest, and if you mean to use it, you had better secure your dose now, for it is doubtful whether you will be with the Prince and myself to the last. I will not stir from his side, happen what may." Morny shook his head with a supercilious smile. "I am not fond of such violent measures," he answered. The supremest comfort Morny could think of for his half-brother when he left him shortly before midnight on the 1st December, 1851, was this:

"Whatever happens within the next few hours, you are sure to have a sentry at your door when you awake to-morrow morning." The episode of the packet of poison remained an absolute secret between the Prince, Persigny, and Morny until several years after the establishment of the Empire, at which time Persigny told one of my grand-uncles of it under the following circumstances. Persigny had at Chamarande a dog to which he was greatly attached. Though not very old, the animal fell ill, and in spite of the vet.'s careful treatment seemed to suffer much. It would take neither food nor physic from any one's hand but Persigny's. At last its death was decided on. "I poisoned it myself," said Persigny, when telling the tale. "I poisoned it myself, with one of the three doses of poison I had had in my possession since the middle of 1851. They were originally intended for the Emperor, myself, and a person I need not name, in the event of our failure." (In the note relating to this conversation, my uncle insists, with how much justification I know not, that the unnamed person was Miss Howard, afterwards Comtesse de Beauregard.) "On the 30th November, 1851, I offered that third dose to Morny, who tried to shake the Prince-President's courage by telling him that he had secured a safe retreat for him if matters should go wrong, in fact, almost persuaded him to avail himself of the retreat before matters did go wrong. Morny refused to have recourse to such desperate measures. I had forgotten all about my having the poison, though not the fact of my having bought it, until quite lately. I have still two doses left; they may be useful some day. Who knows? What did the Prince-President say to Morny's refusal of the poison?" Persigny went on, in reply to my uncle's question to that effect. "the Prince-President said nothing but merely smiled, and he has never alluded to the incident up to the present. Though you know the Emperor very well, you evidently do not know this. The Emperor's like or dislike of people is altogether independent of the merits or defects of these people; it is altogether independent of the ascertained or surmised corresponding sentiment with regard to himself on the part of these people. Put it in this way, if you like. Where his affections are concerned, the Emperor plays throughout with gold, though he may feel absolutely convinced that those with whom he plays are staking worthless counters."

Then Persigny apparently went off at a tangent, for he suddenly asked, " Have you ever seen the Emperor and his cousin, Prince Jérôme, together? I do not mean in public, but in private." My uncle admitted that he had not. "You know," said Persigny, "that Napoleon III., like Napoleon I., addresses his near relations in the second person singular when they are by themselves, and that his relations do the same?" "Yes," assented my uncle, "I have heard the Emperor and Princesse Mathilde do it in my presence." "Well," remarked Persigny, "although the Emperor addresses his cousin Jérôme in the second person singular, the latter always answers in the second person plural." "Out of deference, perhaps," suggested my uncle, though he knew better. Persigny laughed outright. "All the respect Jérôme has for the Emperor will go into a very small compass indeed. No, it is not respect on Jérôme's part; it is resentment at a quarrel they had shortly before the advent of the Prince to the Presidency. When Jérôme made his appearance at the Elysée after that, he adopted the less familiar and affectionate form, and he has never departed from it since. The Emperor, who in reality has been a second father to him, continued to address him as before, just as if nothing had happened. If the truth were known, the Emperor still lives in hopes that his cousin will resume the old style, for, I repeat, the Emperor, where his affections are concerned, plays with gold, knowing full well, as he may, that those with whom he plays stake counters. He is not deceived regarding Jérôme's goodwill to himself, to the Empress, and to the little boy just born; he has not forgotten Morny's attempt to discourage him on the eve of the *coup d'état*, but if ever blood was thicker than water it is Louis Napoleon's, and he goes on loving those whom he has loved, and will go on loving them whatever they may do."

It would be idle to pretend that Louis Napoleon cherished such affection for all his allies in the struggle he was waging, or even that he admired them all and attributed their aid to their personal regard for him. Napoleon III.'s character was curiously complex: he could admire without the least respect for the object of his admiration; he could respect without the least admiration for the object of his respect; he could love without the least admiration or respect for the object of his love or liking. One instance will make my meaning clear, it is not at all pertinent to my present subject, but, in virtue of my being a mere gossiper, I claim the right to take my illustrations wherever I find them. Napoleon III., in spite of his scepticism with regard to men, sincerely respected Drouyn de Lhuys, but did not like him; the statesman, on the other hand, was too sterling and upright to respect his sovereign's devious political ways, but he liked him. "Drouyn de Lhuys and I," said the Emperor one day, "we each give away to the other what we are individually most in want of ourselves."

It is very doubtful whether Louis Napoleon ever contemplated enlisting André Marie Dupin among his allies, either before or after his advent to the Presidency. Though virtually a stranger to the soil of France, the Prince knew every man of note on it, and from their past judged how far they could and would be useful to him in the immediate future. There could be no possible mistake in that respect in Dupin's case. Wherever he could do so without absolute risk of liberty and life, young Dupin had shown himself a bitterly hostile opponent to Napoleon I. and his reign. In a *Manual of Roman Law* he had lampooned the great captain as Tiberius while presenting the great captain's victim, the young Duc d'Enghien, under the traits of Germanicus; he had bespattered the fallen giant after his abdication at Fontainebleau, and insulted him during his imprisonment at St. Helena. True, he had also defended Michel Ney against the acrimonious indictment of that other able lawyer Bellart, who, moreover, owed a great deal to Napoleon I. which Dupin did not; but whatever merit might have accrued to him from this act of independence under the Restoration, he spoilt it by his prominent position ten years later among the mourners at Bellart's funeral. Not one but a half-dozen eminent men openly reproached him with his political apostasy. "You do not seem to understand that the defenders of Michel Ney were longing to hear the *De Profundis* recited over his executioners," he replied, and evidently considered the epigram sufficient to condone as well as to explain his insult to the memory of the martyred victim of one of the foulest crimes perpetrated under the pretext of dynastic necessity.

Dupin's belief in the omnipotence of epigram, as a moral veneer for political as well as other immorality, was to a great extent justified by his thorough knowledge of and his supreme contempt for the majority of his countrymen, and especially for those actively engaged in politics. He knew that in France one well delivered epigram is sufficient to start a man on a prosperous career, sufficient to hurl the man at whom it is levelled from the pedestal he has climbed with infinite trouble and perseverance. And seeing that he had not his equal in the facility for coining them, not even in Talleyrand, that his peer in that respect, Rivarol, had been in his grave since the beginning of the century, Dupin had never been very sparing of them. From that moment, however, he began to sow them broadcast, taking care not to hide his light under a bushel, for modesty was not Dupin's besetting sin. Rather than plead and not be reported, he refused to plead at all, which in fact, he did when asked to defend Béranger a third time. Of course, he did not say so in as many words, but no one was his dupe, because every one was aware that, as an exceptional measure, the Government intended to exclude reporters from the trial. Nevertheless, almost every one thought it perfectly natural that Dupin should not care to waste his truly marvellous epigrammatical and histrionic talent on empty benches and even without a chance of having them conveyed second hand to the public who were so eager for them; so that when in 1832 he was elected to the Presidency of the Chamber of Deputies the public took care that he should have no cause of complaint on that score. They flocked to the Palais-Bourbon as their successors flock to the Académie at the reception of a new member, and they were invariably better rewarded for their journey than the latter. They flocked to the Palais-Bourbon as the cultured Parisians of to-day flock to the Comédie-Française, to roll on their mental palates the epigrams of Dumas *fils* and Edouard Pailleron, sublimely indifferent to the goodness or badness of the cause on which those epigrams are expended. Dupin spared neither friends nor foes. When seated in the presidential chair, perched atop of that storied platform, and with that deep-toned silver bell in front of him, he had only subjects for vivisection, whose mental sores he laid bare with one deft turn of his scalpel. The patient might be in the opposite political camp or in his own, the epigram when on the tip of Dupin's tongue had to find vent. It fact, it is difficult to determine to which party Dupin belonged, for he lashed them all in turns. Like Thiers, he is a political acrostic. Thiers' whole spells "personal ambition," Dupin's "rapacity." His average income at the bar during the Restoration was about 80,000 francs, an enormous sum in those days, never exceeded at that time by the most brilliant legal luminaries, Berryer included. But Berryer had the improvident habit of remitting part of his clients' fees now and then; nay, in one instance, remitted the whole of such a fee lest a client's daughter, whose dowry had been swallowed up in her father's lawsuit, should go husbandless. Dupin exacted his to the uttermost farthing and was not always satisfied then, as the Napoleonic generals whom he defended under the Restoration and the three Englishmen who helped Lavalette to escape, could have testified. Earning, as he did, 80,000 francs per annum, it was but natural that he should have refused elevation to the Bench under the Restoration at half that stipend, but no sooner had Louis Philippe ascended the throne than he accepted a procurator-generalship. It would, he knew, pave the way to the Presidency of the Chamber with a salary of 100,000 francs; and the functions would, moreover, leave him free to resume his practice at the bar, as did M. Jules Grévy forty years later on. For nearly eight years, Dupin filled the presidential chair, and he would have probably filled it till the end of Louis Philippe's reign but for a combination between Thiers and Molé, both of whom had got tired of his repeated onslaughts, and by their tactics prevented his reelection at the opening of the session of 1840. Molé in his fall dragged Dupin with him.

This was the man who after an interval of ten years was chosen once more to direct the debates in the Chamber of Deputies, and whom the would-be historians of the *coup d'état* have unanimously left in the background. It is because these writers, even M. de Maupas, whose work I translated myself, have not had the unenviable but nevertheless salutary advantage of attending for days and days during several years the proceedings at the Palais-Bourbon, and that, therefore, they do not know and fail to guess what a President of the Chamber may and often will do in the pseudo-exercise of his legitimate duties. I have had that advantage, and do not hesitate to say that a President of the French Chamber can mar or make a ministry even more effectually than the majority which supports such a ministry. Although I had never seen Dupin at work, I felt convinced the moment I read the innumerable anecdotes and heard the absolutely unpublished stories about him that as "an artisan" of the *coup d'état* he ought to rank next to Persigny and even before Fleury, which is not saying little as the reader will find directly. It matters little or nothing to my present purpose that his share of the work was performed unconsciously, or, if not unconsciously, against his own inclination, at any rate at the beginning of Louis Napoleon's presidency; for I feel almost certain that not for one instant did he then harbour the thought or desire of smoothing the latter's road to the imperial throne. That he did smooth it is incontestable, and that is why I have dwelt at such great length on him, although the writing of his biography would have been attractive to me under any circumstances. He, a professed Republican—for after Louis Philippe's fall he resumed that appellation once more—made the Republic, its parliamentary adherents, its ministers, and for that matter the whole of the legislature, ridiculous in the eyes of France; and ridicule kills in France, "especially when directed against a civilian," as Louis Napoleon himself admitted. By making the Republic ridiculous, he bred the wish in the minds of Frenchmen to have done with the *régime*. That was, roughly speaking, his share in the preparations for the *coup d'état*.

How he did it must be told in as few words as possible, for I have already outrun the space originally intended for Dupin. One day the Protestant Minister, Athanasius Coquerel, was trying to prove that the Republican system was based on the Gospel. "Nonsense," exclaimed Dupin. "I have yet to learn that Christ said 'My republic is not of this world.'" On another occasion, Victor Schoelcher, who only died a couple of years ago, having said in the course of one of his speeches "We enjoy the happiness of living under a Republic," he was violently interrupted by the members of the Right. Astonished, the speaker turned to the President for an explanation. It came at once. "No one is questioning the fact of the Republic; they are only contesting the fact of the happiness," remarked Dupin. "Persigny is no doubt the author of the *coup d'état*," said the Emperor to my uncle when the news of Dupin's death came (1865); "yet, but for Dupin, there would have been a difficulty in performing the piece; he discredited the rival authors and their companies, and finally shut up their theatre."[1]

Napoleon III. was right; Persigny was virtually the sole author of the *coup d'état*. That his

[1] In my various conversations with M. de Maupas and others, I have never been able to ascertain with any degree of satisfaction to myself whether Dupin's attitude in the early morning of the 2nd December, 1851, was a carefully rehearsed one or forced upon him by the knowledge of his powerlessness to resist the troops that had invaded the Palais-Bourbon. All my interlocutors, but especially Maupas, always turned the subject. Nevertheless, from evidence gathered from other and entirely disinterested quarters, I am of opinion that Dupin knew what was going to happen. While Baze and Leflô were arrested and led away, Dupin was left unmolested in his apartments at the Palais-Bourbon, nay, free to roam about. When, a few hours later, about three score of Deputies managed to effect an entrance to the House, owing to an oversight of Espinasse and Saint-Arnaud, and asked Dupin to preside over their sitting, he declined and wished them good morning. Maupas scarcely devotes half a dozen lines to his share in the proceedings; the fact remains that after the establishment of the Empire, he was on very friendly terms with the Emperor. What was his reward? Not the mere public one of a senatorship with its 20,000 or 30,000 frs. per annum, but a substantial private one, I feel convinced.

name has been cast into the shadow by that of
the principal actor of his piece is due to the fact
that the actor was perhaps greater as an actor
than the author as an author. The same thing
has happened on the stage with the authors of
Our American Cousin, *Rip van Winkle*, *Adrienne
Lecouvreur*, *L'Auberge des Adrets;* in fact in all
cases where the interpreter's genius surpassed
that of the playwright. But, however great the
author, if his piece be a spectacular one, like the
coup d'état, he must in addition to his principal
interpreter or interpreters, have various stage-
managers, and notably able editors and journalists
who, the editors and journalists, will, without
revealing the actual plot of the play, gently
stimulate the interest of the public until the play
be ready to stir the public into enthusiasm or
disgust. Cavour found his stage-managers in
La Marmora and Cialdini, his editors and journalists almost everywhere; Bismarck had von Roon
and Moltke to rely upon in the one capacity,
and a score of eminent men throughout the
Fatherland to propagate his views by means of
the printing press. Journalists and captains
were virtually ready to Cavour's and Bismarck's
hands. Cavour and Bismarck bore honoured
and historic names which inspired confidence;
their collaborateurs offered themselves. Persigny
had no ancestry to boast of, and his name was
only known in connection with two miscarried

adventures and to a small minority. It is doubtful whether his name inspired any confidence at all. Yet, in spite of these drawbacks, he found two men of inestimable value to his undertaking, or to speak by the card, he at once guessed their capabilities when chance or design threw them across his path. I am referring to Dr. Véron and Colonel (afterwards General) Fleury.

I doubt whether the former's name is known, at any rate in connection with the political events preceding the Second Empire, to one out of every thousand Americans or Englishmen. I doubt whether that of the latter is more than a name to one out of every hundred; yet both these men contributed powerfully to Louis Napoleon's elevation to the throne; but unlike Dupin's, their support was given consciously and with a full knowledge of what might be the result. Emile Fleury was absolutely disinterested in the matter, but he had an innate sense of the fitness of things, and considered that a king should enact the king, a usurper have the daring, the lawlessness and grandeur of a usurper. Louis Philippe, it must not be forgotten, was as much of a usurper as Louis Napoleon, but he lacked the daring, lawlessness and grandeur of a usurper. His fall from the throne was not a fall, but a tumble. He himself was probably too old to head a struggle for his crown, but his four sons were all in the prime of life, and not one stretched forth a hand to save that crown, if not for their septuagenarian father, at any rate for their ten-year-old nephew. That this tame submission to the will of the mob was profoundly distasteful to the whole of the French army there can be not the slightest doubt, albeit that the contempt for the mob and the disapproval of the princes' tameness manifested themselves at the time and subsequently in very different ways. Here is a practically unknown story from the lips of General Talandier, the same to whom I referred in the first chapter, as having stemmed, when but a colonel, the tide of insurrection on the occasion of Louis Napoleon's attempt at Strasburg. "Fleury," said the general, when alluding to the former's share in the *coup d'état*, "well, Fleury felt what most of us did, that it was no use fighting for those who would not fight for themselves. That most of us were of that opinion I could prove to you by a dozen instances. One, however, will do. During the month of February, '48, I commanded the 4th Brigade, which was quartered at the Ecole Militaire. When I learnt the news of Louis Philippe's departure, I sent for the seven colonels under my orders, for there were three regiments of the line, three of cavalry, and a battery of artillery. I proposed to gather up our little army and to take up a position at Passy and to bring back the king if possible. All but one colonel refused."

And we must bear in mind that this was before the Duc d'Aumale's want of action became known. The enthusiastic co-operation of the army in the *coup d'état* requires no other explanation than that. All the tales of the fabulous sums of money given on the eve of it to Morny, Maupas, and Saint-Arnaud—to the latter especially, as bribes for the army—are so many fabrications. To begin with, the army did not want bribing, and least of all the garrisons in and around Paris. Apart from the magic influence of the name of Napoleon, to which I have already alluded, and to which I shall have to allude again directly, the army had grievances of its own to avenge on the people. The defeats of their predecessors in the Revolution of 1830 and the defeats of their fellow-soldiers in the Revolution of '48—defeats attributable to no fault of theirs—were rankling in their minds. Their subsequent victories in June '48 and June '49 were not of a kind to efface the humiliating recollections of those defeats. If the truth were known, they were all but too eager to try conclusions with the turbulent scum of Paris, and especially with the National Guard. Secondly, if bribery with money had been necessary, Louis Napoleon could not have done it, for he had not the wherewithal. I have more than one impartial authority (Maupas' evidence might be suspected) for my positive statement that the sum of money in the possession of Louis Napoleon at 10.30 P.M. on the 1st December '51 did not exceed 65,000 frs., 50,000 of which had only arrived two or three days before from England, with a polite but very firmly worded intimation: "This will be the last remittance under existing circumstances." The real significance of the sentence quoted I have explained elsewhere;[1] with regard to my statement that the 50,000 frs. were nearly the whole of Louis Napoleon's resources, I have no less an authority than that of the late Baron James de Rothschild, on whose bank the draft from London, and made payable to Persigny, was drawn. At least such is my reading of a note in my uncle's handwriting and relating to a conversation on the subject with Baron James. My uncles frequently called on him,[2] and though, of course a busy man, he was rarely too busy to decline chatting for a little while on matters not pertinent to their call. It was during one of these chats that Baron James delivered himself of the following, but I have no clue to the origin of the topic. "All these cock-and-bull stories about the wholesale bribing of the Paris garrison on the day of the *coup d'état* would be vastly amusing, if they did not undermine the respect of the soldier for his officers—consequently, discipline. Some one in authority should give them a flat contradiction once for all. The

---

[1] *An Englishman in Paris*, vol. ii. chap. iii.
[2] *My Paris Note-Book*, p. 4.

Emperor cannot do it for many reasons; besides, no one would believe him if he did. I could do it, but people would believe me even less than the Emperor, and yet I could give them proof positive for what I might state, for I know almost to a few thousand francs how much money Louis Napoleon had in his possession on the night of the 1st December. He received 50,000 frs. from England two days before, I saw the draft ten minutes after it had been presented and I do not believe he had another 20,000 frs. to save his life. Where could he have got the money from? Miss Howard had given all she had to give; Princesse Mathilde had stripped herself of every bit of available property, portable or otherwise long before that. From the Bank of France, which it is said, advanced him ever so many millions, or to put it correctly, was compelled by him to advance these millions in return for some privilege? He had no privilege to give, and people might just as well say that we advanced him the money. Nay, the latter hypothesis would sound more plausible, for we, at any rate, could have done as we liked without consulting any one; the Bank of France could not have done so, for the Republicans kept a strict watch upon every one likely to be useful to the Prince-President. He had not even the power to transfer a horse from the stables of St. Cloud to his own. I have an English groom in my service who was at St. Cloud during the three years of the Presidency. One day Louis Napoleon visited the stables in company with an Englishman, and the stud-groom, also an Englishman, trotted out a splendid chestnut to show them. 'Send that horse to me in Paris,' said the President. 'I can't do that, sir,' replied the man respectfully; 'the horse belongs to the Republic.' I am giving you the story in the very words used to me. Besides, if the Prince had all these millions of the Bank of France in his cash-box—some say it was five, others ten—why should he have wanted that miserable 50,000 francs from London? for although the draft was made payable to Persigny, there is no doubt that the money was intended for Louis Napoleon."

No, the army did not want bribing. After three years of constant contact with the heir of Napoleon I., it was ready to do any and everything at that heir's bidding, seeing that only a month after his advent to the Elysée, on the day mentioned in the note about Changarnier, the mere sight of him had aroused the troops' enthusiastic cries of "Vive l'Empereur!" Their co-operation was a foregone conclusion from that day forward, but it wanted intelligent organizing and intelligent leading, and some of the officers had to be shown that Louis Napoleon was not such a "vile civilian" as Cavaignac and his partisans had tried to make him out; not such a "melancholy parrot" as Changarnier delighted in calling him when he found the melancholy parrot developing a tendency to utter sentences other than those he had tried to drum into him.

The task of proving to the army that this vile civilian and melancholy parrot was "a gentleman from the crown of his head to the sole of his foot, and every inch a king," as Lord Normanby, an enemy, said of him, devolved upon Colonel Fleury. Fleury did more than that. It is no exaggeration to say that from the beginning of '49 till the beginning of '52 he was the virtual Minister for War, no matter who was the holder of the portfolio nominally; or to put it in the pertinent words of Persigny, than whom no man was more anxious to acknowledge the services rendered by Fleury, "he was the Minister for the Civil War we foresaw as the result of the Prince's action." It was Fleury, who during these three years selected the regiments to be successively quartered in Paris, and sent them back to the provinces thoroughly imbued with the idea that the imperial *régime* was the best for the physical welfare of the army at home, for its prestige both at home and abroad; it was Fleury who pointed out the officers for promotion, and recruited Saint-Arnaud and Magnan in Algeria, a by no means easy task in spite of the feeling of discontent generally prevalent at the last public act of Louis Philippe's fourth son. Truly, the sudden departure of the Duc d'Aumale, his quiet resignation of the governor-generalship of the colony without his striking one blow for the recovery of his father's throne had bred universal dissatisfaction among the officers in Africa, but the recollection of the Duc's splendid courage and leadership remained; and though the officers had withdrawn their allegiance from him, they were, perhaps, not quite prepared to transfer it at a moment's notice to an " individual "—the term is not mine—of whom in spite of the glamour of his name, they knew comparatively nothing, who had, moreover, been systematically vilified by the two immediate successors to the Duc, namely Changarnier and Cavaignac. This feeling of hostility to Louis Napoleon in the African contingent of the French army only wore off by degrees; as late as 1852, there were still some slight traces of it left [1]; for the Prince-President could not counteract it there by the charm of his personal presence. Fleury, however, was not only a valiant soldier and a thorough man of the world, but a far from despicable organiser, and what was better still, a skilful diplomatist. Even Thiers had to admit this, though reluctantly, after his journey to St. Petersburg at the end of 1870, when Fleury had vacated his post of ambassador only a few months. Alexander II. not only referred constantly to Fleury's diplomatic capacities, but almost plainly hinted that if a sense

[1] See my *Paris Note-Book*, p. 313.

of a soldier's duty had not compelled Fleury's departure, the sequel to Sedan might have been different from what it was. To the outside world of '48, however, Colonel Emile Fleury was nothing more than a brilliant, dashing officer with a splendid record for personal valour, but not otherwise distinguished from a host of similarly endowed African campaigners, except for a greater fund of amiability and an utter absence of buckram, brusqueness and conceit. It is doubtful whether the newly elected President of the Republic chose Major Fleury—he was only a major then—as a member of his military household for any but his social qualities. Fleury was a *viveur*, so was Louis Napoleon. Fleury was fond of woman's society, Louis Napoleon was too fond of it. Fleury was a constant visitor to the green room of the Comédie Française and other theatres. Louis Napoleon, while an exile in London, was frequently seen at the wings, especially when there was a pretty actress in the cast. "It appears, *commandant*, that you go behind the scenes," said the President shortly after his accession when a discussion arose about the prosperity of the House of Molière. "You must have some one to represent you worthily, Monseigneur," was Fleury's ready answer.

But beneath the jovial and apparently careless *bon-vivant*, Persigny had detected the sterling clever emissary necessary to his purpose. It was

Fleury who went to enlist Saint-Arnaud, but Persigny had probably pointed him out. The men who helped to make the *coup d'état* were all, with the exception of one (Dupin), without fear, for Morny, though refusing to take the dose of poison offered to him by Persigny, had given proofs of his courage on the battle-field; only Fleury was without reproach. "One cannot force a cathedral door with a toothpick, and in a fight, provided one knocks one's adversary down, the ledger of the National Debt (*le grand livre*) is as good as a Bible," said the Emperor one day when referring to those who had helped him. I have written the sentence in English, but it was delivered half in English, half in French. It was a habit of Louis Napoleon to use two and sometimes three languages in as many sentences. "I do not like my thoughts to sit fretting at home because they do not happen to have the exact clothes to go out in"; he remarked on another occasion, in explanation of this habit. Persigny knew all about Saint-Arnaud without having been told. Both men had led a chequered career. Saint-Arnaud, though belonging to a very good family, had been a commercial traveller, an actor, a fencing-master, and Heaven knows what else besides, before he entered the army a second time. Persigny had followed many occupations, and none for very long, after he exchanged the dragoon's uniform for the dress of the St.

Simoniens and the latter garb for that of everyday life. Saint-Arnaud and Persigny had no doubt met at some period of their lives, but it would not have done for a simple civilian to sound a general of brigade and Knight Commander of the Legion of Honour on so dangerous a subject as that of his co-operation in the *coup d'état*. So Persigny sent Fleury, whom, as a negotiator, he knew to be immeasurably superior to himself. "I can send Fleury into a quagmire of intrigue with a pair of dancing-pumps on; he will come back as clean as a new pin and with the object I want; Persigny with his jack-boots would get up to his waist in the mud and bring back the object utterly unfit for use. It is because the one would have made the journey with his eyes and ears wide open; the other with his eyes fixed on the sky watching for visions and only listening to the promptings of his own fealty and loyalty to me. Fleury always spoke and acted like the envoy of a Cæsar; Persigny, in spite of himself, conveyed the impression of his having been sent by a Catiline. Intrinsically there may not be much difference between the motives of these two, but history says there is, and history often spells 'prejudice.'" This was Louis Napoleon's estimate of the respective characters of his two principal collaborateurs.

None of the precautions so essential in the case

of Saint-Arnaud were needed in that of Dr. Louis
Véron. At that time, Dr. Véron was the proprietor of the *Constitutionnel*, and what was better
still, from the Prince-President's view, the sole
arbiter of its policy. The influence of the
Constitutionnel itself can best be measured by a
couple of sentences from Lamartine with regard
to it. "The Republic has produced nothing
better in the way of a daily paper. The *Constitutionnel* is a clan of men of wit encamped one day
on the Boulevard, the next in the Rue de Rivoli,
watching the Revolution as it passes by, and looking at men and things with the smile of dilettanti
and through an opera-glass." The chieftain's
name had long before that become a household
word with the Parisians, and Paris then as now
dictated to the rest of France. There had
been proprietors of nostrums before Dr. Louis
Véron, but never such a one as he; there is not a
single device in the way of advertising resorted to
by the present vendors of patent medicines that
was not suggested by him. The genius for booming his wares, himself and those whom he wished
to befriend, he brought to bear on the management
of the *Revue de Paris* and on the direction of the
Opéra, though with different results. The periodical was a comparative failure, simply because
the public were not quite ripe for exceedingly good
literature of a lighter kind, in monthly doses;
secondly, because there sprang up in the mind, if

not in the heart of Dr. Véron himself, a formidable rival for his affections, namely, the opera, which in the course of five years he raised to a pitch of prosperity such as it had never attained before nor has attained since. Dr. Véron ought to have been a happy man and have clung to the Muse that virtually made him a prominent figure, by the side of such celebrities as Meyerbeer and Scribe, Auber and Adam, Hugo, Balzac and Dumas, with whom, of course, no one attempted or pretended to compare him intellectually, but with whom, nevertheless, he associated on a footing of social equality; basking as far as the public was concerned, in the reflected glory of their fame. That however was not sufficient for him. Though he commanded social distinction long before similar distinction was accorded to great operatic impresarios in other lands, he flung operatic management to the winds to become a factor in politics. He was bitten by the mania which in those days gripped some of the most brilliant luminaries of the literary firmament, Lamartine, Hugo, Dumas, Sue, &c., &c. Unfortunately he chose to make his political *début* under the guidance of Thiers; in other words, he bought the *Constitutionnel* and made Thiers its master, and Thiers rewarded him as he had always rewarded, and rewarded to the end, all those who made themselves the stepping-stones to his ambition; with ingratitude and promises which were not only never realised, but never intended to be realised.

It must not for one moment be supposed that Dr. Véron sat fretting over his political disappointments. He simply consoled himself for them by making money, for making money was a supreme enjoyment to him. But he was no miser. I knew Dr. Véron personally during the last ten years of his life, and, though too young to judge critically, I remember many acts of his kindness to the poor. Truly, as I remarked elsewhere, he did *not* do good by stealth and blush to find it fame, but he did good for all that. My uncles were frequent visitors at his house, for though he had relinquished the active profession of a surgeon almost at the outset of his career, he was fond of the society of his former colleagues and proud of his medical degree. I never saw Lord Brougham in the flesh, but whenever I come across a portrait of the eminent English statesman, my thoughts always wander back to Dr. Véron. I dare say the likeness exists to a great extent in my imagination. I have never tested it by putting their portraits side by side. I doubt, however, whether the two men had much in common mentally and morally, except their overweening vanity. Lord Brougham, I have been told, often made himself ridiculous in private life; I feel certain that Dr. Véron rarely if ever did either in private or in public. Long before he flung Thiers overboard he must have known that the latter was furthering his own political ambition and none but his own, by means of the *Constitutionnel,* but until Véron felt himself capable of personally navigating the ship, and until he had sighted the America of his own ambition, he submitted to Thiers' whimsical dictatorship.

That moment of independent action struck shortly after the advent of Louis Napoleon to the Presidency, to which advent the *Constitutionnel* had contributed at the instigation of Thiers. He had made up his mind to be Louis Napoleon's successor at the expiration of the latter's four years of office, the period provided for by the new Constitution. In order to prove this, I append one of the Emperor's remarks on the subject to my uncle. "Shortly after my election to the Presidency, Thiers asked me one morning what official costume I was going to adopt, and when he heard that I was wavering between the uniform of a general of division and that of a general of the National Guard, he said, after a few moments, 'Take my advice, adopt neither the one nor the other. I feel convinced that the nation will be delighted to see its *civic* chief magistrate adopt civilian dress. Besides, if you were to adopt a military costume, your successor might be awkwardly situated if he could not do the same.' It was telling me in so many words," concluded the Emperor, "'I'll be succeeding you in four years, and I cannot very well put myself in a general's uniform.'" All these designs of Thiers were knocked on the head one day by an article in the *Constitutionnel*, entitled "Two Dictatorships." It was written by the father of M. Paul de Cassagnac, and simply announced that the *Constitutionnel* had gone over with arms and baggage to Thiers' enemy.

By that time the paper had already an enormous circulation—of course for the France of that day. Véron increased it still further by grouping around him all the literary men of note. He did more. He instituted a daily dinner at his house and a weekly gala one, both of which became the active centres of the propaganda of the Napoleonic cause. In the course of these chapters I shall be enabled to show the influence of the drama, music, and pictorial art on the history of France; I need therefore not insist upon it here. In fact, except M. de Maupas, not one of Louis Napoleon's *collaborateurs* has ever denied Véron's share in the *coup d'état;* and much as I owe to Napoleon III.'s Minister of Police, I feel bound to say that his evidence is tainted with jealousy. M. de Maupas never reconciled himself to the fact that there were ten thousand men in France who could have given the Prince-President the same intelligent co-operation he gave, and that chance befriended him in being selected for the task. There were not a half-dozen Vérons. General Magnan, assuredly more clever as a soldier than was M. de Maupas as a prefect of police, never advanced such pretensions of being unique in his way. Colonel de Béville, who performed his share in the affair with a tact, determination and skill equal to those of General Magnan, was as modest as he. The undercurrents of the Second Empire, on the threshold of which we now stand, will show that save Fleury, not a single one of Louis Napoleon's henchmen was capable of improving what he had helped to create, and least of all among them M. de Maupas. But, like Louis Napoleon, I also must change my dress while preparing to enter the Tuileries. Henceforth, at any rate for a considerable time to come, I accept the part of Court chronicler; not a slavishly blind one, the reader may feel assured. Like Latour, the famous eighteenth-century pastelist, I will endeavour to be impartial alike to master and servants. If at the end the master should still stand out as a great though very faulty man, it will be because the servants were faulty without having an atom of his greatness.

CHAPTER IV

AMONG the notes written by my elder granduncle within the twelvemonth preceding his death, I find the following: "We went to see the arrival of Alexander II. at the Northern Railway, and while waiting on the platform, caught a glimpse of the Emperor. At that distance he looked ill and careworn—more careworn than ill. I feel convinced that among that chosen gathering within, and that vast crowd without, the station, there were not two men feeling more wretched than the Czar of all the Russias and the Emperor of the French, whom to honour these crowds had assembled. But I fancy that the Emperor feels even more wretched than the Czar, for although they both know that they may at any moment become the victims of assassins, the latter is borne up by the knowledge of being hemmed in by a serried phalanx of blindly devoted friends, while the former is painfully aware of being surrounded by envy and intrigue. 'I can count the friends who would sacrifice their lives for me on the fingers of one hand, and still have two fingers left to snap at my enemies,' the Emperor said the other day in a tone of bravado which, however did not deceive me or himself as to its underlying bitterness. I think the Emperor is mistaken in the number of those who would fight for him as long as they had a drop of blood left. Conneau and Rouher, and half-a-dozen others I could name, would stand by him, like Fleury, Persigny, and Princesse Mathilde, no matter what happened. At the same time, there is no doubt that since Mocquard's death[1] he feels more acutely than he did before the envy and constant antagonism of which he is the object on the part of Jérôme. Mocquard was the only one who could manage that cur (*ce chien hargneux*), for he was his equal in knowledge, and did not mind flinging his knowledge over-

---

[1] François Mocquard was Louis Napoleon's private secretary from the moment the latter became a candidate for the Presidency until his (Mocquard's) death. My grand-uncle's estimate of his mental attainments was somewhat exaggerated; for though a very talented lawyer and a clever literary man, he was *not*, intellectually, Prince Jérôme's equal. My uncles' partiality was due to their sincere friendship for Mocquard, who was a constant guest at our home, and whom I liked almost as well as did my uncles. The origin of these three men's attachment to each other was their common and fervent admiration of Queen Hortense, and their unbounded sympathy with her third son. I am under the impression that the substance of a great many of my uncles' notes relating to things absolutely unknown even to the Emperor's immediate *entourage*, was communicated by Mocquard, though I have no absolute evidence to that effect. I shall avail myself frequently of them, especially in this chapter.

board to come to close quarters with him physically. If Mocquard had had his way, he would have made an end of him seventeen years ago, and Louis Napoleon would have been rid of the most cowardly and at the same time most unscrupulous enemy he had had in his life." The last sentence of this note must be taken literally, for it is an absolute fact that on the morning of the 7th of December, 1851, hence on the Sunday after the *coup d'état*, Mocquard would have shot down Plon-Plon like a mad dog if the Prince-President had not placed himself in front of his cousin at the risk of his own life. The incident is absolutely unknown, but I have chapter and verse for what I state. The Prince-President was very indignant, and ordered Mocquard to apologise. Mocquard not only refused to do so, but turned on his heel and left the room. When Plon-Plon was gone, the Prince went to Mocquard and repeated his order—" unless," he added, " you can give me a valid reason for this utterly unprovoked attack." " I will neither apologise nor give you a reason, Monseigneur," replied Mocquard firmly ; " sooner than do either, I would leave you and the Elysée for ever. But mark this, the time will come when you will be sorry for my miscarried attempt." The Prince did not insist, and to the day of his death he never knew what had goaded Mocquard into that apparently unprovoked assault. Mocquard himself kept the secret of it for many years, but at the time of Plon-Plon's marriage with Victor Emmanuel's daughter he told it to my grand-uncle, and after the above particulars, gave him the reason for the attack; pledging him to secrecy only with regard to it, and not with regard to the cause. " I meant to kill him," said Mocquard, "and have been sorry ever since that I did not succeed. From the Tuesday till the Friday morning (December 2—5, 1851), he was seen everywhere except at the Elysée, by the side of the cousin to whom he already owed so much. When I say everywhere, I mean among the adversaries of the Prince. And when, on that Friday morning all further resistance seemed obviously hopeless even to the most determined of the Prince's adversaries, Plon-Plon girded his loins for another effort. He actually went to the offices of the *Presse*, and in conjunction with Emile de Girardin drew up a kind of manifesto inciting people to further revolt. While the matter was being put in type, Plon-Plon waited in an adjoining room. He was correcting the proofs when two members of Girardin's staff came in and told him that the army was master of the situation. Thereupon Girardin informed them of what was being done in the next room, and before he had ceased speaking, Plon-Plon came in, proofs in hand. ' Then you mean to say,' he exclaimed angrily, ' that you accept the whole affair as an accomplished fact—that you decline to sign this protest?' 'And you,' was the counter-question of one of the new-comers, 'and you, will you sign the protest?' 'That's different, my position forbids me doing so.' 'In that case,' remarked Girardin quietly, taking the proofs from Plon-Plon's hands, 'in that case, there is no need for these proofs, for I was under the impression that you were going to sign at the head of us all.' Saying which, he tore up the proofs and flung the pieces into the waste-paper basket. I have got them in my possession with the corrections and two additional sentences in Plon-Plon's handwriting. I have had them since the evening of that day. It does not matter how I got them. I pasted the pieces together, and keep them under lock and key."

The suppression of that one fact could have made but little difference to Louis Napoleon's estimate of Plon-Plon's character, nor did it. The Prince knew that his cousin and his uncle would shrink from nothing to gain their ends—namely, the imperial crown for the former—and the knowledge embittered his life from the moment he set foot in the Tuileries. Until then his life had been perfectly safe from their attacks, for they had nothing to gain by his death and everything to lose. It is generally supposed that the new Emperor endeavoured to surround himself with the *noblesse* of the old *régime* from a feeling of vanity, and for the purpose of conciliating that *noblesse*. Nothing is further from the truth, at any rate, while the Emperor was a bachelor. To begin with, Napoleon III. was the least vain of all men in this respect; if anything, his vanity lay the other way; he prided himself upon being a parvenu among the crowned heads of Europe, and somewhat ostentatiously applied the epithet to himself. Secondly, he felt convinced that no amount of favour and goodwill shown to a fraction of the Faubourg St. Germain would insure him either the political or social countenance of the rest. But he thoroughly agreed with the axiom of Napoleon I., "Qu'il n'y a que la noblesse qui sache servir," and he wished to take his Mamelucks, his Roustans, from among them. "I believe in my star, but I am afraid of the satellites," he said one day to my uncle, shortly after he had taken up his residence at the Tuileries. My uncle endeavoured to talk him out of it, albeit that he himself believed the fear to be justified, and then the Emperor told him a story, which if invented by a Palais-Royal farce-writer would stamp that writer as one of the greatest masters of his craft, though at the same time the public might object that their credulity had been put to too severe a test.

"You remember," said the Emperor, "that on the 2nd December [1852] I removed to the Tuileries for good and that there was a State dinner in the evening. Nor need I remind you of the debt of gratitude I owe to my cousin the Princesse Mathilde. Well, I considered it my duty to acknowledge that debt semi-publicly, and took the opportunity of doing so that night. Through an oversight of the reporters, the papers reproduced the spirit, perhaps, though not the substance of my words. I took her in to dinner, and before we sat down, I said, loud enough to be heard by everybody, ' My dear Mathilde, for the present your place is on my right hand ; when you vacate it, it will be to take the one still nearer to my heart.' The papers had it, ' My dear Mathilde, you will take the first position here, on my right hand until there is an empress.' In reality, there was not a pin to choose between the significance of the two sentences. The moment I had spoken the words, I noticed a scowl on my uncle's face, and during the whole of the dinner, he scarcely addressed a syllable to me, and answered me gruffly when I spoke to him. Next morning, Fleury came in as usual, before I had seen any one, for Mocquard had nothing special to communicate to me that day. I have always considered a few minutes' chat with Fleury as a stimulant to help me through with the business of the day. Fleury has got a tell-tale face, and the moment I looked at him, I knew that something funny had happened. ' Funny, indeed, sire,' he said, in answer to my remark ;

'I doubt, however, whether your Majesty will think it as funny as I do. Your Majesty's uncle has been simply foaming at the mouth since last night, and goes about yelling that you have no business to marry, that such a marriage would interfere with his son's rights. Just before he left, he held forth to me for about ten minutes. I was under the impression at first that he was joking, but I assure your Majesty that he was terribly in earnest. At last I succeeded in putting in a word. "But assuredly," I said, "your Majesty does not expect the Emperor to remain single all the days of his life?" "That's just what I do expect," he shrieked; "for my nephew is as much fit to marry as were Louis XIII., Louis XVI., and Peter III. of Russia." With this he turned on his heel, leaving me absolutely breathless with astonishment. I did not know whether to laugh or to be indignant; but laughter got the upper hand, for I may frankly confess that the idea of comparing your Majesty as a would-be husband with the somewhat physically deficient spouses of Anne of Austria, Sophie of Anhalt-Zerbst, and Marie-Antoinette was too much for my risible nerves. I stood absolutely roaring with laughter in the middle of the room. Since then, I have been thinking what a capital comedy the idea would make, if properly worked out and the scene laid among the aristocracy, or better still, among the wealthier middle classes. Just imagine, sire, the havoc that might be wrought by a man, a comparatively young man, like your Majesty, whose heirs, for purposes of their own, had spread the report that he was "a saint *malgré lui*," he being all the while "a jovial sinner *par conviction*"; just fancy a man going about with the reputation of a Louis XIII., and the appetites of that monarch's father and that monarch's son rolled into one.'

"Thus far the Emperor's remarks," says this lengthy note. "The most curious part of the whole affair, though, is this. The Emperor seemed entirely ignorant of the sequel to his uncle's contemptible aspersions, and I had not the courage to enlighten him, lest I should still further endanger the already sufficiently strained relations between the ex-King of Westphalia and the head of the family. Fleury's conception of the play to be founded on the subject was partly realized in a prologue a few days after its communication to the Emperor. I was dining with Véron on the 6th December in the company of Velpeau, Ricord, Tardieu and Trousseau, when Véron happened to say that the sooner the Emperor got married, the better it would be for the welfare of the country and the stability of the dynasty. Including our host, we were nine at table; four of us, myself among the number, cordially agreed with Dr. Véron, but our four eminent colleagues kept absolutely silent, and apparently by common consent. This was the more remarkable, inasmuch as the subject had been started quite spontaneously. Nor were they seated together, and they had certainly not discussed the matter between their arrival and our sitting down to dinner. Their silence was so puzzling that Dr. Véron appealed directly to Velpeau. 'What is your opinion, cher maitre?' he asked. 'Ma foi,' was the answer, 'I am reluctant to give an opinion. The Emperor's marriage would undoubtedly be beneficial to the country and consolidate the dynasty, provided'— and here he paused—' provided it were blessed with children. But will it be so blessed? If I am to believe all I have heard for the last three or four days, it will not be thus blessed, unless'—and here he paused a second time— 'unless the foulest aspersion that has ever been cast upon a man's virility is positively without foundation.' Ricord, Trousseau, and Tardieu had nodded their heads in approval while Velpeau was speaking. To cut the story short, the ex-King of Westphalia's assertion as to his nephew's unfitness for marriage had already reached the ears of the foremost members of the Medical Faculty, and they believed in it."[1]

I am not quite prepared to endorse my uncle's opinion with regard to the Emperor's ignorance

---

[1] Until the birth of the Prince Imperial, the belief was firmly shared by numberless Frenchmen of all classes; and even Bismarck was not proof against it. Those who care to read between the lines of his *Political Correspondence* of 1855 must inevitably come to this conclusion.

of these rumours. On the contrary. In spite of my uncle's assumption of that ignorance, I am inclined to believe that these rumours had reached the Emperor's ear even at the time of the conversation recorded above. Nay, more, I feel convinced that these rumours prompted his marriage with Mdlle. Eugénie de Montijo. I say prompted, not hastened; for every note on the subject in my possession goes to prove that until that moment the idea—mind the mere idea—of placing Mdlle. de Montijo by his side on the imperial throne had not as much as entered his mind. We have heard a good deal about the violent passion of Louis Napoleon for the supremely beautiful Spanish girl from the moment he set eyes on her—which must have been before he was President of the Republic, for they both stayed at adjacent hotels in the Place Vendôme. The passion was no doubt a fact, for Louis Napoleon had always a great amount of love-passion lying idle and only waiting for investment. In that respect he was unlike Goethe and like Jean-Jacques Rousseau. The author of *Wilhelm Meister* was for ever trying to work up a love-passion for an object; the author of *La Nouvelle Héloïse* was for ever endeavouring to find an object for his love-passion. Jean-Jacques, however, contented himself with one investment at a time; Louis Napoleon, on the other hand, had nearly always "a great many irons in the fire." In after years, Bismarck called him a "a crowned Werther"; the appellation *minus* the adjective would have applied to Louis Napoleon throughout his life. The "violent passion" he had conceived for Mdlle. de Montijo did not prevent the conception of an almost equally violent passion for Mdlle. Madeleine Brohan, who shortly before that had made her first appearance at the Comédie Française; while concurrently with the existence of these two passions, the victim suffering from them was "on ne peut mieux" with Rachel, Miss Howard being at that period "la maîtresse en titre." The latter, we may take it, had to be satisfied with the crumbs that fell from the lord's table—unless the board happened to be spread in the provinces, on which occasions she was the sole and therefore principal guest—*et pour cause*—although the entertainment was a secret one. Not so secret, however, as to prevent the particulars of it leaking out and offending the "unco' guid," as was the case during the presidential journey to Tours in 1849. Accommodation had to be found for the already numerous suite of the newly-elected Prince-President, and the house selected for Miss Howard was that of M. André, the Receiver-General, a strict Protestant, whose family and himself were temporarily absent from the capital of Touraine and on a visit to the Pyrenees. M. André considered that his home had been sullied by the presence of "such a woman "—the quotation marks are not mine—and wrote to that effect, winding up his letter as follows: " Have we, then, perchance, gone back to the period when the Mistresses of Kings flaunted their scandals in the various cities of France?" The letter was addressed to the then Prime Minister, Odilon Barrot who, like Thiers, aspired to succeed Louis Napoleon as President of the Second Republic, but who had not the pluck to show it to the man for whom it was really intended. Ferdinand Barrot, his brother, who throughout Louis Napoleon's career was a sincere friend, and had defended him before the Court of Peers after Boulogne, when his elder brother had declined to do so, placed the epistle before the President. The President penned an answer to it, ostensibly in a letter to the Prime Minister himself, but with a request that a copy of it should be forwarded to the uncharitable Receiver-General. I need only quote one sentence from it. After reminding M. André of Christ's words in connection with " the Woman taken in Adultery," the writer went on : " As for myself, I plead guilty to having looked to illicit ties for the affection of which my heart stands in need." Odilon Barrot, who had not had the courage to present the indictment, shirked sending a copy of the defendant's plea to the accuser which, after all, was only one of extenuating circumstances, not a denial of guilt.

The plea itself, however, was a specious one, for

it is no libel on Louis Napoleon's memory to say
that those illicit ties were mostly slip-knots which
now and then, as in the case of Miss Howard,
threatened to become halters. Like François I.
and Henri IV., Louis Napoleon was "entiché de
femmes et de corps et d'esprit;" like François I.
he would, had it been feasible, have roamed the
streets of Paris after dark in search of adventures,
without a sigh of regret for the pomp and splendour
of the Tuileries which from the very beginning were
irksome to him, inasmuch as they interfered with
his theory of "free selection," and with his ideas
of "physical affinities." For we must not deceive
ourselves: love—I cannot, or will not, find another
word—with Louis Napoleon was merely an affair
of the senses; a practical illustration of part of
Chamfort's cynical definition of it—" le contact de
deux épidermes." This is so absolutely true that,
in after years, the lawful spouse could invariably
bring him back from the too ardent pursuit of a
strange goddess by merely adopting the tactics
said to have been adopted by Phryne before the
Areopagus. For this, as for all other things I
may have occasion to state, I can, if necessary,
give chapter and verse.

Louis Napoleon, then, as I have said, would have
liked to roam the streets of Paris after dark in
search of adventures. Of course, as the Emperor
of the French, or even as President of the Republic,
such perambulations in the fairly-well lighted

thoroughfares of the capital were impossible ; but during his short stay there in 1831 when he was altogether unknown by sight to the Parisians, he could indulge in his mania to his heart's content. Like François I., Louis Napoleon did not care whether the woman who attracted his attention was a duchess or a dairymaid, provided she came up to the standard of beauty he had in his own mind! If anything, he preferred *la bourgeoise* and *la grisette*—there were *grisettes* in those days—for " all women yield through curiosity rather than from passion, and the courtship of a man of the world is a novelty to the woman of the middle and lower classes," he said on one occasion. It was his mother's dictum, when Queen of Holland : " in the eyes of the *bourgeois* there is no such a being as an ugly duchess," applied to the female members of that section of society. " Since our French dandies have begun to dress and to behave like grooms, in imitation of the English aristocracy," he said, years later on, " our *grandes dames* no longer elope with their grooms ; there is not sufficient contrast between them and their husbands.' There was a considerable deal of method in Louis Napoleon's amorous madness. Now and again, though, and the method notwithstanding, it led him into terrible scrapes, as we shall perceive throughout these pages. It led him into terrible scrapes, just as Napoleon I.'s amorous propensities would have done, if he had not constantly acted upon a maxim of his own coining, to the effect that "Love is the occupation of the idler, the diversion of the warrior, and a danger to the sovereign."

In 1831 Louis Napoleon, in spite of his preoccupations about the French throne, was virtually an idler—a *flâneur*—though evidently not the kind of *flâneur* so tersely described by Balzac, the *flâneur* whose apparently idle lounging is a science, viz. the gastronomy of the eyes. For it is very doubtful whether the *flâneur* proper as distinct from the literary man and painter would have attempted to cultivate that science in the Quartier Mouffetard and round about the Place Maubert sixty-five years ago, when that neighbourhood was even less savoury than it is now. And yet it was to that unsavoury neighbourhood that the twenty-three-year-old Prince repaired nightly for more than a month before the disturbance on the Place Vendôme (May 5th, 1831); it was in a thieves' den that he spent most of his time while Louis Philippe, who had given him and his mother permission to stay for a short period in Paris, was under the impression that he was ill in bed, although Casimir-Perier (the grandfather of the late President of the Republic) knew better; for he had given orders to the Prefect of Police not to lose sight of Hortense's son. Young Louis Napoleon was arrested on the 7th or 8th of May, and conveyed to Sainte-Pélagie. That much is certain, for Raspail, the eminent savant, saw him there and gave a description of his mode of life. But the particulars of this arrest never fully transpired; beyond the fact that the Prince was *not* arrested at home, the outer world knows nothing up to the present day, and but for the following note, I should have been just as ignorant. Whether I have read the note aright or not is a question I dare scarcely decide for myself.

"The news of Eugène Sue's death reached here a couple of days ago, and of course, the papers are full of biographical articles and reminiscences. In spite of all these, I question whether more than a dozen people are personally affected by his disappearance. But Véron, whom I met yesterday, was decidedly upset, albeit that the cause of his emotion is, to say the least, curious. 'To think,' he said in a subdued tone, 'that not one person in a thousand will give Sue a second thought after he, the individual, has read the articles about him. And yet it seems but yesterday that the whole of France was ringing with his name, that people were absolutely frantic to know what he ate and drank, how he dressed and spent his time. If such is the case with a man of his talents, what will it be with men of less talent, but who, nevertheless, have also tried to benefit their fellow-creatures?' And he pulled a very doleful face, at which I burst out laughing, for I could plainly see that he was thinking of his own posthumous reputation. He evidently read my thoughts, for he smiled. 'Ah, well,' he remarked, 'we all have our little weaknesses.' Then he suddenly added, 'I wonder what the Emperor thinks?' 'The Emperor?' I repeated in surprise; 'the Emperor has no need to regret or to mourn for Eugène Sue, for Sue certainly did not behave in a friendly way to him. Even if Sue's republican convictions were as strong as he represented them to be, which I doubt, he ought to have remained silent at the *coup d'état.*'[1] 'I was not thinking about that,' replied Véron; 'I was wondering how he takes the death of the novelist who immortalised him as Prince Rodolphe in *Les Mystères de Paris.*' I stood staring at him. 'I see, you do not understand,' he said. 'Come along, and I will tell you.' We sat down at Tortoni's, and then he told me that when Louis Napoleon was arrested in May,

---

[1] My uncle was right. Eugène Sue was the godson of Louis-Napoleon's mother and of her brother, Eugène de Beauharnais, whose Christian name he subsequently took, although it was not given to him at his baptism. The fact of his being the godson of some of Louis Napoleon's relations ought to have imposed a certain reserve with regard to the Prince, even if his, Sue's, socialistic tendencies, Republican opinions, and sympathy with the poor had been less suspected, and justly suspected, than they were. (See *An Englishman in Paris*, vol. I. ch. II.) Even the people in whose interest he professed to act made fun of him when he became a candidate for a seat in the Chamber of Deputies. But on the strength of his two great novels, Sue determined to pose as a benefactor to suffering humanity, although he himself had not the least intention of assuming such a *rôle* when he began *Les Mystères de Paris*. Accordingly, when on the 2nd December, 1851, Morny placed his

1831, he was not only *not* arrested at home, but that he wore a blouse and a cloth cap at the time. 'To the best of my belief,' Véron went on, 'it was on the outskirts of the Quartier Mouffetard, but of that I will not be certain, for Sue, who told me, was not certain himself.' 'Then it was Sue who told you?' I asked. 'How did he know?' 'That I cannot tell you, I do not know; but I am under the impression that he got the story at the time from ex-Queen Hortense herself.' I remembered that in spite of Sue's tuft-hunting in the Faubourg St. Germain in the early thirties, he went to see his godmother once or twice; it was not quite so clear to me why Queen Hortense should have told him the particulars of her son's arrest, and I pointed this out to Véron. 'The same thought struck me, and I can only account for it in one way,' replied Véron. 'Part of the story was sure to leak out—these things always do; for when Louis Napoleon was transferred from the Palais de Justice to Sainte-Pélagie, he still wore

name on the list of Deputies to be arrested, and when the President put his pen through the name, Sue, still determined to enact the victim, voluntarily constituted himself a prisoner at the Fort de Vanves. When the "Bill of Exile" was promulgated, he was again disappointed, for the President had effaced his name a second time. Sue professed himself offended at this clemency, and went into exile of his own accord. As may be seen from all this, Louis Napoleon remembered that Sue was his mother's godson, Sue did not. Louis Napoleon's behaviour in this instance bears out the words of Persigny, quoted in a previous chapter, namely, that Louis Napoleon gave his affection to people irrespective of its being returned or not.

the clothes in which he was taken. The officials of the prison must have seen the Prince in them, and they had no incentive to hold their tongue. Queen Hortense, I need scarcely tell you, was too clever not to have anticipated this; so in order to explain her son's disguise, and to find at the same time a colourable excuse for his constant excursions to the Quartier Mouffetard, she invented the story of his having gone there to get materials for his contemplated studies on pauperism. I feel certain that at the time Sue himself was taken in by the story, and when ten years later, *i.e.* after the publication of the opening chapters of of *Les Mystères* in the *Débats*, M. Considérant, the editor of *La Démocratic Pacifique*, gave him, as it were, the cue as to the aim of his novel, he took the hint, and made Rodolphe a philanthropist, a redresser of wrongs, and so forth. Honestly speaking, I do not believe for one moment that Sue started his novel with such an idea. He no doubt recollected the incident of the Prince's arrest, and from the very outset had the Prince in his mind's eye when sketching Rodolphe, but that was all. Nor do I believe that the Prince went to the Quartier Mouffetard for philanthropic purposes. Some years ago—it must have been shortly after the attempt at Boulogne—I went twice to the Quartier Mouffetard. It was during the trial of Prince Louis, and the illustrated papers, in spite of the prohibition of the Government, published several more or less striking portraits of her. It was Canler who took me there, and at our second visit he stopped to speak to a woman of about twenty-eight or thirty, who, in spite of the evident traces of debauch, was still very handsome. Suddenly he took from his pocket the portrait of Prince Louis, and, after having torn off the line at the bottom, showed it to her. 'Do you know this young man?' he asked. The woman's eyes positively started from their sockets. 'Mais oui, je le connais,' she gasped; 'c'est mon amoureux; il n'est donc pas mort? Oh, comme je voudrais le revoir.' 'Ce n'est pas lui,' said Canler softly; 'c'est quelqu'un qui lui ressemble. Votre amoureux est mort en prison.' That same night Canler told me how years before he had discovered accidentally that this was the woman who had attracted Louis Napoleon to the Quartier Mouffetard in '31."[1]

I have given this long note for many reasons, irrespective of its interest as an item in the history of fiction. I wished to prove by something more than mere assertion that in at least one respect Louis Napoleon was like François I., *i.e.*, in the fascination the latter exercised over women.

[1] Canler published some interesting memoirs in the sixties; but the incident related above is not so much as mentioned. It could be said, though, that Canler was not only an ardent Imperialist, but a sincere admirer of Louis Napoleon personally, and who, probably considered it more loyal to hold his pen. At the same time I feel convinced that Dr. Véron, who had no reason to dislike the Emperor, did not invent the incident.

Moreover, the note, coupled with the utterances of the Prince immediately preceding it, will convey a fair idea of his moral estimate of the female sex in general. To the full as ill-favoured by nature as Mirabeau, Louis Napoleon had been just as successful with women, and in many instances with women of standing in society. At the very moment when Mdlle. de Montijo appeared on the scene, a woman was to a certain extent supplying the first sinews for the war the guerdon of which was to be the imperial crown of France. And, in spite of all that has been said, Miss Howard was neither born in a garret nor bred in a kitchen. She may not have been a gentlewoman by birth and breeding in the best acceptation of the word; but she was by no means the utterly vulgar, ignorant, and debased creature people have tried to make her out. She was the courtesan *de grande facture et de grande allure*, not highly educated, perhaps, but with a natural charm and tact that made up for the lack of education. Great statesmen did not hesitate to solicit her help when Louis Napoleon even as President became inaccessible to them; great statesmen's emissaries did not consider it superfluous to sound her with regard to the new Emperor's opinions on very weighty measures. If my statements on these points are challenged, I will give proofs which it will be difficult indeed to controvert. She had hosts of wealthy admirers, and was possessed of considerable means. She sacrificed both admirers and means for the man who had accosted her one night as she was leaving a friend's house, just as he had accosted the girl belonging to the dregs of the Paris population. The sum she lent Louis Napoleon was far short of the legendary eight millions of francs, but it amounted to more than £40,000. And let it be remembered that, by Miss Howard's own admission not one cent of that money was borrowed or lent under a promise of marriage, although the contrary has been so often asserted as to make one tired of contradicting it. Miss Howard was too sensible a woman to have ever fostered such a hope. In her bitterest denunciations of Louis Napoleon she never taxed him with having deceived her in this way. "The awkward, sallow-faced, lank-haired adventurer was as much a hero to her as was the Moor to Brabantio's daughter," said Alexandre Dumas the elder one day. "But here the likeness ceased," he added, "for Miss Howard was not a Desdemona; hence she did not see the necessity of eloping with or marrying her hero in order to make him all her own. When I say 'to make him all her own,' I am speaking figuratively; she knew his habitual inconstancy too well. Nevertheless she loved her 'Poléon' as ardently as Desdemona loved Othello."

Louis Napoleon, though not a vain man, was

well aware of the passion he had inspired. His previous as well as actual love affairs—the use of the plural is necessary—must, moreover, have convinced him that his powers of fascination were not on the wane. What more natural, in his case, than that he should wish to test them on the young Spanish girl whom accident had thrown across his path, and who was unquestionably one of the most beautiful women of her time.

Says La Fontaine:

> Filles de sang royal ne se déclarent guères
> Tout se passe dans leur cœur, ce qui les fasche bien,
> Car elles sont de chair ainsi que les bergères.

If ever a man knew these three lines by heart, and felt inclined to act upon the strong hint conveyed in them, it was assuredly Louis Napoleon. Besides, he was, above all, a thorough worldling, and as such may have entertained a strong suspicion that it was not altogether accident that had thrown Mdlle. de Montijo across his path, but that in view of his well-known susceptibility to woman's charms, she wished to try her powers upon him. Frankly speaking, Mdlle. de Montijo's surroundings would have warranted the suspicion. There is a French proverb which bids men to beware of the young girl whose cradle has been a travelling trunk, and whose finishing school a *table d'hôte*. Though still very young when Louis Napoleon first met her, Mdlle. de Montijo had already travelled a good deal; the best hotels in the larger capitals of Europe had sheltered her and her mother within their walls, at a time when young girls of her station and of her faith were generally entrusted to the care of some religious sisterhood to fit them for their future social duties. The fame of her beauty had spread through many lands; she rarely appeared anywhere without a throng of admirers, but she might have said, with Esther Eccles in *Caste*, "There is not a husband among them"; for though many aspired to the pleasure of her society, none aspired to the honour of her hand. Her elder sister had married a descendant of the Duc de Berwick, for whom the ancient dukedom of Alva had been revived. "The Duc d'Albe is a lucky man," said an *habitué* of the greenroom of the Comédie Française to Augustine Brohan, when discussing the marriage. "Very lucky indeed," was the answer, "for the Comtesse de Montijo might have made him marry both her daughters by a special dispensation of the Pope." "But that would be impossible, mademoiselle."

Nothing is impossible to Madame la Comtesse de Montijo where the happiness of her daughters is concerned." "Yes, I am told she is a very clever woman, and that she has travelled a good deal." "Yes, and never without her samples. She is like the mother of the Gracchi, always showing her jewels, and Prosper Mérimée has been deputed to furnish a fresh description of their virtues every now and again. He ought to be able to do it. He knows the mine where they were found."

The celebrated actress was perhaps more outspoken than the majority of her contemporaries, either male or female; at the same time, there is no doubt that her words embodied the opinion of that majority with regard to the matrimonial scheming of these two. The author of *Colomba* and *Carmen* was even then strongly suspected of dictating the replies to the numerous affectionate epistles received by Mdlle. de Montijo, and especially to those addressed to her by Louis Napoleon; for not her most ardent admirers pretended that the mantle of Mme. de Sevigné could have fallen on her, but it was reserved for her imperial husband to find the suspicion fully confirmed. The blow came in the shape of a letter on the occasion of the Empress's first visit to Scotland after her marriage. These visits were frequently repeated, and we shall see the reason why as we proceed. It was not a love-letter that caused the disenchantment, it was, perhaps, the reverse of a love-letter, but oh, what a falling off in style was there!

Nevertheless, it was not the great display of wit in her correspondence nor the conspicuous absence of it from her conversation that prevented Mdlle. de Montijo's admirers from taking a decisive step.

Unlike the body, a woman's mind need not be clothed in the most brilliant raiment in order to produce a lasting impression. Mdlle. de Montijo frightened her admirers by her lack of mental simplicity. To see a girl assume the *rôles* of Lydia Languish, Becky Sharp, and Lady Teazle —as Miss Ada Rehan reads the latter part—in the space of twenty-four hours is apt to breed misgivings in the mind of a man intent on matrimony and not on *marivaudage*,[1] however young and deeply smitten he may be. If, in addition to this, the parts are invariably over-acted, the misgivings are apt to develop into something more positive. The girl who poisons herself in despair at an ill-requited passion is an object of admiration and pity; the girl who for similar reasons attempts to poison herself with a bottle of blacking, "because," by her own confession, "she was in too great a hurry to get something more effectual," becomes an object of laughter. "But," observed a cynic who heard the story, "it would have taken her less time to die from strychnine or prussic acid; the time lost going to the chemist's could have been made up in that way, apart from the disagreeably gastronomic experiment of swallowing blacking and of having her soul mistaken for that of a nigger. Perhaps she does not mind having her soul mistaken for that of a nigger. She may have been reading

---

[1] It means "superfine flirting" after the style of the comedies of Marivaux, who excelled in portraying that kind of courtship.

that story about a nigger's deathbed that appeared lately in *The National Era* at Washington."[1] And if after that pseudo-heroic attempt at self-destruction "for love's sake," she had only shown herself a little more considerate for the feelings of those who happened to love her, the attempt would probably have been set down to the romantic freak of a somewhat "too emancipated girl." But no such consideration was ever shown by her, as the following story, which is one out of a dozen, will show.

In those days, the railway to within a mile or so of Chantilly had just been opened and caused a great influx of female visitors from Paris, who until then had abstained from going, owing to the scarcity of comfortable accommodation and the difficulty of returning on the same day. But there was still a journey of between three and four miles to the racecourse, and the supply of hackney vehicles at the arrival of trains was never equal to the demand. Under these conditions the provident among the males took care to engage a conveyance beforehand. One of Mdlle. de Montijo's most sincere admirers—in fact, the only sincere one, and who would probably have set prejudice with regard to her at defiance by an offer of marriage—had made such provision. But when the damsel arrived, escorted as usual by a bodyguard of elegant *viveurs*, she and they took

---

[1] The speaker was not an American but an Englishman—Lord Hertford.

possession of the vehicle without as much as saying "by your leave." There was just one seat left when the lady espied the Count de Galva—for whom the blacking had been swallowed. Overjoyed at seeing him once more, she offered him the vacant seat, regardless of the claims of the purveyor of the conveyance, who, too well bred to show his annoyance, pretended to look upon this as a joke, and in a spirit of bravado kept up with the vehicle on foot. Count de Galva remonstrated with Mdlle. de Montijo; the remonstrance did not prevent her from offering the vacant seat to a second favourite on the return journey. The sincere admirer did not run by its side this time; he never spoke to her again. "That carriage," he said, years after, for he only died in '84, "that carriage ought to have been bought by Wilhelm I. as the carriage of Napoleon I. was bought by Madame Tussaud; without it there might not have been an Empress Eugénie; without an Empress Eugénie there would probably have been no Franco-German War; without a Franco-German War there would have been no German Empire."

There is no doubt that this and other stories reached Louis Napoleon's ear, and yet no hint seems to have been given to Mdlle. de Montijo to be more reserved in her intercourse with the *jeunesse dorée*, although she was already then a frequent guest at the Presidential entertainments;

for it is very certain that after the episode just related the flirtations went on as strongly as ever. This alone would prove that Louis Napoleon had not the faintest intention of making the handsome Spanish girl his wife either in the near or remote future. Nay, to speak frankly, the presumption is that he intended to make her the reverse of his wife. From the frequent allusions in his conversations, we may take it that Louis Napoleon knew his history of France by heart, and no part of it so thoroughly as its *chronique galante*. From personal experience he knew that there were dozens of Mesdames de Nesle and Mesdames Poisson about and scores of Mesdemoiselles de Nesle to realise their mothers' schemes. He was neither as handsome nor yet as powerful as Louis XV., but he may have paraphrased his mother's dictum once more to himself, and concluded, "Qu'il n'y a pas de laid monarque pour une aventurière." The Countess de Montijo and her daughter had persistently disregarded the last of the three precepts laid down by Beaumarchais for woman's guidance;[1] they had failed to command consideration, and if Louis Napoleon looked upon Mdlle. de Montijo in the light of a consort at all, it was in the light of a consort *de la main gauche* and not *de la main droite*. If proof of this were wanted, it would be found in the fact of his

---

[1] Here are the three precepts, "*Sois belle si tu peux, sage si tu veux, mais sois considérée, il le faut.*"

having as good as solicited the hand of several royal princesses during the period—the twelve months immediately preceding his marriage—when he was supposed, and not unjustly, to be simply frantically in love with Mdlle. de Montijo. Cælebs in search of a wife was nothing to it. The Dowager Duchess of Baden (Stéphanie de Beauharnais), the Duke of Leuchtenberg (another relation on his mother's side), and Don Francis d'Assisi (the husband of Isabella of Spain) were successively but fruitlessly appealed to by him to provide him with a spouse. Finally, just a month before the public announcement of the Emperor's betrothal to Mdlle. Eugénie de Montijo, he applied to Prince Hohenlohe for the hand of Princess Adelaide, and a week later the Queen and Prince Albert were still discussing a letter from Prince Hohenlohe on the subject. The new Emperor's offer was kept a profound secret at the time, at the urgent request of Prince Hohenlohe himself, who feared that the prospect of being Empress of the French might prove too dazzling for his daughter, while he, her father, was in no way fascinated by it. From his point of view the proposed union was not desirable; he had misgivings about the settlements, and objected, moreover, on the grounds of religion and morals. The Queen herself, with that truly womanly charity that credits the reformed rake with the best of conjugal intentions, did not oppose the alliance, although, with a kind of prophetic instinct, she alluded feelingly to the fate of Marie-Antoinette and her successors on the throne of France. Prince Albert tried hard not to let his personal dislike of Louis Napoleon influence his counsel— a dislike, by the by, he shared with nearly all the Coburgs.[1]

After all this, what becomes of the stories of the over-mastering passion of Louis Napoleon for Mdlle. de Montijo, and of his plighted troth to her? The stories are virtually true; yet, I repeat, up till the beginning of January, 1853, the Emperor had not the least intention of making her his wife. Had his request for Princess Adelaide's hand, or for that matter, for any princess's hand, been accepted, he would have simply broken his pledge, and substantial compensation would have been forthcoming—that is, if Mdlle. de Montijo, *faute de mieux*, had not accepted the position of a La Vallière, qualifying meanwhile for that of a Pompadour; for Louis Napoleon was like Louis XV. rather than like Philippe

[1] Want of space prevents my giving all the particulars of this affair, which for many, many years afterwards were only known to a half-dozen persons at the outside, namely, the Queen, Prince Albert, Napoleon III., Prince Hohenlohe, Lord Palmerston, and Walewski, who had sounded Palmerston on the subject. It was Palmerston who suggested the Emperor's letter to Prince Hohenlohe. Walewski, who was a friend of Dr. Véron, at whose house he once lost 96,000 francs at a single game of lansquenet, told his host, and the latter told my uncle. I feel almost convinced that the whole truth is not even known now, except to the Queen. As

d'Orléans, and would not have said, "Je ne donne pas d'audience sur l'oreiller."

As it was, the announcement caused a panic, though not an unforeseen one, for the Emperor's *entourage* had been, if not consulted, at least apprised of his intention. That *entourage* was, as we shall see in the next chapter, heterogeneous to a degree; yet, dissimilar as were all these men in taste, birth, breeding, and disposition, all but one disapproved of "this *in extremis* matrimonial choice"—the expression is not mine. To all of which objections the Emperor, *faisant bonne mine à mauvais jeu*, and with commendable chivalry to his betrothed, replied: "Quand on a sous la main ce que l'on aime, ce n'est pas la peine d'aller chercher ce que l'on n'aime pas." "The Emperor is right," said Dupin—the only one who approved, though reservedly, the choice—"the Emperor acts more sensibly in marrying the woman he likes than in eating humble pie to

---

for my statement about the dislike of the Coburgs of Napoleon III., it is not founded on hearsay only. Leopold I. of Belgium disliked him heartily, and for very good reasons. Duke Ernest, Prince Albert's brother, hinted very plainly in his *Memoirs* that Louis Napoleon was a coward, which was not a fact. Duke Ernest was a guest at the Tuileries on the 14th January, 1858, and was present at the Opera when the Emperor entered his box after Orsini's attempt. The Emperor did certainly not "indulge in incoherent gesticulation from sheer fright"; on the contrary, he was outwardly very calm, but even if he had indulged in such gesticulation, it would have been more courteous on the part of his guest not to have recorded the fact.

some German princelet for his daughter with feet probably as large as mine. At any rate, when the Emperor kisses his wife, it will be from choice and not from compulsion."

The Faubourg St. Germain—*i.e.* the old *noblesse* —made common cause with the Orleanists' salons in their scathing comments. They conveniently overlooked the fact that they were the descendants of the most corrupt society the world had seen since the Roman Empire, so corrupt that before the Revolution the fact of having a Frenchwoman among his ancestors disqualified a man for investiture with the knighthood of one of the Teutonic orders. There was no attempt at investigation, the fact itself was deemed a conclusive proof that plebeian blood had been introduced. Prince Puckler-Muskau, who had a French mother was debarred from entering the Knights-Templars on that account. The Faubourg St. Honoré—the *noblesse* of the First Empire—also forgot their own origin. The bourgeoisie of the Chaussée d'Antin was more disgusted still, and in its comments hit the Faubourg St. Honoré smartly on the head, though perhaps unwittingly. They in reality considered it a slight that the Emperor had not chosen one of their daughters. "Eugénie de Montijo is after all the granddaughter of a trader like ourselves. One of our girls would have done as well. The First

Empire was built up with the blood of stable lads, coopers' 'prentices, and what not. The Second Empire might have done worse than take a little of the blood a cut above that of the stable lads, &c." The Faubourg St. Antoine would have applauded such a step; though they would, in spite of their democratic prejudices, have preferred a daughter of the old *noblesse*. In default of a foreign princess, they would have preferred a Frenchwoman of no matter what class, and they jeered at that part of the Emperor's manifesto which described Mdlle. de Montijo "as being French at heart." The bourgeois Voltairien jeered at another allusion in that proclamation—viz., "the virtues of Josephine." "It is a strange present to put into a girl's *trousseau*," he said, but perhaps they can only afford one shift, and they have given her a Nessus-shirt, which will not come off.

When it came to selecting the Empress's future household, the difficulties were still greater; the Faubourg St. Germain as well as the Faubourg St. Honoré declined the honour of a position at Court for their womankind. The Emperor quoted Ovid. "Ardua molimur; sed nulla nisi ardua virtus," and paraphrased Juvenal in reference to a lady who declined in a somewhat offensive way. Her own reputation was not altogether spotless. "Ardeat ipsa licet, tormentis gaudet amantis" is the correct quotation. Napoleon made it "Ardeat ipsa licet, ibidines aliarum juvant."

Not that the Emperor was bent upon the rigidly virtuous woman, but he was perforce obliged to make advances to her. With what result will be apparent in the next chapter.

CHAPTER V

"During the week that passed between the public announcement of the Emperor's forthcoming marriage with Mdlle. de Montijo and the celebration of the marriage itself, civilised Europe simply went mad with excitement, and the whole of this excitement was virtually transmitted to Paris like a telegraphic message." This sentence was written less than six weeks after the event, and on the writer's return from a dinner party at the Tuileries. It forms part of one of the notes given to me by M. de Maupas, shortly after I had translated his *Story of the Coup d'État*, and I have every reason to believe that their author was an English nobleman—I repeat, an English nobleman, and not a commoner, so it could not have been Mr. (afterwards Sir) Richard Wallace. If I were even more certain of his identity than I am, I should feel compelled to withhold his name; this much I may however point out to my past as well as future critics that, in spite of all their efforts, and they were assuredly many, they have never been able to convict me of a false statement with regard to the main facts contained in either of my previous books, and I doubt if they will be more successful in the present instance. I will now return to the note in question which proceeds as follows.

"The excitement has not abated ; if anything, it appears to be on the increase, and especially is this the case with the immediate *entourage* of the Imperial couple. The whole of to-night's entertainment looked to me unreal, something like a banqueting scene of an opera, and I should not have been surprised to find the capon under my knife to consist of cardboard and my 'goblet of sparkling wine' 'full of emptiness,' with a rim of cotton-wool to represent the foam of the champagne 'that was not there.' I fancy, moreover, that this feeling of unreality, which obtruded itself on me at intervals, exists permanently among the majority of the new Imperial household, and is not altogether absent from the minds of the Emperor and Empress themselves, although they play their *rôles* with consummate skill and ease, especially the Empress ; but the marvellous self-control of both is calculated to deceive every one except perhaps those who, like myself, are constantly on the watch. Different is it with the majority of their chamberlains, courtiers, servants, though not with the *dames d'honneur*. In spite of the former's phenomenal *aplomb* and their irreproachable *tenue*, they 'give themselves away' more frequently than the latter, for the slightest noise seems to startle them, and they are constantly glancing at the doors and behind them, as if expecting some sudden catastrophe which will fling them back into the humdrum existence from which they have just emerged, or worse. ' *Mon ami,*' said Vély Pasha, to whom I communicated this impression ; '*Mon ami,* you are right, and I may compliment you on your powers of imagination which enable you to enter into their feelings. To me, or to a Russian[1] of my age, that kind of look presents nothing unusual ; it is the kind of haunted look which you may notice on the face of nearly every Turkish or Russian Court official after a more or less successful palace-revolution, when he expects at any moment the doors of the apartment to be flung open and a company of soldiers to lay hands on him and his fellow guests. In a few months from now this look will gradually disappear, especially if the more cordial recognition of *le fait accompli* or of *les faits accomplis,* both of the Empire and the marriage, be forthcoming from the Courts of Europe. The Emperor is moving heaven and earth to obtain this recognition. Will he succeed ? I fancy

---

[1] Vély Pasha was the then Turkish ambassador to France. He was, I believe, of French extraction, and exceedingly well-informed.

he will. His most formidable opponent at present is King Leopold, who is spreading all kinds of reports about him, some true and others not true, with regard to his warlike intentions. Of course, Leopold is working for his own parish; in other words, he is afraid concerning his own throne, and would, moreover, do a good turn to his nephew, the Comte de Paris. It is Leopold who has been trying for the last twelvemonth to persuade Queen Victoria that the restoration of the French Empire means a perpetual danger to England. It was Leopold who put a spoke into the Emperor's wheel when the latter asked for Princess Adelaide's hand; and Palmerston, in spite of his own cleverness and his dislike of the late Louis Philippe and his family, was unable to checkmate Leopold in that respect. What he did prevent, and will continue to prevent, is the attempt to poison the Queen's mind politically against Louis Napoleon. He found an unexpected ally in Wellington, who, shortly before his death, went to the Queen or sent her word to the effect that though Louis Napoleon might be unscrupulous he would not go to war with England. I know that you do not share either Palmerston's or Wellington's opinion, but you will find that both were right. Whatsoever happens, the Emperor will not go to war with England, and that for various reasons; although I have not the least doubt that a war with England would be popular at any time in France. To begin with, a war with England would mean a naval war, and Louis Napoleon fosters no illusions on the subject of the French navy,[1] even if he could find a plausible pretext for such a war. The only question which the Emperor can take up at present in a hostile spirit is that of the Holy Places, and in that direction the interests of England and France appear for the moment identical. I say appear identical, inasmuch as both England and France would prevent Russia laying hands on Constantinople on the pretext of protecting the Christians in the East. In reality, those among you who suspect the Emperor of a desire for war are not altogether wrong, but they mistake his main motive which is not the aggrandisement of France at the expense of this or that power. What he desires most is a showy, but for all that Platonic alliance, an alliance that will cast a glamour on his newly revived dynasty, or, to be correct, on himself and the Consort whom he has chosen in direct defiance of all tradition. Such an alliance, unfortunately, cannot be contracted

[1] The Emperor could have fostered no illusions on the subject, seeing that a twelvemonth after this conversation—viz., at the outbreak of the Crimean War—Marshal St.-Arnaud had to be conveyed to the scene of operations on a tug, while the Spahis, his particular escort, had to be satisfied with *La Belle Poule*, the vessel that had brought Napoleon's remains from St. Helena more than twenty years before.

à propos de rien, there must be a real or supposed adversary against whom to combine, and accident has befriended him in making Nicholas not only the most convenient enemy, but the sole enemy against whom an advantageous alliance, from the Emperor's own point of view, may be contracted. Just work out the problem for yourself,[1] always bearing in mind that the alliance itself is the thing, and that it must afford not only the greatest number of chances of success from a military standpoint in case of need, but at the same time the greatest

[1] The author of the note did not work out the problem, at any rate not on paper; but it only requires a moment's thought to admit the justice of Vély Pasha's remarks. There were only two European powers to attack at that moment, Austria and Russia. To beard the former on the pretext of freeing Italy from her yoke, as was done in 1859, would have been too dangerous for the home peace of France, for the clergy never mistook the final aim of a free Italy—namely, the occupation of Rome, and the clergy had especially to be reckoned with at the beginning of Napoleon III.'s reign. Besides, a war with Austria would have only given the Court of the Tuileries the advantage of an alliance with the Court of Turin, and Adelaide, Queen of Piedmont, who was an Austrian archduchess, was not sufficiently important to counteract the prejudices of Europe with regard to Mlle. de Montijo and her surroundings, even if she had consented to do so, which is extremely doubtful. To court the alliance of Prussia or Austria in a war against Russia would have been equally futile. Prussia was in those days under the tutelage of Nicholas, whose wife was the sister of the King of Prussia himself and of the heir-presumptive. Queen Elizabeth of Prussia (the wife of Frederick William IV.) would not have paid a visit to the Tuileries; Princess Augusta—afterwards Empress Augusta—would not have been allowed to go, if she had wished. Francis Joseph was a bachelor, and, moreover, under too recent obligations to Russia for her assistance in the suppression of the Hungarian insurrection.

amount of social prestige obtainable. By which I mean that it must provide the most unexceptionable sponsor for himself and the Empress in the face of Europe. If you do work this out for yourself, you cannot fail to come to the conclusion that Queen Victoria is not only the most desirable ally, but, in fact, the only available one. A show of active goodwill on Queen Victoria's part will put an end at once to the equivocal situation of the Imperial couple, it will reverse at once the unspoken sentence of ostracism delivered mentally against the Empress by the female members of the reigning houses of Europe; it will, in fact, be tantamount to a presentation *en règle et en masse* at one of the 'drawing-rooms' at Buckingham Palace of all the adventurers and adventuresses among whom we happen to be seated at this moment."

"I looked closely at Vély Pasha," says the author of the note, "in order to discern how much of all this was thrown out as a bait, and how much of it was founded upon knowledge. Two months ago (December, 1852) I had been told by a friend from London that they considered Louis Napoleon's somewhat too conspicuous concern about the Holy Places and the Latin Christians in the East as fraught with danger to the peace of Europe, and at any rate, as premature. But no motive like that advanced by Vély Pasha had been assigned to it, for the simple reason that a marriage with Mlle. de Montijo was only decided on about the middle of January. Before that time the new Emperor's contemplated action in the matter was attributed to his wish to court favour with the clerical party. The new Empress however is also suspected of decided ultramontane tendencies, and both may be wishing to kill two birds with one stone. Be this as it may, there is no doubt about Vély Pasha's absolutely correct view of the actual situation. Directed against no matter whom, the first war of the Second Empire will be waged for the sake of securing to the Empress a different footing from that which she occupies at present.

"Candidly speaking, the present footing is the reverse of agreeable. The *grandes dames* of the Faubourg St. Germain, to whom the highest positions in the Empress' household were offered, laughed the idea to scorn, as their grandmothers and mothers had done to a certain extent when Napoleon I. made similar overtures to them at his marriage with Marie Louise. Napoleon I. foamed at the mouth, and swore at all those 'belles dames qui font les renchéries et ne veulent pas paraître à ma cour!' and threatened to make them obey.

"He succeeded in a little while, because after all, the daughter of the Hapsburgs was as good as they, and there could be no comment on her past. His nephew, who has his temper under better control, and is less brutal and more witty, simply smiles and makes scathing remarks in the shape of epigrams. 'We ought not to have offered Mme. la Duchesse de . . . the post of dame d'honneur,' the Emperor said about seven weeks ago. 'She is too busy at night to undergo any kind of fatigue in the day.' Another of the refractory dames he called ' une Pénélope à rebours '—*anglicè*, a Penelope who inverts the task of Orestes' wife, 'vu qu'elle defait pendant le jour ce qu'elle a accompli pendant la nuit.' But epigrams, however brilliant, are not calculated to bring about the wished-for *rapprochement* between the women of the Tuileries and those of the Faubourg St. Germain. Some of the male members of the old nobility are showing a tendency to rally round the new *régime*. It will not do, perhaps, to scrutinize their motives too closely. Some are influenced by pecuniary considerations, others by personal ambition.[1]

"But whatever these motives may be, they do not appear to be strong enough to affect the minds of

---

[1] Shortly after the re-establishment of the Senate (January, 1852) its members passed a bill conferring upon the Emperor the right of granting senators an annual gratification varying from 15,000 to 30,000 francs. The Emperor had the nomination of 150 senators, Dupin was one of the first to be appointed. But as the author of the above note remarks, all the new converts were not influenced by money considerations. The Duc de Guiche, the playfellow of the Comte de Chambord and to whom the Comte's aunt had left £40,000 per annum, could not have been thus influenced. This was the future Duc de Gramont, who rushed France into the war of 1870.

the womankind of the new converts. They, the womankind, continue to stand aloof; their fathers, husbands, and brothers attend the Imperial receptions and entertainments by themselves. This makes it awkward for the six or seven true gentlewomen by whom the Empress is surrounded, for, in spite of Vély Pasha's wholesale condemnation, all the women are not adventuresses, but the men, with the exception of the contingent from the Faubourg St. Germain, and a *very few* others have all a more or less shady past, and that notwithstanding their high-sounding titles, which, in the majority of cases are real enough. 'I do not know a single individual here who in any other country would pass muster as a commonly honest man.' Thus wrote Finch, the English ambassador to the court of Elizabeth of Russia, and his sentence will almost hold good with regard to the civil members of the Emperor's household, for, as I have said, with the exception of the new comers from the Faubourg St. Germain and a few others, such as, for instance, Walewski, Mocquard, and Ferdinand Barrot, they have all been involved in discreditable money transactions. The *vieille noblesse*, though clean in that respect until now, will not remain clean long, for albeit that the Empire is very young, there is the smell of booty in the air, and, unless I am utterly mistaken, the smell will even corrupt what has been hitherto the most invulnerable section of the

French nation, the French army, by which, of course, I mean the higher grades.

"As it is, these civilians are, as yet, the most interesting to the dispassionate observer, especially those who for reasons which it is impossible to guess and rarely possible to ascertain, have been pitchforked into high places. The number of civilian craftsmen who 'staged' the *coup d'état* is pretty well known; they are Persigny and Maupas; yet, to see these new-fangled dignitaries strut and pose, to hear them talk, one would really think that each of them had borne the whole brunt of the affair. There is a minister [1] who would fain have us believe that he furnished thousands upon thousands to defray the expenses of the *coup d'état*. As it happens, I know for a fact that the *coup d'état* was carried out with very little money, one might say without any money, for the President had not sufficient to settle the notes that were sent in afterwards for the refreshment of the troops, though the whole amount did not exceed 15,000 francs. I have heard this boast on the part of this minister for the last three months, and the other day while at luncheon with Véron, I happened to mention it. Sophie, his housekeeper,[2] was in the room, and as she is an old and trusty servant, the like of whom

---

[1] At the especial request of many sincere friends and advisers I have suppressed nearly all the names from this note.

[2] She was a famous character. I have given a short account of her in *An Englishman in Paris*, Vol. I., Chap. iii.

one rarely sees off the stage, she often gives her
opinion on men and things without being asked.
' He lend the Emperor money!' she interrupted,
' vraiment la plaisanterie est trop bonne. Voyons
monsieur' this turning to her master : ' you know
well enough that he would not lend a *traître sou* (a
red cent) to any one to save him from starvation.
Does not monsieur remember his coming in one
morning after he had been to see the President,
and his telling monsieur how nicely he had been
received? Thereupon he told monsieur,' this
particularly to me, ' that the President had
offered to make him a minister. " Why didn't you
accept?" asked monsieur. " I would have done
so," he answered, " but I was afraid of his asking
me to lend him some money." ' It's quite true,'
Véron burst out laughing. ' I had forgotten all
about it.'

" There is also an equally brand-new chamberlain, who goes about bellowing that as long as
he remains at the Tuileries not a hair of the
Emperor's head will be hurt, that, in fact, he
will be the French Roustan to Napoleon III.,
while it is well known that a few months
before the *coup d'état* he said repeatedly to
every one who would listen to him that ' Louis
Napoleon ought to be got rid of,' and that ' the
man who would put a bullet through his head
would deserve well of his country.' "

I have given this note *in extenso* because I feel

convinced, from collateral evidence, both from English and French sources that it contains the explanation of France's share in the Crimean War. My reasons for not producing that evidence are simply want of space. By this time Napoleon III. had become fully alive to the necessity of counteracting the unfavourable impression produced throughout Europe by the *faits et gestes* of his courtiers, which doings formed the main topic of the despatches sent by the various ambassadors to their governments. To check, still less to put an end to, these doings was at that moment absolutely impossible, for the simple reason that such an attempt would have entailed the banishment of the whole of his family from the Tuileries and perhaps from France; for those whose foremost aim and duty it should have been to preserve the by no means unsullied records of the Bonapartes from additional stains, seemed bent on besmirching these records still further, and to this charge there is scarcely an exception. The ex-King of Westphalia and his son, not content with their political burrowing and their undermining of the influence of their nephew and cousin as a monarch and the head of their house, must needs discredit him and his court by flaunting their vices in the face of France and consequently of Europe. One does not expect men to be saints, but when a septuagenarian or nearly such, like the ex-King of Westphalia, never stirs without his mistress by his side the word "Satyr" is apt to crop up to people's lips. "The apple does not drop far away from the tree;" says a German proverb, and the son was worse than the father; so bad, in fact, that Palmerston, who was throughout Louis Napoleon's friend, stopped him at once when he hinted at a marriage between his cousin and Princess Mary of Cambridge (the present Duchess of Teck). I had the story some years ago from the lips of Ernest Renan, whose admiration of Prince Napoleon's mental qualities seems, curiously enough, to have blinded him to the man's utterly moral worthlessness. Renan's informant was the Prince himself who, it should be said, was as cynically frank about the rebuffs he received in life as about his successes. Though at the time of the Emperor's suggestion the Anglo-French commercial treaty was scarcely thought of, "free trade" was in the air, especially shortly after the Exhibition of '55, at which time the conversation between the Emperor and the English statesman must have taken place. "A marriage between your Majesty's cousin and Princess Mary, sire," Palmerston replied in answer to the suggestion; "I am afraid that's out of the question. The Prince is somewhat too much of a free-trader, and though England may be pleased to see most duties abolished, I doubt if she will want to do away with conjugal duties." The Emperor smiled and dropped the subject.

And be it remembered that Palmerston was a man of the world in the widest sense of the word, and neither a hypocrite nor strait-laced. But even Victor Emmanuel, who was of much coarser fibre and not scrupulous where the gratification of his passions was concerned, hesitated to give Princess Clotilde in marriage to Plon-Plon. It wanted all the eloquence of Cavour[1] and all the great issues at stake to reconcile him to the idea; that is, if he was really ever reconciled to it, which invincible reluctance I shall be able to prove by and by.

And though there is no doubt that Plon-Plon was the worst offender, the whole of the Emperor's family, with the exception of Anna Murat, afterwards Duchesse de Mouchy, vied with each other to bring the dynasty into contempt. Princesse Mathilde's unfortunate marriage justified to a certain extent, perhaps, her *liaison* with Niewerkerke; it did not justify its brazen-faced obtrusion on the public. The Caninos, Cameratas, Pepolis, Murats, and Morny all followed suit, and followed suit with a vengeance. Their amorous intrigues were, after all, the least of their offences. They all soiled their hands with money transactions; they lent

---

[1] To students of history, this statement need not be insisted on. The ordinary reader, curious in such matters, I may refer to Cavour's correspondence, and particularly to the despatch sent by him to Victor Emmanuel from Baden on the 28th July, 1858, after his (Cavour's) interview with the Emperor at Plombières.

their names to bogus companies, and both in the love-affairs and money transactions, the Emperor, when exposure became imminent, had to bear the brunt of their misdoings to avoid public scandal. What the writer of the note quoted in the beginning of this chapter predicted came to pass, and in a very short time; the corruption even spread to what had been until then the most invulnerable section of the French nation— viz., the higher grades of the army. Shortly after the establishment of the Empire, Saint-Arnaud became involved in Stock-Exchange speculations which, rightly or wrongly, led to the accusation on the part of Colonel Comeneuse that he (Saint-Arnaud) had abstracted £4,000 from the War-chest. They fought a duel in a room in the Tuileries itself, and Colonel Comeneuse was killed. In this instance the Emperor's proposed mediation was of no avail.

Every now and then, though, there was a comic side to the Emperor's part of mediator, financial stopgap and universal peacemaker; especially when complications of a somewhat flighty nature had to be adjusted, in which case the sovereign was made the scapegoat for the doings of both parties, sometimes with his will, more often against it. One evening, just before dinner, an ordnance officer of the Emperor, a dashing, good-looking captain of cavalry, entered the Apollo drawing-room with a semi-mysterious look of mischief on his face. A few minutes afterwards he retired to a recess near the window, accompanied by some of his fellow-officers, all young, to whom he showed, somewhat ostentatiously, an envelope containing a small engraving or woodcut, the sight of which aroused shouts of laughter, more or less suppressed. That, of course, was sufficient to excite the curiosity of the female guests, some of whom approached on tiptoe and begged to be allowed to look. The request having been granted, they retreated more or less confused, although in reality there was nothing absolutely shocking about the picture. There was, however, enough to whet the appetite of those who had not been gratified with a glimpse and who were meditating a journey to the window-recess when the chamberlain on duty announced that dinner was on the table. Among these was the young and sprightly wife of an old and rather stern general who was, moreover, exceedingly jealous. It so happened that the possessor of the picture had to take her in to dinner, which gave her an opportunity of preferring her request more urgently. The officer deftly slipped the envelope into her hand and she, more deftly still, slipped it into her dress without being seen by any one. Next morning, almost before the Emperor was out of bed, the ordnance-officer asked to be admitted. The sprightly young matron, unable to restrain her impatience had cast a furtive glance at the picture, and the jealous husband had caught her in the act. She was obliged to give the name of the donor and she gave the name of the Emperor—informing the young officer during the evening of what she had done, and leaving to him the task of "setting matters straight," which he had not much difficulty in doing, for the Emperor was amiability personified and delighted in a Boccacian joke. The general himself never applied to the Emperor for confirmation of his wife's story. He probably felt flattered at the sovereign's having singled her out in this way; although he himself as well as every one else must have known by that time that the Emperor was not prone to commit what we may euphemistically term *farces platoniques.* The *sans-gêne* of the culprit in appealing to the Emperor to get him out of his scrape; and the *laissez-faire* of the victim in not appealing to the Emperor for an explanation supply a sufficiently conclusive instance of the tone and sentiments then already prevailing at the Tuileries with regard to womanly reserve and conjugal fidelity.

As time goes on and the dynasty becomes apparently more consolidated at home and abroad, this original attitude of *sans-gêne* with regard to the Emperor will assume a form which even the least observant cannot fail to notice, for there lies one of the germs of the

Franco-German War. As yet, however, we are at the period immediately before and after the outbreak of the Crimean War, when Napoleon III. is still the sole dispenser of the good things, when the adventurers around him are not sufficiently daring, but above all not sufficiently accredited in the eyes of France which eventually they are to bleed in every vein, to help themselves. The " Haussmann- izing " of Paris, that theoretically honest, beneficent and gigantic idea is, as yet, only in its infancy, and has not been transformed into a system of shameless robbery and into a precedent for systems equally shameless. In one word, the sovereign is as yet the sovereign, consider- ably hampered by his past, it is true, and often yielding where he ought to resist, but not the puppet of the most gangrened society that ever existed on the face of the civilized earth, as will be seen later on.

Meanwhile the struggle in the Crimea was running its course; the battles of the Alma, Inkermann and Balaclava had been fought, but with the exception of a State visit from the Queen to the French ambassador in London in 1854, the Anglo-French alliance had not been productive of the results which according to Vély Pasha were the chief motive of this alliance on the part of Napoleon III. I quote once more from one of the notes given to me by M. de Maupas, but unlike the first, this one appears not to have been written at one sitting.

"The French are almost apathetic with regard to the news from the seat of war. There was no enthusiasm at the tidings of the victorious engagements, and for once in a way the magic of the word *gloire* seems to have failed in its effect, not only on the masses but also on the better classes; and this, notwithstanding the efforts of the newspapers to work the oracle. This lukewarmness on the part of the nation is not due to the fact of 'the glory being divided;' as some of my English friends who were here a few days ago, suggest. It is due to the impression generally prevailing that France is taking the chestnuts out of the fire for England to munch; in other words, that France is being made the catspaw of England. And the impression is shared by the court itself, for of course, no one outside the court circles and very few within have a definite idea of the real reason that prompted the Emperor to contract this alliance—for I begin to think that Vély Pasha was absolutely correct in his surmises. If so, the Emperor and Empress must be greatly disappointed, for as yet no invitation from Windsor has reached the Tuileries. That both are clever enough to hide their disappointment there is not the shadow of a doubt; at the same time, the Empress, who is a Spaniard and consequently impulsive, may have dropped a few words expressing her dissatisfaction with things as they appear, while still hiding her real thoughts, and these words have no doubt been magnified and spread about. The Empress is slowly gathering round her a coterie—as yet it is not a party—whose avowed mission, or rather pretension it is to take a share in politics. Their targets at present are Jérôme and his son, which puts the Emperor in an awkward position, for, not to mince matters, I believe the Emperor is afraid of Jérôme's son and I am not the only one who fosters this belief. Lord Cowley said as much the other day.

"Success at last! The Emperor and Empress are going to England about the middle of next month.[1] The visit, from what I hear from those who do know, will be the upshot of a cleverly enacted comedy within a comedy. How far it will deceive those who, in spite of themselves perhaps, have been drawn into the cast, I am unable to say, but two of the principal actors, the Emperor and the Empress, have every reason to be satisfied. It appears that some months ago the Emperor expressed his intention to Lord Clarendon to take command of the army in the Crimea. Clarendon quietly told the Emperor to abandon the idea, and the matter was not referred to again until within the last fortnight or three weeks, when the

---

[1] This part of the note must, therefore, have been written in March, 1855. The remaining part seems also divided by a short interval.

Empress, at one of the receptions, took Lord Cowley aside, and with tears in her eyes, communicated to him that the Emperor had reverted to his original intention and was determined this time to carry it through. ' I cannot and dare not dissuade the Emperor; if I did, there might be an outcry against me;' the Empress said, or words to that effect. The Empress also as good as said that in this instance her usual influence over the Emperor would be of no avail, that in fact she did not have much faith in any one's influence except perhaps that of the English court. Two or three days afterwards Cowley had a private letter from England on the same subject and stating that both Walewski and Countess Walewski had expressed a similar opinion. Cowley gives one pretty clearly to understand that he did not for one single moment believe in the Emperor's genuine intention to go to the Crimea, or in the Empress' belief in that intention, at the same time he is quite willing to admit that the Emperor would have gone if the invitation to Windsor had not been given. As that, still according to Cowley's admission, was a contingency to be avoided at all costs, he also set to work to procure the invitation, but whosoever else is, Cowley is not the dupe of the comedy."

"The visit to England, it appears, has gone off most admirably. If it was a comedy, the London crowd, the City Corporation, the public

bodies have seconded the Queen and Prince
Albert in a marvellous manner in the spectacular
part of it. For though Londoners are not more
intelligent than the dwellers in other capitals of
Europe, a good many among the former must
have had an idea, however vague, that all the
traditions of the English Court and the private
life of the sovereign herself were opposed to the
reception *en famille* of this very brand-new
Imperial couple. But the Queen having said A,
her good-tempered Londoners were determined to
proceed to the last letter of the alphabet, and before
they were half through with it, made the comedy
a reality. Of course, the unquestionable beauty
of the Empress has had something to do with
this spontaneity, but if I read the private accounts
which have reached me aright, the Emperor himself did more than any one else to provoke this
enthusiasm by the masterly interpretation of his
part. He adopted the tactics he had found so
effectual at Strasburg and Ham and Boulogne
during his presidential journeys, and without
waiting for people to remind him of his adven-
turous past, he reminded people of it. What
was cleverer still, he did it *dès son entrée en scène*,
as the French would say. As the Royal and
Imperial procession wound its way up St. James'
Street, less than an hour after his arrival, he
stood up in his carriage and showed the Empress the lodgings in King Street he had occupied

when his future seemed dark and dreary enough.[1] That, unless I am mistaken in my own countrymen, 'did the trick.' Next day, the story went the round of the papers, supplemented by other anecdotes from those who had known Prince Louis when he was a familiar figure at the clubs and at Lady Blessington's; the writers vying with each other in laying stress on the indomitable strength of will in adversity of the new Emperor and conveniently forgetting how they had laughed that strength of will to scorn at the time of its display. In short, twenty-four hours after the raising of the curtain upon that particular act of the comedy, the author of the play as well as *all* the actors in it, seeing that every one was satisfied, might have asked one another with Don Basile in *Le Barbier de Séville*—'Qui trompe-t-on ici ? tout le monde est dans le secret.' As it happened, every one was not let into the secret, not even among those who ought to have made it their

[1] History always repeats itself. The first time Napoleon I. and Marie-Louise crossed the Pont-Neuf together, the Emperor stood up in his carriage and pointed out to his bride a house on the Quai Conti. Great was the consternation of the tradesmen on the quay who were under the impression that the whole of their dwellings had been singled out for demolition, and in those days no Municipal Council would have contested the will of the sovereign, who had, however, no such intention. He was simply pointing out to the Empress the house on the fifth floor of which he had lodged, when he came to Paris from Brienne. I remember, when a youth, seeing the tablet which had been placed in front of the house since 1853, in commemoration of the fact. *L'Empereur Napoléon Bonaparte, officier d'artillerie, sortant de l'école de Brienne, demeurait au 5me étage de cette maison.*

business to be—I am referring to the corps diplomatique. Mr. Buchanan, the United States Minister in London, had no idea that all this was a comedy and that the Emperor no more intended to proceed to the Crimea than Mr. Buchanan himself. He was under the impression that this great show of goodwill to the Emperor was a kind of 'God's speed' on his journey to the seat of war. At the reception at Walewski's the Emperor went up to Mr. Buchanan expressing the hope that he would see him at the forthcoming Exhibition, and at the same time mentioning his regret that the United States should not be represented more effectually—from an industrial and manufacturing point of view—at the New Palais de l'Industrie. The fact is, there has been already a good deal of comment on this absence of competition on the part of the United States, and in some quarters it has been construed into a political manifestation of a hostile nature to the Emperor himself, if not against the Empire. To do the Emperor justice, it should be said that he never speaks but in terms of the greatest admiration of America; and he probably feels somewhat sore on the subject, though I am certain that he did not show his annoyance. Mr. Buchanan, with great tact, replied that he was shortly going back to the United States, which would make it difficult therefore for him to accept the Emperor's invitation. 'Steam is a wonderful thing in shortening distances;' said the Emperor. 'True, sire;' replied the Minister with somewhat less tact than he had shown before. 'The distance between Paris and Washington is perhaps less great than between Paris and Sebastopol, whither your Majesty, I am told, is going.' This time the Emperor was visibly annoyed. 'This is entirely my own concern, and no one but myself knows anything about it;' he said drawing himself up and leaving Mr. Buchanan to stare almost open-mouthed at him. I can understand the astonishment of the Minister, but he could not, for the simple reason that he had neglected to keep himself posted up in the 'undercurrents' of the moment, a thing which no diplomatist should neglect. He had unwittingly reminded Napoleon III. that all the cheers, all the speeches, all the bunting, all the State pageantry of the last few days were virtually the result of a false pretence on his, Napoleon's, part, and Napoleon did not like it."

Here ends the note which, together with the one that preceded it, lets in more light on the secret causes of France's share in the Crimean War than any number of so-called political histories. The first war of the Second Empire was undertaken not for political but for social purposes, namely, to give the new Empress the sponsor she lacked to introduce her to the sovereigns of Europe. The second (1859) was waged to save the Emperor himself from assassination; the third (Mexico), perhaps, in order to cover the frauds of Morny in connection with the Jecker bonds, but certainly to conciliate to a certain degree the Papacy, and also to found a French Empire beyond the seas: the fourth for the sake of securing the tottering Napoleonic dynasty to the Prince Imperial. I fancy I have already proved the first of these four contentions; I will endeavour to make good the other three in the course of these pages.

One thing is absolutely certain. Even amidst the excitement caused by the Queen's return visit to Napoleon III., Paris, if not the whole of France, distinguished clearly between the sovereign and the nation over which she ruled. I am enabled to speak about this without reference to notes, for four months after the termination of this visit, I set foot in the French capital for the first time, and although I was but a mere lad, I paid a great deal of attention to the conversations around me, for the simple reason, perhaps, that there was little else to do. The relatives with whom I had come to stay were old bachelors, our home was the habitual resort of a number of men of note, and I had no companions of my own age. I could not but listen, and being blessed—or cursed—with an excellent memory, I remember these conversations, after forty years, as if I had heard them yesterday. And the subject of the Queen's visit and France's relations with England seemed inexhaustible, especially after the return of the French troops from the Crimea ; which spectacle I was privileged to witness three days after my arrival. It was on that occasion that I also caught my first glimpse of Napoleon III. as the troops marched past him on the Place Vendôme after he, the Emperor, had ridden along the whole length of the Grand Boulevards to receive them on the Place de la Bastille. We had a "police-pass," and were allowed to walk in the middle of the road, unhindered by any one. Though I did not speak French as fluently as I do now, I understood everything that was being said. "This is the revenge for Moscow;" remarked my grand-uncle to a friend whom we met.—"You are mistaken, dear friend," was the reply, "it is the stultification of Waterloo and St. Helena." Though I understood the words, I did not understand their sense, and when we got home I asked, for I had been taught to ask. My uncle explained as well as he could to a lad of thirteen and, presumptuous as it may sound, I did understand. From that moment I have never ceased to understand that no amount of diplomatic talltalk or soft-sawder will ever remove from the French mind the dislike of the English. I understood it still better when, a week later, a friend of my relatives, a surgeon-major who had just returned from the Crimea, paid them a visit. He was one of those courteous gentlemen, the like of whom are fast dying out in France, but his courtesy notwithstanding, he had not a good word to say for any of the English officers with the exception of Colin Campbell. He did not for one moment question their bravery and refrained from commenting on their military talents. He was simply dwelling upon their innate, albeit carefully suppressed, antagonism to the French. "The men are different," he said, "they fraternize well enough, especially the Irish and the French. I remember," he continued, "when the more minute accounts of the Queen's visit to Paris came, that there was not a single one whose face did not show the most intense disgust. I understand but little English, but I understood their faces well enough. The English soldiers suffered a great deal more than the French, mainly on account of their inability to make the best of things, and on account of their more naturally cleanly habits, but much of this suffering might have been avoided if the men had been allowed to come into closer contact with ours, for there is no doubt that the British troops would not have been above taking a lesson from our men in many things. But the officers systematically set their faces against this comradeship. Yes, we have done wonderful things, as the result will prove. In a score of years from this day, England will have reaped all the benefit from this campaign, and France will be left in the cold when she wants an ally. The French are grown-up children and easily pleased. It appears that Victor Emmanuel came a month or so ago. That visit will cost France another war."

He said much more, for which I cannot find space here, but I may have occasion to quote now and then from his recollections which he left to my grand-uncles. They are chiefly anecdotal, and refer to the Franco-Austrian rather than to the Crimean War. He had been away nearly two years, and the transformation Paris had undergone during that time struck him greatly. "I suppose it's all right. L'Empire means peace at home. After all, French soldiers would sooner fight for a cause not their own than not fight at all. The Emperor knows this, but he may fight once too often."

CHAPTER VI

THERE appears to be a kind of poetical justice in the enjoyment Americans derive from their stay in Paris, for according to Napoleon III. himself, the idea of transforming the capital *en bloc* and at one time, was suggested to him by one of their countrymen. Truly, all the rulers before Napoleon III. had attempted to improve the capital both architecturally and hygienically, but these improvements were conceived and executed piecemeal, with the result that the city, in the pre-Haussmannic days, was like Mr. Wilfer in *Our Mutual Friend;* it had never worn a complete new suit of clothes. It is doubtful whether Paris had any such ambition; even the proposals in olden times to endow it with a new monument, a public square, or a street having always met with most strenuous opposition on the plea of expense. The Parisians of Louis XIV.'s reign, lampooned and criticised that monarch and his architect Mansart, as their successors lampooned and criticised Napoleon III. and his Prefect of the Seine with this difference, that the subjects of "le Roi-Soleil" merely looked at the financial consequences of the proposed reforms, while the subjects of Louis Napoleon professed to be swayed in their opposition by loftier considerations than those of money only. When Mansart got frightened at the enormous outlay involved in his royal master's plans, and more or less "muddled" in his own accounts, Louis XIV. told him to "go on building; if you run short of funds, I will advance the money; the foreigner is sure to reimburse us."

Napoleon III.'s faith in the foreigner's willingness to pay liberally for the attractions provided for him was probably as strong as that of the Bourbon, but he did not possess the private wealth of the latter to back his faith. Nevertheless, he virtually took a leaf from the *grand monarque*'s book, but slightly transposed the text. "Go on building," he said to Haussmann; "the foreigner will reimburse the funds expended, but you must ask the Parisians to advance them." The two Bonapartes who ruled over France never disguised their admiration for the Bourbons; in several instances they revived the latter's miscarried or uncompleted legislation. Some one having remarked to Berryer: "Louis Napoléon veut faire le lit de Henri IV.;" the eminent barrister replied: "Au moins il ne lui manquera pas de paillasses."¹ Népomucène Lemercier, the greatest dramatist of the First Empire and the sometime friend of Napoleon I., was more direct, though perhaps less scathing in his strictures on the Emperor's imitation of his predecessors, especially in matters of ceremonial. "Vous vous amusez à refaire le lit des Bourbon ; vous n'y coucherez pas," he told him to his face. Lemercier's ire had been provoked by the golden bees on the Imperial mantle of the French Cæsar. He thought they were an imitation of the golden lilies of the *ancien régime* ; while in fact, the golden lilies were an imitation of the golden bees on the mantles of the Frankish kings. But the bees had been forgotten for centuries, until a French stadtholder of the Southern Netherlands unearthed one of these cloaks at Tournay and presented it to Louis XIV. Napoleon I. found it in a cupboard in the Tuileries, and adopted the bees to oust the lilies.

"The voice of the people may be the voice of God," said Napoleon III. one day to my granduncle when alluding to the Parisians' criticisms on his transformation of their city ; "the voice of the people may be the voice of God, but the ditties the people yell, rather than sing are assuredly composed by Satan. When a ruler does nothing for them they shout about *un roi fainéant ;* when a ruler attempts to do something for them, they

---

¹ *Paillasse* means both a pallet and a clown, or mountebank.

misinterpret his motives, unless they invent some which are altogether foreign to his thoughts. At this present moment the opponents of my plans have adopted the cry that I am attempting to do too much at once, and that this attempt is prompted by my wish to hold all Paris in the palm of my hand by means of broad thoroughfares, in which large masses of troops can move freely and cannon play effectually. Another section of society accuses me of wishing to reduce Paris to a mere city of pleasure and make it the resort of all the profligates and idlers—titled and untitled, rich and poor, honest and dishonest—of the whole world. That, according to the last-named critics, is my method for stifling the nation's aspirations towards a higher standard of political liberty. If I had adopted Louis XIV.'s and my uncle's system of improving the capital bit by bit, the outcry and objections would have been just the same, though different reasons might have been alleged for them. You who have read the memoirs dealing with the reign of Louis XIV. and the First Empire know this as well as I do. But neither shouting nor objections will prevent me from carrying out my plans wholesale. I made up my mind to that effect long ago. You asked me just now for a Government situation for one of your *protégés* who is possessed of considerable talents, but if he has talents why does he not use them properly, instead of wasting them in a

Government office at the rate of 1200 francs a year?" asked the Emperor, apparently going off at a tangent.

For a moment or so my uncle was at a loss for an answer, for he had asked himself the same question many a time in connection with the various candidates he had recommended to his Majesty.

"I suppose, sire," he said at last, "that in spite of his talents, he is not clever." "Put it that way, if you like," remarked the Emperor; "I should say because he has got no imagination, for cleverness and imagination may in this instance be synonymous. From your description of the young fellow, I fancy he must be like a young fellow I met with when I was in the United States—alike in every respect save in the possession of a strong imagination. Your young friend knows geometry, mathematics, surveying, and the rest; he has an inkling of architecture; and all that knowledge which argues a considerable application on his part during his college days, he wishes to place at the disposal of the Government in exchange for a stool and a salary of 1200 francs at the Ministère des Travaux Publics (Board of Works). Well, the young American to whom I refer, and to whom I owe the idea of the wholesale transformation I am attempting, knew all these, though probably not so well as your young friend. But

he did not apply to the United States Public
Survey Office to help him to get a crust of bread
on a stipend which would have provoked the
scorn of nine-tenths of the working men in
America. He wanted to live, not to vegetate.
He was bent on making a fortune and a twelvemonth after my first meeting with him he was
worth two or three millions of dollars. He was
poor and looked poor, so poor as to be frequently
behindhand with the weekly payment at the
boarding house in New York where we both
stayed. But he never lost heart. One day he
came in, an hour late for dinner, but with a big
roll of paper under his arm. 'I am very sorry
to be late, but I have got hold of my fortune
to day,' he said by way of apology, pointing to
the papers, which turned out to be the complete
plans of a city for 40,000 inhabitants with its
churches, its public squares, its monuments, &c.,
&c., including even an exchange. It looked like
a fairy city, but the plans were nevertheless carefully worked out; it was the city of the future,
such as I intend to have in France, if I live long
enough. The young fellow had, however, done
more than merely draw an attractive city on
paper; he had bought the site of it—of course
conditionally; entered into contracts with builders,
sanitary engineers, marble masons and landscape
gardeners, and provided with these documents,
applied to a couple of big bankers with a keen

eye for possibilities. They were going to form a
syndicate and the works were to be started at once.
That same evening I had a long conversation
with the young fellow. 'So your town will rise
like Thebes at the sound of Amphion's lyre?' I
asked smilingly, for all this was very new to me.
'Mythology may be reduced to practice some
time,' he answered, 'but I do not suppose we
shall be as magical as all that. One thing,
however, is very certain. The whole of my plans
will be started on the same day, and if possible
will be completed within a few weeks of each
other. We are not going to follow the example
of Europe and build a street or half-a-street of
houses at a time.' Then the Emperor sat still
for a moment or two. "You are considerably
older than I am,' he said at last to my uncle;
"yet you may outlive me. When in days to come
people tell you that Napoleon III. transformed
Paris, you in your turn may tell them that he
owed the idea to an American of whom Europe
has probably never heard, for on the evening to
which I refer, I made up my mind to do what I
am doing, if ever I got the chance. That was
why I asked you once more about your *protégé*,
between whose education and that of the American
there was probably little difference; but the one,
had the true ideas of liberty in his blood, and the
Frenchman has been fed on the tradition that the
Government ought to do something for him, and

yet when the Government is willing to do everything for him he revolts, though at the same time he tries to line his pockets by the very schemes he condemns."

The Emperor was right; in spite of the fierce outcry against his plans everybody took advantage of them to line his own pockets. I am old enough to remember all this; for though I was not thirteen when I came to Paris, at which period the transformation of the capital was virtually in its first stages, it never ceased during the reign of Napoleon III., and as it went on, fraudulent speculation and corruption of every kind in connection with this transformation became more and more rife. With the exception of the Emperor himself, Fleury, Princesse Mathilde, and perhaps Haussmann, *there was not a single person at the Tuileries, whether male or female, and from the highest to the lowest* who did not benefit materially and to a larger or smaller extent by the facilities offered to him by his position for surprising, worming out and intercepting early news of Haussmann's projects. Of course, the knowledge thus acquired had to be used cautiously and according to the possessor's means and opportunities. Few persons had the money wherewith to buy house-property or land in the doomed quarters, and when they had such funds, either of their own or obtainable from friends, they were obliged to proceed warily lest hurry and a show of too great anxiety should "let the cat out of the bag."

The construction of the Pont de l'Alma (though not under that name) was included from the very beginning in the Emperor's and Haussmann's plans. The entire transformation of the village of Chaillot, which for two hundred years previously had enjoyed the title of faubourg, had, however, not been decided upon publicly—although one moment's reflection on the part of those who did think must have shown them that logically, practically and artistically the one measure would entail the other. The Pont de l'Alma was finished about the beginning of 1856, for I remember that I was taken to see it within a few months of my arrival in Paris. And yet, a couple of weeks previously, my elder grand-uncle, coming home one day from the Tuileries, told his brother that the Empress had bought the mansion of Count Lauriston for her mother at a cost of three millions of francs. The fact of such a purchase, involving an outlay which must have appeared enormous to most people, especially in those days when hundreds and thousands of pounds were not mentioned in conversation with the unconcern of to-day, was calculated to impress itself upon the mind of a lad of thirteen and particularly sharp for his age. Nevertheless, he would probably have forgotten all about it, but for the comments to which the purchase gave rise during the next week, which comments were revived about a twelvemonth or eighteen months later when the pickaxe began to do its work in Chaillot. The most lenient conclusion to those comments as affecting the purchaser herself was a consensus of opinion "that she was very clever; as clever as Louis Philippe who invented European complications—in order *to contradict the reports, having meanwhile profited by the fall of public securities and their almost immediate restoration to public confidence.*"

I am not prepared to say whether the compliment to the Empress was genuine or not, but the transaction was unquestionably a profitable one. It would be difficult to compute the present value of the property off-hand; it is certainly worth four times the amount of its purchase price forty years ago. The site of the erstwhile mansion of Count Lauriston and its immense gardens, which were but a small part of the estate of the Comte de Choiseul-Gouffier, have all been built on; the old-world village of Chaillot has become the very modern Quartier Marbœuf; the transformation took many years, but the Empress, as far as I am aware, did not part with her land. A mere ground lease for building purposes is a very unusual thing in France, so we may take it that the palatial dwellings which have been erected on the site of the Comtesse de Montijo's former town residence are part and parcel of the property.

"It is a decent provision for a rainy day," said my grand-uncle in the latter years of the Second Empire, when in spite of his personal affection for the Emperor, or just because of that affection, he began to doubt the stability of the Empire. "A decent provision for a rainy day," repeated Alexandre Dumas the Elder, who happened to be seated by his side, and who neither liked the dynasty nor believed in its duration. "Say an ark for the coming flood and you will be nearer the mark." And forthwith there was a positive flood on his part of historical and literary anecdote in connection with the slowly rising Quartier Marbœuf. I feel perfectly certain that not one of these anecdotes has ever been published, and I should like to give them all, but the space I have mapped out has been overstepped more than once and I must not extend it. At the time of this interesting and impromptu lecture—for it was nothing less, seeing that it lasted for nearly an hour—I was over twenty, and though already then fully confident of my memory had begun to take notes. I have these by me now and they would make two or three chapters. As it is I must confine myself to a very few extracts.

"It is very curious," began Dumas, "that as early as 1842 or 1843 Balzac foresaw the eventual transformation of the village of Chaillot into a fashionable quarter. As usual, he conceived a vast scheme for making money in connection with it by buying up the whole of the land. Equally as a matter of course, no one would embark in the enterprise. They treated the project, as they were in the habit of treating all Balzac's plans, as purely visionary. Visionary they no doubt were, including as they did, the publication of a gigantic edition of Balzac's works in separate volumes, each volume to have attached to it a ticket in a lottery, the prize in which was to be a plot of ground or a mansion. It would take too long to explain the whole of the complex project, but the presentiment with regard to the destiny of Chaillot was right enough. At any rate, one man to whom that presentiment had been communicated, believed in it and almost immediately acted upon the belief—namely, Emile de Girardin. In less than a twelvemonth afterwards he bought from M. May, the chaplain to the English Embassy, the former mansion of the Count de Choiseul-Gouffier, in the grounds of which there stood at that time a Protestant place of worship.

"Contrary to his custom," Dumas went on, "Balzac did not altogether abandon his scheme when he found his initial combination impracticable. He was constantly meditating fresh ones in connection with it, and in the end of '46 or the beginning of '47 he removed to an apartment in the Rue des Batailles, opposite the mansion inhabited by Regnault de Saint-Jean d'Angély under the First Empire. Balzac said he wished to be on the spot to watch events more closely, but there were no events to watch. There were, however, a good many 'houses with histories.' There was the house where Barras died in '29 and where the Government tried to lay its hands on his *Memoirs*[1]; there was the house where for more than twenty years a young girl belonging to a family of the *ancien régime* waited in bridal dress for her supposed bridegroom—I say, supposed, for the man with whom she had fallen in love was a general of the First Republic and First Empire, to part her from whom her parents had locked her up in this then secluded mansion. I have an idea that some one must have told this story years ago to Charles Dickens, who adapted it for an episode of one of his novels.[2]

" I fancy Balzac intended to weave this and other stories connected with the place into one big plot. He hinted as much when he asked me to share the apartment in the Rue des Batailles. But there were many reasons why I did not wish to collaborate with Balzac, and least of all did I wish to live under the same roof with him. His ideas of the comforts of home and mine differed altogether. I do not object to rise early in order to set to

---

[1] By the time this is in print, the English translation of the complete edition of Barras' *Memoirs* will have appeared both in England and America.
[2] *Great Expectations.*

work, but I hate having to dress and go out at unearthly hours in order to avoid process-servers and sheriff's officers who might come to arrest me for debt or to seize my furniture. I never put these officials to any inconvenience in that way. They know that at whatever time of the day they come, my door is always open to them.[1]

"Finding that I turned a deaf ear to his hints, Balzac induced Jules Sandeau to come and live with him. No two men could have been more unlike than these two, but Balzac meant well, and but for him one of Sandeau's best works would, perhaps, not have been written. I am referring to *Mariane* which Sandeau wrote in the Rue des Batailles while still distracted with grief at his rupture with Georges Sand. Sandeau had comparatively few wants and could not understand Balzac's constant worries about money. Balzac, on the other hand, though he tried to cheer Sandeau in his love troubles, only understood them in the abstract. If anything were needed to convince me that Balzac was one of the greatest geniuses that ever lived, it would be his marvellous power of describing feelings which he never experienced.

"At that particular period Balzac had come to the definite conclusion that, in order to impress

---

[1] In order to make Dumas's meaning perfectly clear with regard to his treatment of creditors and that of Balzac, I must refer the reader to *An Englishman in Paris*, vol. i., chapters ii. and iii. It will obviate repetitions on my part.

publishers and induce them to subscribe to his most extravagant terms, it was absolutely necessary to make a great show. Consequently, the rooms in the Rue des Batailles were crammed with the most costly furniture; sumptuous hangings and velvet-pile carpets met the eye everywhere, and scores of wax candles in exquisitely chiselled sconces were distributed along the walls; for let me tell you, the visits of publishers were always timed for the evening. And, until the secret leaked out, the publishers were impressed. The whole affair was a cleverly staged act of a comedy, even to the guests invited for the nonce, who, to show their contempt for all this display of wealth bred from familiarity with it, stood on the silken cushions and spilled the ashes of their pipes and cigars everywhere. Of course the publisher did not dare to haggle with two such pashas of literature; Sandeau playing his part from sheer good nature. At the break of day, though, the apartment became deserted, and when a few hours later, the bailiff rang the bell in the execution of his delicate functions, he was told that M. de Balzac was only a friend of the tenant whom he occasionally honoured with his company."

The scheme conceived by Balzac for buying up a whole neighbourhood was even beyond the private resources of so highly placed a personage as the Empress Eugénie; to form syndicates or limited companies to that effect, would have probably defeated its own purpose, for it would have let too many people into secrets which, I repeat, had in the majority of cases been unfairly obtained. So the favoured recipients of these secrets or merely clever eavesdroppers, instead of combining, determined to work each on his own account. Most of them were unable to raise sufficient funds wherewith to buy the smallest bit of house property; they merely sold their knowledge to the leaseholder of the dwelling, and he in his turn hastened to renew his lease. Of course, he was careful to keep his own counsel, lest the landlord, having too many applications for renewals at one time, should become suspicious and raise the rents. Repeated in six or seven different quarters, although with but one tenant in each, the sale of such information frequently yielded the considerable sum of between 200,000 and 300,000 francs to the vendor, and I could name at least a score of such vendors in the *very* immediate *entourage* of the Imperial couple. Those who were farther removed from the august presence, and to whom, therefore, the information came at third and fourth hand, had to be satisfied with less. But I am not exaggerating in computing the money thus obtained at over one million sterling.

Practically this money came out of the coffers of the Paris Municipality, for it need scarcely be said that the lessees in their subsequent claims for compensation did not forget to reckon the sums disbursed in the purchase of their information, and do what they would, the Municipality were found in the end powerless to resist those claims. The original intention on their part had been to let the majority of leases "fall in" before commencing operations in this or that quarter. Under such conditions the ground alone would have had to be paid for. The lessees, with their fresh leases locked in their desks, simply sneered at the Municipality's announced intention to exercise patience. They believed the Civic Fathers to be ignorant of the negotiations they the lessees had just concluded with their superior landlords. The Civic Fathers were not as ignorant as the lessees thought them, and in spite of the obstacles thrown in their way repeated their intention to wait, although the period of waiting might be prolonged. Thereupon the lessees forced the Municipality's hand. They set up claims to the effect "that the intention to evict them at the expiration of their leases constituted an act of actual eviction entitling them to damages."[1] And preposterous though the contention seemed and seems, its validity was finally admitted by the highest tribunal in France.

This decision paved the way for a system of

[1] I have condensed the claim into non-legal language, but taken care to preserve the spirit of the plea.

wholesale exaction and jobbery, the like of which it would be difficult to find in the annals of any modern community in Europe. Equally difficult would it be to find parallels to some of the claims for compensation except in the librettos of Mr. Gilbert and kindred writers. To begin with, there was the claim of the owner of the ground and dwelling, or of the ground only through which the new thoroughfares were to pass. He was simply extortionate in virtue of his ownership. One case in point must suffice. One of these owners had as good as sold a plot of ground to a firm of hydraulic engineers for 75,000 francs, which sum he professed to be glad to accept. Pending the signing of the documents, he got wind of M. Haussmann's project of cutting a new thoroughfare across what was still his property. He declined to ratify his bargain with the engineers, and eventually claimed 1,800,000 francs. The valuation jury awarded him 950,000 francs. Then there was the claim of the principal tenant, who, as a rule, occupied the ground-floor part of the premises, including the shop. He could not claim compensation for being disturbed in his actual tenancy, inasmuch as the Municipality had announced its intention not to disturb him; nevertheless, he claimed in virtue of the decision of the Court of Cassation, to which I alluded just now; and moreover magnified his claim on the plea of the prospective harm his heirs and successors would suffer. "But," objected the leading counsel for the Municipality, "if my instructions are correct, the claimant's lease which has just been renewed will not expire for another twelve years; the claimant is close upon seventy, his wife is but a few years younger. They will scarcely remain in business until they are eighty; and although they are unquestionably entitled to damages in virtue of the judgment of the Court of Cassation that judgment makes no provision for the hypothetical injury done to heirs or mere business successors. Besides the former in this instance do not exist at all, seeing that the claimant is childless, and will in all probability remain so at his advanced age." To which the claimant's counsel made rejoinder: "My learned brother should not take it for granted that my client will go childless to his grave, because my client himself is far from cherishing such convictions; he belongs to the Hebrew race, and the miracle that was vouchsafed to Abraham and Sarah may be repeated in his favour, unless my learned brother wishes to imply that the age of miracles is past."

Finally, there was a category of tenants, mostly occupants of sets of apartments who claimed compensation on purely sentimental grounds. To recapitulate their alleged grievances one by one would lead me too far afield; one gentleman pleaded that his invalid daughter could see from the windows of the apartment from which he was to be dislodged, the steeple of the church where her mother worshipped when a girl. The majority indulged in "tall talk" about "the roofs that had sheltered their fathers and the spot where their children's cradles stood." And though in reality three-fourths of those who talked thus had not even been born in Paris—for barely one-third of the Paris population are natives of the capital the valuation jury generally admitted their claims; ostensibly in order "to teach the Government a lesson;" in reality because each of their decisions created a precedent by which they in their turn hoped to benefit at some future time.

Thus much about the doings of the valuation jury and claimants while they were both left to their own devices, expectations of immediate or contingent spoil, and so-called political independence. The latter feeling, however, was soon raised to the boiling-point by newspaper articles and pamphlets. Of one of these pamphlets I would say a few words, inasmuch as it was the work of the late Jules Ferry, at that time an obscure, and probably deservedly obscure, barrister, like so many other shining lights of the Third Republic that was to be. It was most widely circulated; I doubt, however, whether throughout the whole of France there were a hundred people who read it from beginning to end; most people giving up the attempt after half a dozen pages, for it was dull to a degree, and what was worse, dull without being convincing, and, as the Emperor said, "dull under false pretences." Its great sale was due to its clever title: a perversion of the title of the French version of Hoffmann's *Weird Tales—Les Contes Fantastiques d'Hoffmann*. M. Ferry had altered this into *Les Comptes Fantastiques d'Haussmann;* but the happy thought was due to two of Dufaure's secretaries, MM. Duval and Delprat, M. Ferry's friends, who had hit upon it during a conversation at an Orleanist's social gathering, and made a present of the idea to the future Prime Minister, who died as President of the Senate. "After all," remarked Napoleon III., when he had read the *brochure*, "I am glad that M. Ferry's pamphlet is so dull: if it had been as brilliant as its title, M. Ferry would be in the painful position of having to bring an action for libel against his face and appearance." The remark was spiteful, but absolutely just. In those days Ferry was a cantankerous likeness of Offenbach. Later on the likeness grew less apparent, and the cantankerousness more. I used to meet him frequently on the boulevards in company with Hérold, the future Prefect of the Seine under the Third Republic, and the son of the celebrated composer of *Zampa* and *Le Pré aux Clercs*, who had been a friend of my grand-uncle. I liked Hérold, who had one of the most wonderful memories I have ever met with, but I always avoided him when Ferry was with him. My grand-uncle, seeing them together one day, exclaimed, "Here goes Zampa's heir in custody of a gendarme."

M. Ferry charged Haussmann with having purposely underrated the cost of his proposed improvements. "That is nominally true," said the Emperor, "but in reality Haussmann has not underrated the cost of the improvements, he has only underrated the greed of the Paris *bourgeois*, just as he would have underrated M. Ferry's impudence if he had attempted to transform him into a fair critic and a gentleman." The Emperor was right once more: the greed of the Paris tradesman and *bourgeois* burdened the budget of the capital with sixteen millions sterling in as many years, and this in addition to the reasonable indemnities which might have been claimed in virtue of the judgment of the Court of Cassation. At least 15 per cent. of this money stuck to the fingers of more or less unscrupulous lawyers, retained by shady and still more unscrupulous agencies, which for a minimum commission of 10 per cent. on all the sums wrung from the Municipality, set the machinery of the law in motion on behalf of the smallest and utterly unimportant shopkeepers—such as dairymen, fruiterers, greengrocers, coal-sellers, &c.—all of whom, but for these agents' instigation, would have removed to adjacent streets or adjacent premises without losing their customers. The organisation of these agencies was little short of perfect; their recruiting of fraudulent auxiliaries strategic to a degree. One of these pseudo-*hommes d'affaires*, with the successors of whom Paris swarms even at present, managed to get hold of about ten quires of old paper bearing the Government stamp. Each of the sheets served for the making of a lease supposed to have been granted in 1850. He himself never put pen to paper: he simply sold each of the sheets to the various agencies in need of them at the rate of 10,000 francs apiece. The £100,000 sterling thus earned were all lost in Stock Exchange speculations, and after the fall of the Empire he boasted of what he had done. When the Commune exploded, he came to London and set up business as a wine-merchant: he is now leading a miserable and precarious existence in another capital of Europe.

Ante-dated leases, made with the connivance of both subscribers to such documents, were, after all, but one wheel in the huge mechanism of fraud. The agencies provided false inventories, false balance-sheets, false sets of account-books, false stock in the shape of blocks of wood, neatly wrapped up and suitably labelled; they repainted and redecorated the shops of their clients; and for many weeks before and after the time appointed for the regulation visit of the valuation jury, the establishment was crowded with customers from morn till night, which sham customers were attended to by equally sham assistants, hired at the rate of three francs per day. In fact, no stage-manager of genius ever arranged his scenic effects with greater forethought than they.

It would be rash to pretend that all the lawyers these agencies employed were their accomplices; there were some honourable exceptions, and they were their dupes. One of the latter was pleading one day in behalf of a grocer in a moderate way of business. Confidently flourishing the day-book of his client—for the agency frequently left the choice of a barrister to the claimant himself—he began to enumerate the customers, and asked for considerable damages. The counsel for the City of Paris interrupted him. "My learned brother need not trouble himself," he said; "I know that day-book, by heart, it is the grocers' day-book; it has done duty already several times." As a matter of course, the "learned brother" grew very indignant, and proceeded to refute the allegation. "I am sorry to insist," replied his opponent, "but if you will turn to page 73, you will find my initials." The bare fact was this. During a previous trial, the amounts inscribed in that day-book, and quoted in support of an exorbitant claim, had struck the counsel for the City of Paris as being too exaggerated. A vague suspicion of the truth had dawned upon him then, and he had asked to look at the day-book itself, and while pretending to add up figures had quickly initialed the page. He felt almost convinced that he would meet with that account-book again. But, though it seems scarcely credible, the claimant got his damages.

On the morning after this decision, the Emperor, contrary to his habit, was up betimes, and when Fleury went in to have his usual chat, he found him dressed and ready to go out. A few minutes later, Haussmann, who had evidently been sent for, made his appearance. "You and I are going for a walk, *mon cher préfet*," was Napoleon's greeting. "I am afraid I only know my Parisian subjects theoretically, and I wish to get a little more practical knowledge of them. I will take another leaf from my uncle's book; he used to go for walks in the morning with Duroc, and he told my mother that one of these strolls was worth a hundred reports from Fouché. That was after he had been plainly given to understand that a ruler must pay through the nose for any and everything he wants for his personal use and gratification, and a still more extravagant price if the object he desires be intended for the benefit of the nation at large. I will tell you how it happened. He and Duroc were walking along one early morn, when in the window of a very small *bric-à-brac* shop my uncle noticed a bronze statuette, the companion of which was in the Louvre. 'What is the price of that bronze?' he asked the dealer, who was perched aloft on a ladder, dusting the front of his place. 'Don't worry me,' growled the man, without troubling to look down or come down; 'you will find it too high for your pocket.' My uncle, who was in an amiable mood just then, insisted. 'Well, suppose I say four hundred francs, what then?' was the grudging answer. 'Then I should take it,' shouted my uncle; for the dealer had not stirred. This time he looked down and caught sight of my uncle's face. He descended immediately, but gave no further sign of having recognised him. His tone, however, altered. 'I said "suppose," monsieur; I was only joking; in reality it is two thousand francs.' 'Very well,' remarked the Emperor, 'I will take it at that.' 'I am afraid I cannot let you have it,' objected the man. 'A gentleman who saw it a few days ago told me that its companion statuette is in the Louvre, and if the authorities have set their minds on having it, I will not part with it for less than five thousand francs.' 'Do you know who I am?' said my uncle. The man stammered and turned pale. 'I see you do, and I mean to make you stick to your bargain. There is no more reason why you should rob the nation at large than that you should rob a private individual. I mean to have it at the price you asked me.'

"My uncle had the statuette, but I am not of my uncle's mettle. I cannot force the Parisians to sell their houses at the price they would sell them to a private individual; but I must find a way of meeting craft and greed. Direct contact with the Parisian may suggest a way. That is why I wish you to go for a walk."

CHAPTER VII

If Napoleon III. had been the most arrant coward on earth—and he was the very opposite of a coward—Orsini's attempt on his life would have been calculated to convert him into a man of courage. I am at all times reluctant to enter into a man's religious belief or absence of belief, but the intended victim who had escaped from such an attempt as that of January 14th, 1858, could only come to the conclusion that he bore a charmed life. If religiously disposed he would simply attribute his escape to a direct intervention of Providence; if a fatalist like the Emperor was supposed to be, his fatalism would be intensified a hundredfold, and henceforth he would advance on the road mapped out for him by that Fate—not only mentally blindfolded, but disdaining to take the ordinary precautions of the sightless. That this was absolutely the case with Napoleon III., I shall have no difficulty in proving as I proceed.

The attempt of January 14th, 1858, was the fourth directed against Louis Napoleon's life during the ten years that had passed since his memorable interview with Lamartine. Whatever illusions he may have entertained with regard to the *rôle* of the police as a protector in the three previous ones, he could not possibly have remained in such a "fool's paradise" where the fourth was concerned. It is more than doubtful, though, whether Louis Napoleon deceived himself at any time or was deceived as to the collective power of the police to frustrate the designs of the would-be assassin, or to hamper or detect the doings of secret societies. In a former book I have given a conversation between him and my grand-uncle on the subject,[1] and everything leads me to believe that he became more sceptical upon all these points as time went on. He knew that he could count upon a few Corsicans such as Alessandri and Griscelli to defend his life at the risk of their own; he knew that they were intelligent to a degree, absolutely loyal to him, and as absolutely unscrupulous with regard to the rest of the world; but he also knew that of the so-called organisation at the Prefecture of Police they were things apart; that, if anything, they despised that institution which in its turn hampered them on

---

[1] *My Paris Note-Book*, ch. II., London: Wm. Heinemann; Philadelphia: J. B. Lippincott & Co.

every occasion, either from sheer professional jealousy, or in order to court favour with its chief for the time being, or to plot for the return to office of a former one; each of these chiefs fancying himself a Fouché, a Réal, a Desmarets and a Dubois rolled into one; though in reality the whole of the five prefects who held office during the second Napoleonic period—namely, Maupas, Blot, the two Piétris (Pierre-Marie and Joachim), and Boitelle—had not together as much brain as the famous Duc d'Otrante by himself or as one of his principal coadjutors.

This does not mean that the five men I have just named were devoid of intellect or that their lieutenants such as Hyrvoix, Lagrange, and the lieutenants of the latter, Canler, Claude, Jacob and others, were incapable. Far from it. They all had a great deal of talent; nay, Canler and Claude were geniuses in their own way, but neither they nor their official superiors had sufficient genius or talent for the dual task, circumstances and the prevailing spirit of intrigue imposed upon them. They were confronting the enemy with the fear of being shot in the back by their own men, or to put it mildly—of being deserted by them at the most critical moment. They were not only called upon to look to the safety of the dynasty and its actual chief, but had to guard against their being dislodged from their own position by the plotting of their predecessors, or the machinations of their would-be successors. "They are dancing on the tight-rope the whole of the time they are in office," said the Emperor, speaking of his prefects of police a few months after Orsini's attempt; "they are dancing on a tight rope the whole of the time they are in office, and you cannot expect the tight-rope dancer to pay any attention to what is going on below or around him. He has quite enough to do to look to his own balance even if the rope on which he is performing is rigorously left alone by his rivals; and in this case it is not. Carlier tugged at the rope of Maupas, Maupas tugged at the rope of Piétri, and Piétri in his turn tugs at the rope of Boitelle. I did think," he went on after a moment, "that Piétri after his own nasty tumble would not try to endanger the safety of others, especially after the care I took of him, but it appears I was mistaken. After all," he commented with a smile, "they are only doing what I did myself; I tugged at the rope on which Louis Philippe was performing: Louis Philippe and his father before him tugged at the rope of the Bourbons; the Bourbons tugged at the rope of my uncle; the d'Orléans are tugging at mine and so on till the end of time."

This conversation, for which I can fix no date, seeing that the note which relates to it bears none, must have taken place, as I remarked, shortly after Orsini's attempt, but how long after

I cannot say. Boitelle, Persigny's friend and erstwhile fellow-soldier, had replaced Piétri (the elder), who had shown a most lamentable want of foresight which caused great loss of life, much suffering and would have caused the death of the Emperor and the Empress but for a miracle. I am not exaggerating; the carriage that conveyed the Imperial couple and General Roguet, the Emperor's aide-de-camp, was literally riddled with projectiles; no less than seventy-six of these were subsequently found imbedded in the panels and other parts; one of the horses wounded in twenty-five places was killed on the spot, the other had to be slaughtered; the three footmen and the coachman were all severely hurt; General Roguet's deep, though not fatal, flesh wound just below the right ear bled so profusely that the Empress's dress was absolutely saturated with blood as she entered the opera. Finally, a bullet had gone right through the Emperor's hat. I am only referring to the Emperor and his immediate *entourage* on that night; the total number of wounded was 156, at least a dozen of whom died of their injuries.

Yet the whole of this butchery might and could have been prevented, for there is not the least doubt that the French authorities were warned in time both of Orsini's departure from London, of his contemplated journey to Paris and of his fell purpose. Billault, the Minister of the Interior,

Piétri, the Prefect of the Police, Lagrange, the Chief of the Municipal Police, and Hébert, the superintendent specially entrusted with the service *des hôtels garnis*—in other words with the surveillance of the visitors to Paris and of those residents without a fixed abode—were aware of the presence of Pieri and Gomez in the capital, if not of Orsini's. Nevertheless, both remained perfectly free until the mischief had been done. We lay no stress on the passage of Morny's speech at the opening of the Chamber stating that the provincial branches of the secret societies were looking forward to some upheaval in mid-January, which upheaval would be followed by important movements. These periodical announcements were part of the policy of the Second Empire during the first ten years of its existence. They were intended to strike terror into the hearts of the peace-loving population, and to make them rally still closer round a dynasty which was supposed to hold the revolutionaries and republicans—the terms were almost synonymous in those days—in check by exposing and forestalling every one of their plans. In spite of everything that has been written and said on the subject, it is a moot point whether there was one secret society in France of sufficient weight or dimension to constitute a serious danger to the dynasty, or whether the Emperor or any of his most confidential advisers believed in the existence of such. But at the particular period of which I treat an openly avowed belief in them was still part of the system. Four years later (1862) the system is absolutely reversed. The secret societies are supposed to have vanished from off the face of the land—their disappearance being due of course to the strong and energetic government which leaves no cause for dissatisfaction anywhere. The alarmists who would still believe in secret societies must be dissuaded from their belief by the most delightful but at the same time most effectual means France has at her disposal to that effect, namely the stage, and the Emperor himself takes the initiative in this direction. He commissions M. Camille Doucet (the late lifesecretary of the Académie who died recently), the then official superintendent of theatres, to find the Aristophanes who will make people laugh and, in making them laugh, disarm their fears. M. Doucet applied successively to Théodore Barrière, Louis Bouilhet and Amédée Rolland,[1] all of whom attempted the task but without success and who each received 6,000 frs. for his trouble. What they failed to accomplish, though, was achieved in another way by Alexandre Pothey, one of their

[1] Théodore Barrière, the famous author of *Les Faux Bonshommes*, *Les Filles de Marbre*, and co-author with Henri Murger of the dramatic version of *La Vie de Bohème*. Louis Bouilhet, the friend of Gustave Flaubert. Amédée Rolland, the founder of the satirical journal *Le Diogène* and a well-known playwright, though not known in England or America.

friends, in his satire of *La Muette*; the name of the secret society which baffles all the researches of the police. There is no evidence that Pothey ever saw Napoleon III. in private, yet his satire bears a remarkable likeness to the story told by the Emperor to my grand-uncle.[1]

Sceptical though the Emperor may have been with regard to the existence of secret societies in France, he could not pretend to ignore the existence of at least one outside France. Many years before his advent to the imperial throne he had become affiliated to the *Carbonaria*, and it was the *Carbonaria* which through Mazzini and Orsini claimed the fulfilment of the project to which he had subscribed at the time of his admission. That project of which Lord Castlereagh had already a copy in 1813 and which before that had been submitted to George III. aimed at the establishment of an Italian Empire, limited by the Alps on the one side and the sea on the other three, with Rome as its capital and an Emperor chosen from either the reigning families of Sardinia, Naples or England.[2]

In 1858 the most powerful living subscriber to this document was unquestionably Napoleon III.,

---

[1] *La Muette* made Pothey famous. He was originally a wood engraver. His best-known book however, is *Le Capitaine Regnier*, a precursor of *Le Colonel Ramollot*.

[2] Both the act of affiliation and a copy of the project were seen by Monsignor Louis Gaston de Ségur, Arch-Canon of Saint Denis during the Second Empire.

Emperor of the French. But, powerful though he was, he dared not dispatch 300,000 men across the Alps in discharge of a purely personal obligation, which was moreover contracted in his pre-imperial days. We need not inquire whether Louis Napoleon's compact with the *Carbonaria*, dating as it did from so many years previously, was generally known in France. I was a lad of fifteen then and, as I have had occasion to remark, constantly thrown into the society of my elders, nearly all of whom were more or less behind the scenes. I remember having heard vague allusions to the danger the Emperor ran "from the knife of the hired assassin;" I heard the names of Mazzini, Karl Marx, and Bakounine in connection with conspiracies, but until four or five months before the attempt of January the 14th none of these conversations tried to establish the existence of a vast organisation to deprive the Emperor of his life. The three principal attempts up to that time, including that of Kehlse, were supposed to have been instigated by small groups, not necessarily Italians. My uncles' friends argued that the nine serious attempts on Louis Philippe's life and the one on the Duc d'Aumale were apparently not dictated by questions affecting the King's foreign policy; that with the exception of Fieschi all those would-be regicides were Frenchmen; but they observed also that the fact of Kehlse, Sinabaldi, Silvani and the rest being foreigners did not

absolutely imply either a far-reaching conspiracy
or a conspiracy from without. The plotters were
as likely to be Republicans or Legitimists as Italian
revolutionaries. Soon after the *Coup d'État* there
had been an attempt to kill Louis Napoleon by
means of an imitation of Fieschi's infernal machine;
the attempt was nipped in the bud, but the presumption was strong against the partisans of the
Comte de Chambord. In short, until within four or
five months before the butchery in the Rue Le
Peletier, neither my uncles nor their friends, not
even Joseph Ferrari, who was an Italian by birth
and intimately acquainted with the doings of
Mazzini,[1] seemed to be certain that the Carbonari
were collectively at work in this respect.

But there was a sudden change of opinion.
One day my younger grand-uncle came home
looking very serious, and during dinner told
his brother that there had been an attempt to
decoy the Emperor. He did not say more that
night, and I discovered afterwards that at that
moment he knew no more. I specially recollect
one thing in connection with this brief statement.
I was told not to breathe a word of it to any one.
The injunction was absolutely superfluous seeing
that I had been taught at a very early age to
keep a silent tongue; moreover, that I had
scarcely a companion of my own age to whom

[1] See *An Englishman in Paris*, vol. II., and *My Paris Note-
Book*, ch. iii.

to talk even if I had felt disposed. The next day more particulars transpired, or to be exact, more rumours found their way to our home, for no one could or would vouch for the truth of what he had heard and repeated. The word "decoyed" as used by my uncle was, however, a misnomer. The Emperor had simply walked into a trap set for him by a woman with his eyes open, for he had been warned that it was a trap. He had been drugged and would have been abducted but for the intervention of another woman. All these stories though varying in detail agreed as to the main fact; there had been a carefully concocted plot to get hold of the Emperor and to convey him to the frontier, whether to imprison him as a hostage or to do away with him eventually was not stated. Not a single word of this, though, found its way into the French press, but the Belgian papers published different versions of the affair in the guise of fairy tales. In spite of the vigilance of the police and the customs, some copies were smuggled into France. The veil which fiction had woven around the original personages was too transparent for the public not to recognise them at once; nevertheless, people might have looked upon the whole as an ingenious fabrication but for the indiscretion of the Marquis de Boissy, a senator and the jester in ordinary to that august assembly, just as the late Comte de Douville-Maillefeu was the jester in ordinary to the Chamber of Deputies under the Third Republic.¹ M. de Boissy was always putting questions to the Ministry, and when the rumours just alluded to became rife he insisted upon their being denied or confirmed by the Emperor's ministers. No such denial or confirmation being forthcoming, M. de Boissy exclaimed; "The Emperor, Messieurs les Sénateurs, is not sufficiently careful in his intercourse with the fair sex. Out of sheer consideration for us, for himself, and for the country, His Majesty ought not to place himself at every moment in the power of this or that adventuress." M. de Boissy was not called " to order " by the chair, and although in those days no reports of the Legislature were allowed to be published the story of the unanswered interpellation and of M. de Boissy's remark got wind. People not only concluded that the fairy tales of the Belgian papers contained a solid foundation of truth, but that the repeated attacks on the Chief of the State were something more serious than the individual acts of a Ravaillac or a Louvel. Shortly after that came the affair of the Rue le Peletier.

I am not speaking without authority when I say that the Emperor in spite of his profound concern

---

¹ The Marquis de Boissy married the Countess Guiccioli, who played so important a part in the latter years of Byron's life.

for the innocent victims of that outrage would have felt pleased to see the perpetrators of it escape. He knew that neither their arrest nor execution would influence by a hair's breadth the course the *Carbonaria* had mapped out in order to force their erstwhile member to fulfil the pledge he had given. And the fulfilment of this pledge meant war with Austria, for no reason affecting the interests of France herself at that moment, with Austria against whom Prussia, in spite of her many years of warlike training, did not dare to draw the sword as yet, with Austria who with France was the protector of the temporal sovereignty of the Holy See. The lesson of the Crimean war had not been lost on Napoleon III. In spite of the glory that had accrued to French arms, the Emperor was aware that the war had not been popular with the majority of the French nation, who strongly suspected the motives that led to it, especially at its conclusion when there was no territorial or other compensation for the great sacrifices they had made. And in the Crimean War the Emperor had had the support of the clergy, which he felt certain would fail in a war for the liberation of Italy; for not the humblest rural priest fostered the faintest illusion with regard to the final upshot of such liberation as far as Rome was concerned. And although the idea of freeing their Latin brethren from the hated yoke of the Austrian was no doubt attractive to some Frenchmen, the prospect of the humiliation of the Papacy as pictured by the priest throughout the land was hateful to nearly all.

That is why the Emperor felt sore with the police for not having prevented the catastrophe, and not, as has so often been alleged, because of the danger to which their neglect had exposed him. Truly, this danger had never appeared so formidable as then ; the erstwhile *Carbonaro* had fondly imagined that the *Carbonaria* would stop short at taking his life—that all its former attempts had been intended to force his hand, not to render that hand powerless in death ; and to a certain extent he had logic on his side. Louis Napoleon's death would have dispelled for at least a decade all reasonable chances of a free and united Italy. Mazzini's contention, assumption, or boast—call it what you will—that " Napoleon III.'s death would have been followed by another republic which would have come to the aid of Italy," to which boast Orsini gave utterance at his trial, will not bear a moment's investigation as regards its second postulate. But the truth of the first was patent to everybody and more than patent to Louis Napoleon himself, who, notwithstanding his fatalism and his marvellous escape from the jaws of death, was too logical to court deliberately a second risk of a similar nature. The Prince Imperial was not two years old, and his father knew but too well that the sight of an infant king in its cradle, and shown by its mother, was no longer sufficient to keep revolutionary passions in check as it had been two hundred years before, during the Regency of Anne of Austria. If at any period he had been at all sanguine about the results of such an exhibition, the somewhat analogous experiments of the Duchesse de Berri (July 1830) and of the Duchesse d'Orléans (February 1848) were amply calculated to disabuse his mind in this respect, apart from the fact that in spite of his great love for his wife, he was not quite prepared to credit her with the heroism that beards a revolution. The Emperor, therefore, knew that the first and foremost condition of his son's succession to the throne was the prolongation of his own life. Four and twenty hours after the bloodshed in the Rue Le Peletier, he had been categorically told that his life depended on the following steps on his part[1]: 1st. The Pardon of

[1] I have heard it stated over and over again that on the morning after the affair in the Rue Le Peletier the Emperor sent for an old friend of his mother, a Roman exile who had been living in Paris for many years and who had been implicated forty-three years before in the conspiracy against the Holy See. Queen Hortense had told her son that if ever he was in trouble to apply to this friend. Though close upon seventy at that time, he was in direct communication with the *Carbonaria* and had not left off conspiring. It was he who imposed the three conditions mentioned above, and a few days later announced to the Emperor that fifteen months respite would be granted for the other two. Personally I am under the impression that this intermediary between the Emperor and the *Carbonaria* was the lawyer Domassi, the same who, in 1815, when a prisoner in Rome, was the guest of Monsignor Pacca, the Governor of the Holy City, at whose own table he ate. I feel certain that his name was mentioned several times in my hearing,

Orsini; 2nd. The Proclamation of the Independence of Italy; 3rd. The Co-operation of France with Italy in a war against Austria.

There was no alternative but acceptance[1] and even then the *Carbonaria* made a show of generosity in relieving Louis Napoleon of one of his pledges, the pardon of Orsini. They were afraid probably that the execution of that first pledge would entail the non-fulfilment of the other two; for at the first mention of his contemplated clemency, the Emperor was confronted by the whole of the French clergy in the person of Cardinal Morlot, Archbishop of Paris. This prelate told him distinctly that powerful as he was in France "your Majesty is not sufficiently powerful to do this. By God's admirable grace, your Majesty's life has been spared, but a great deal of French blood has been shed, and that blood demands expiation. Without such expiation, all idea of justice would be lost. *Justitia regnorum fundamentum.*"

When the words were reported to him at our

but I have not a single note to confirm my impression. On the other hand, my uncles maintained that the man for whom the Emperor sent was the Comte Arèse, the same who had been brought up side by side with Prince Louis and whose father was on most intimate terms with Queen Hortense. Comte Arèse is said to have told the Emperor that, in addition to Orsini, forty other Carbonari had been selected to repeat the attempt, if Orsini's should fail.

[1] A few days after the attempt the Prince Regent of Prussia (subsequently Wilhelm I.) wrote to Prince Albert as follows: "Napoleon's dilemma was summed up in two words: War or the dagger; not a French dagger, but an Italian one."

home—I remember the scene as if it were to-day—Ferrari leaped from his chair, and exclaimed: "They have come direct from Rome. The priests flatter themselves that the *Carbonaria* will insist rigorously on the redemption of the whole of the three pledges, and that short of that the society will take the Emperor's life. Well, the priests are mistaken. A human life counts for nothing with the *Carbonaria* and they will sacrifice Orsini's as being for the moment less valuable than Louis Napoleon's to the cause of Italy's freedom. Remember what I tell you."

His interlocutors could not help remembering, for his prediction was realised to the very letter. A couple of days later, the Emperor paid a secret visit to Orsini in his prison, and though no one knows till this day what transpired during this interview, Orsini after that became an altered man. He who had opposed a stern and stubborn silence to M. Treilhard's questions made virtually a clean breast of the whole affair. He supplied the most minute particulars of the organising of the plot in London, and it was by the Emperor's special permission that Jules Favre was enabled to point out the lofty sentiments that impelled the deed. Louis Napoleon had virtually accepted the executorship of Orsini's political testament.[1]

---

[1] I had the confirmation of this visit from the lips of the late Marshal Canrobert, who had the particulars from General Fleury who accompanied the Emperor.

By this time the Emperor could have had but few, if any, illusions left with regard to the efficiency of his police to protect him and his subjects against such outrages as that which had spread consternation throughout the land. The renewal of his compact with the *Carbonaria* had, however, given him a respite of fifteen months, for he felt confident that under no circumstances would they prove false to their word. And fifteen months to a man of his temperament, who trusted to the events of an hour to carry out the plans he had meditated for years, who had even postponed the Coup d'État from week to week, fifteen months to such a man, just escaped from a supreme danger seemed little short of eternity. Fifteen months might be productive of a chapter, nay, of a whole volume, of accidents; meanwhile he could breathe freely; the sword of Damocles that had been suspended over his head since his accession to the throne had gone to the grinder's.

What, then, was the Emperor's surprise when within the next three months he was informed secretly by one of his chamberlains that another plot against his life was being hatched by the *Carbonaria*. There could be no doubt about the society's share in the matter, seeing that a portrait of Orsini, very rare at that particular period, served as a token of recognition among the conspirators, several of whom were in Paris.

Piétri had been succeeded by Boitelle, and the chamberlain's revelations which had been preceded by insinuations virtually took the shape of an indictment against the new Prefect of Police. At first the Emperor had been disinclined to attach much importance to these communications, although he gave Boitelle a hint of the rumours that were abroad, without divulging, however, his own source of information. But when the Chamberlain handed the Emperor a portrait of Orsini, said to have been borrowed from one of the conspirators, the Emperor sent for his Prefect and placed the documentary proof before him. The latter was not in the least disconcerted. "If your Majesty will tear off the sheet of paper that covers the back of the portrait, the value of the documentary evidence will strike your Majesty as original." The portrait was signed by Boitelle himself. "In fact," said the Emperor when telling the story; "Boitelle while dancing on the tight-rope of office is compelled to do as the others do. Though honest to a degree he has to invent tricks to keep his balance, and like the others he has but little time to spare to look around him. That kind of dual observation can only be accomplished successfully by a Fouché, and even my uncle had only one. Fouché danced on the tight-rope and every now and again knocked the enemies of the Emperor on the head with his balancing-pole; my prefects allow my enemies to get hold of the balancing-pole and with it to drag them easily off their rope. That is the difference between my police and those of Napoleon I." Eighteen months later, and that notwithstanding the apparently satisfactory issue to France of the war in Italy, the Emperor might have held the same language with regard to the superior officers of his army.

After all this, there is no need to insist upon the real motive—as distinguished from the alleged one—that led Louis Napoleon to undertake a war against Austria. What is, perhaps, less intelligible is the Emperor's anxiety for his cousin's marriage with the daughter of Victor Emmanuel, notwithstanding the King's scarcely concealed repugnance to sanction such a union. I will endeavour to explain this anxiety directly, though I am by no means confident of success, but I must first quote a note of my granduncles, dated January 1859.

"The King, though brave to a fault, dreads 'scenes' with his womankind. He had been more or less afraid of Queen Adelaide; he was afraid of Rosina Vercellana long before he made her Contessa di Mirafiori; he appears to be more afraid of Princesse Clotilde than he was of the late Queen and is of Contessa Rosina, although the Princess is but sixteen. But she takes life very seriously and has strong religious feelings, in both of which views and feelings she is backed up by her former governess, Signorina Foresta. There being no mother these two are of course much thrown together, and the opposition to the marriage derived considerable and additional force from this constant companionship. Victor Emmanuel was on the horns of a dilemma, but Cavour got him out of it by positively 'bundling' Signorina Foresta out of the palace and ordering her to leave Piedmont within the space of twenty-four hours. Ferrari tells me that Cavour, in spite of his mild and benevolent looks can be very rough and arbitrary. The only one who is not afraid of him is Garibaldi, who on one occasion said that, Prime Minister or not, he would fling him out of the window if he began bullying. "Be this as it may," Ferrari went on, "Prince Napoleon was talking to Victor Emmanuel when the latter was called out of the room and told that Signorina Foresta had been got rid of. A moment or so afterwards the King returned, his face beaming with satisfaction. 'There has been a lot of worry about this marriage of yours,' he said to Plon-Plon, with whom ever since his visit to France in 1855 he had been on terms of boon companionship. Plon-Plon nodded his head affirmatively. 'Well, we'll settle the matter at once,' he said, and before Plon-Plon could ask any further questions, he rang the bell and sent for his daughter. A few minutes later the Princess entered the apartment, and the door had hardly closed upon her when her father pushed her into Plon-Plon's arms. 'I have told you that you are to marry Napoleon,' he laughed, 'and here he is; kiss one another and let there be an end of the matter.'"

That is how Victor Emmanuel got over his scruples or pretended to get over them, for to the end of his life he never forgave himself for that marriage. "I shall be able to account to my Maker for the blood I have spilled for the cause of Italy's freedom," he said shortly before his death; "I shall never be able to account for the tears and the martyrdom I have inflicted upon an innocent woman for this same cause; and that woman is my daughter."

The Emperor felt as conscious of the magnitude of the personal sacrifice he was exacting at the hands of Victor Emmanuel and his daughter as they felt themselves; but he was practically powerless. Cavour and not Napoleon had set his mind on this marriage; and in spite of everything that has been written and said during the last thirty years, Cavour in the execution of his own designs was more unscrupulous and inexorable than Bismarck. To those who have studied the private character of the great Chancellor it becomes exceedingly doubtful whether he would have ever *deliberately* wrecked a woman's existence in the furtherance of his political plans. The stern-looking Teutonic giant with the fierce moustache, beetling eyebrows, and somewhat gruff voice was and is "all heart" where women, children, and animals are concerned; the benign-looking, "bespectacled," pot-bellied Italian who might have sat as a model for the mildest of Dickens's characters appears to have been unaffected by such sentiments. The causes of the difference in that respect between those two great statesmen must be looked for, perhaps, in their earlier lives. The first serious love-affair of Otto von Bismarck made him a happy husband and father; the first serious love-affair of Camillio Cavour made him a disappointed man. Henceforth, there seems to be no room either in his mind or heart for anything but ambition; ambition, it is true, of the loftiestkind, but ambition which at the same time shrinks from nothing, not even from murder, to attain its end. It has not been left to posterity to detect the hand of Cavour behind the murderous plots of the *Carbonaria;* at least two of Cavour's most eminent contemporaries, neither of whom liked Napoleon, spoke out plainly on the subject. Prince Albert, writing to Leopold I. in the beginning of January 1858 on the slippery policy of the Emperor and his confidential relations with Piedmont, said: "I quite agree with you that the dread of assassins is an important factor in all this, and that Cavour does his utmost to keep this fear alive; in that way he has his nag thoroughly in hand, makes it advance when he likes, and applies the whip now and then by telling him that he has discovered one or more new plots against his life." To such a man the misery of a girl of sixteen at being bound to a libertine of the worst description for ever, was absolutely of no consequence whatever. Cavour knew of Prince Napoleon's influence over his cousin, and of his hatred of the French clergy; he also knew of the influence of the French clergy, an instance of which he had just experienced in Cardinal Morlot's opposition to Orsini's pardon; he was determined that the one influence should counteract the other and he carried the day.

The barest enumeration of the incidents of the Franco-Austrian campaign is out of the question here. There are at least a hundred books professing to treat these incidents historically; I have read several of these works, I have skimmed a great many more. As far as I can recollect there is not one which has fulfilled its real historical purpose of showing the reader that the disaster of Sedan was foreshadowed in the victory of Magenta. It is simply because the historian proper travels from his starting point—Cause—to his goal—Result—in a railway train, which mode of locomotion prevents him from examining the intervening ground invariably bestrewn with valuable personal anecdotes. In one of Disraeli's earlier novels—I do not remember which—there is a father who recommends his son to read biography and autobiography, by preference the latter, rather than history. I read that novel when I was a mere lad, and have never seen it since, but I promised myself to profit by the advice. I have not neglected history, but have taken it as the English take their melon, after dinner—*i.e.*, after I had my biographical fill of the men and women who played a part in that history. Most people take their history as the French take their melon, viz. before their biographical meal. Accident has, moreover, befriended me by placing at my disposal a number of notes not available to others, and it is from some of these that the evidence will be forthcoming not only as to the rotten state of the French army during the Franco-Austrian campaign, but of Napoleon's knowledge to that effect at the very beginning of the campaign; which knowledge went on increasing until the end, when he could but come to one conclusion, namely, that in spite of the glory that had accrued to it, the French army would be as powerless to keep the foreign foe at bay on its own territory as the police had been powerless to protect his life from the attempts of the assassin. Fate and only Fate had stood by Napoleon's side, and to Fate he would have to trust throughout.

The Emperor left the Tuileries for the seat of war at 5 P.M. on the 10th May, 1859; at 7.30 A.M.

on the 4th May, hence, six days and a few hours before his departure, Lieutenant de Cadore, one of his Majesty's orderly officers, handed Marshal Vaillant an autograph letter from his sovereign informing the old soldier that he had ceased to be Minister of War. A little less than four years before that period the Marshal in a confidential gossip with a friend, had confessed his inability either to accomplish or even to initiate the desired reforms in the army, the necessity of which was painfully patent to him. The Marshal was essentially an honest man, so honest, in fact, as to accuse himself frequently of dishonesty without the smallest foundation for such an accusation. The Emperor must have been more or less aware of this incapacity of which, moreover, Vaillant made no secret;[1] yet there was no attempt on His Majesty's part to replace the admittedly incapable by the admittedly capable, for it would be idle to pretend that all the captains of the Second Empire who did not come to the front were vainglorious mediocrities. There were men who, though not endowed with genius, were nevertheless exceedingly well-informed and ornaments to their profession; unfortunately for the Empire, they lacked the qualities that told most with the party of the Empress, viz., the courtier-instinct, and promotion was withheld in consequence.

[1] *An Englishman in Paris*, vol. II., ch. viii.

General (afterwards Marshal) Niel was neither a Moltke, nor anything like a Moltke, but as an organiser he was probably superior to most of the then prominent men. His subsequent failure to reorganise the French army was due first of all to his early death; secondly, to the opposition he encountered on all sides during the short spell he had his hand on the helm. And there were many men as able as he who were not even vouchsafed this little chance.

Lest this should appear an unfounded charge against the Empress and her party, I hasten to give proof of what I advance. Coupled with the news of the victory of Solferino came the particulars of Niel's magnificent share in the events of that day and the semi-official announcement of his elevation to the rank of marshal. Tidings of that promotion seemed almost the only drop of bitter in the overflowing cup of sweet. "Can you account for this infatuation (*engouement*) of the Emperor for Niel?" she asked her interlocutor. "It is very easily accounted for, Madame," was the reply; "General Niel is highly gifted; he speaks on most subjects not only with ease but with knowledge; he is a living encyclopedia; he is, moreover, a man of solid parts as far as education goes. The Emperor, being surrounded by men whose ability is as often denied as affirmed (*contestée et constatée*), no longer applies to them when in need of in-

[...]tion. Niel supplies it without a moment's he[si]tation." "Thank you for the others, for the p[ortr]ait you have just drawn of them;" remarked th[e] Empress, and dropped the subject.

I repeat, there were many men like Niel in the French army. Why did not the Emperor replace Marshal Vaillant by one of them long before that? Why, having waited so long, did he dismiss him so abruptly at the twelfth hour? The eleventh had gone by, for a great part of the forces was already in Italy.

The first question must remain unanswered until I treat of society at the Tuileries and at Compiègne. The second I will answer at once.

Vaillant was deprived of his portfolio at a moment's notice because he had become imbued with the idea that an incapable Minister for War, pocketing the emoluments attached to his office, ought to atone for his incapacity by saving the moneys of the State. He had positively sent three of the divisions belonging to Canrobert's *Corps d'armée*—namely those of Bourbaki, Renault, and Trochu—across the Alps *with insufficient clothing, without stores of any kind, without cartridges, and almost without guns.* "Pray ask the Emperor," said Bourbaki to the officer sent by Napoleon III. to take a preliminary view of the situation; "pray ask the Emperor whether his Minister for War is a traitor or whether he has fallen into a state of idiocy?" "A French army has made its way into Italy before now without shoes to their feet and without shirts to their backs; but the sight of a French army going to confront the enemy without cannon and without cartridges is an unprecedented sight"; concluded Trochu when making his report to the same envoy.

This was before a blow had been struck, before a shot had been fired. On the 1st June (three days before Magenta) the Emperor was within an ace of being taken prisoner by the Austrians at a distance of about a hundred yards from the French outposts, which outposts themselves were not three hundred yards away from the encampment of Failly's division. This narrow escape did not occur during an engagement, but while his Majesty was peacefully trundling in a shandredan on a country road—I believe from Bicocca to Vespolata. At the battle of Magenta MacMahon himself fell among a detachment of Austrian sharp-shooters, who luckily for him mistook him for one of their generals.

Is it wonderful then that the Emperor's illusions with regard to his army were gone? Is it wonderful that being the fatalist he was, he rushed madly into the war of 1870, trusting to his star and to his star only? For that such was the case I shall have no difficulty in proving by and by.

CHAPTER VIII

There is one fact connected with the Second Empire which the nobodies who have lorded it over France since the Empire's fall have not been able to explain away. I allude to the unprecedented prosperity the country enjoyed during these eighteen years. All their attempted explanations to that effect are lame and more than lame; they cannot even limp along; they are positively paralysed by subsequent facts. The impartial observer, whether he be a Frenchman or a foreigner, who happens to have lived in France under the *régime* of Napoleon III. and under that of the Third Republic cannot help pointing out that during the first-named period the peasant, and for that matter the townsman too, had his "fowl in the pot"; a condition of things which was considered by Henri IV.—not a bad king as kings went in those days—the height of a country's welfare.

The answers to such a remark come glibly

enough, and in many instances they are partly epigrammatic, partly philosophical. " Before the War of Secession in America," replied a pseudo-Republican to me, " the slaves on the southern plantations were better fed and cared for materially than many of the free-born citizens." I was not in a position to contradict him, for I know little or nothing about America, and although I had a notion that he knew as little, I was angel enough not to tread where he had rushed. Nor do I know whether the erstwhile slaves are better off to-day than they were before their emancipation. This much I do know: the political bondsman of the Second Empire regrets the " fowl in the pot," and is by no means consoled for its absence by the thought that the bird has taken flight on the wings of political rhetoric.

"That 'fowl in the pot' on which you lay so much stress," retorted another Republican, "was simply the 'goose with the golden eggs'; the nation was eating both her interest and her capital." That, I maintain, is an absolute falsehood. It could be proved over and over again, if it were necessary, that the war expenses and the war tax of five milliards of francs were paid out of the savings of the population during the previous fifteen or sixteen years, that scarcely an acre of ground was either mortgaged or sold during the two or three years after the Treaty of Frankfort by those who invested their money in these loans. To adduce such proofs would lead me too far astray. I may mention, however, that in many of the smaller provincial centres these loans were almost entirely subscribed in what appeared to be newly minted gold and newly issued banknotes, both of which tenders, though, turned out on closer examination to have been minted and issued six, seven, eight, and twelve years before. The money had simply been lying idle during the whole of that time in the linen presses of the peasantry and the *petite bourgeoisie* in accordance with a system that has prevailed in France ever since the peasantry and *petite bourgeoisie* had anything to save, a system which will not be entirely abandoned within the next century, if then. If further proofs were wanted of the unexampled prosperity of France between 1855-70, they would be found in a comparison of the reports of the Poor Law Board (*Assistance Publique*) during the Citizen Monarchy and the Third Republic with those of the Second Empire. A judicious critic of the Second Empire has truly said, "Si Napoléon III. ne fut pas le Napoléon de la Gloire, il fut au moins le Napoléon du *louis d'or*."[1]

It would be sheer folly to pretend that there

---

[1] The *louis d'or* existed long before Napoleon III.'s time. In former days it represented twenty-four francs; under the present monetary system twenty francs. But few, except the wealthier classes, ever spoke of it as a unit. The lower classes and the *bourgeoisie* called it a piece of twenty francs, and treated it as it were

was no poverty in France during the Second Empire. But from various causes the attitude of "Fortune's favourites" towards the indigent was different from what it is to-day. The self-sufficient, pompous, quasi-virtuous big-wig of the Third Republic flatters himself that he owes his position to talents, energy, and perseverance. Though he can be lavish at times, he is rarely generous; he contents himself with being just—according to his own lights. In the majority of cases he has never had the handling of large sums of money until he wheedled himself or was pitchforked into parliament, diplomacy, or office, and what is worse for the poor, he knows his position to be insecure, and that, therefore, he must make hay while the sun shines. A change of ministry may at any moment relegate him to a very chilly corner, and a change of ministry is the only certainty that can enter into his calculations.

It is doubtful if the big-wig of the Second Empire ever entertained these fears of relapsing into obscurity and straitened means. Whether talented or not, he was less impressed with his own "high and mightiness" than the Republican. Those whom I have known were almost inclined to laugh in their sleeves at the idea of a

<small>with a kind of reverence. It is only during the Second Empire that the word became general. The familiar sight of the coin in almost every one's pocket reduced its prestige in the vocabulary of the nation.</small>

providential mission on the part of Queen Hortense's son, let alone at their own share in such a mission. Not a few grinned behind the backs of the worshippers at the Napoleonic shrine, but until a short time before the collapse all had great faith in the cleverness of the high priest, and above all in his " star." And inasmuch as he, the high priest, convinced that his "star" would never fail him, gave freely, without stint, almost too lavishly, and certainly too indiscriminately, the majority of his Court followed suit in this respect as in every other.[1]

And in spite of the Republicans' frequent assertions to this effect, Louis Napoleon's charity was *not* the result of political and dynastic

[1] After the fall of the Empire, thousands of begging letters were found at the Tuileries, nearly all of which were annotated in the handwriting of the Emperor himself, mentioning the sums that had been sent in reply. He spent on an average £140,000 per annum in this way thus £2,500,000 during the eighteen years of his reign. When we consider that this same man left an income of less than £5,000 to his widow, the reader will agree that the words lavish and indiscriminate are not misplaced. We are not concerned here with the private fortune of the Empress, for although it is true that she pledged her jewels in the beginning of September, 1870, in England, in order to face the immediate expenses for herself and her small band of followers, *it is by no means certain that necessity compelled that step.* With regard to the late Emperor's invincible belief in his "star," here is another proof. By his will, drawn up while he was still on the throne, everything was left to the Empress not the smallest provision having been made for the son whom he loved with a deep-seated, almost idolatrous affection. It was because Napoleon III. felt confident that his "star" would prolong his days until he had seen that son firmly established as his successor on the throne. In that case there would have been no

calculation. It proceeded from the wish to enjoy life himself and to make every one around him enjoy it; for he was essentially the *bon-vivant* in the widest and most beneficent acceptation of the term; the *bon-vivant* whom Marivaux had in his mind's eye when he said, " Pour être assez bon, il faut l'être trop." His charming ways, his amiability in all things, his disinterested generosity, his appreciation of humour, even when it was directed against himself, have never been surpassed by any monarch; and as a consequence, perhaps, no monarch—Charles II. included—has contributed more to his own downfall than he. One instance of this amiability which under the circumstances might well be called culpable neglect to checkmate his enemies in time, must suffice here. On the 3rd November, 1863, Thiers and many other avowed opponents of the Empire resumed their seats at the Palais Bourbon. Morny, in his opening speech as President of the Chamber, alluded in graceful terms to the reappearance of some of his former parliamentary colleagues. " I rejoice to see them once more, and have no doubt about the loyalty of their intentions," he said.[1] The next morning Morny paid a visit to

necessity to provide for him, and it would have been but right that the Empress should enjoy the revenues. But for that will the Prince Imperial might be alive and on the throne of his father, for he would certainly not have gone to Zululand.

[1] In 1857 the number of those opponents was five; in 1863 it had increased to twenty-three.

the Emperor, who complimented him on his eloquence. "Nevertheless," added Napoleon with a smile, "it strikes me that your reference to the election of M. Thiers was a little—well, a little too intense. You are reported to have said, 'As for myself, I rejoice,' etc., etc. Does not 'rejoice' convey a little too much?" Morny pointed out that he had referred to former colleagues with whom he had then been on the best of terms, and so forth. "Yes, yes," retorted the Emperor gaily; "I had better make up my mind to it, I am surrounded by enemies. There is no doubt about it, you are an Orleanist; decidedly, you are an Orleanist."

The note relating this incident is couched in somewhat critical terms, an unusual tone for my grand-uncles to adopt.[1] It goes on as follows: "I do not like the way things are drifting at the Château (Tuileries). Every one there seems to be master except the master himself. Politics are discussed in the interval between two dances by men and women who have no more idea of such matters than our cook has of anatomy, dissecting, and operating. I dare say our cook would indignantly refute such a charge of ignorance by triumphantly pointing to the fowl she has trussed or the joint she has trimmed, and it would be vain on my part, I suppose, to make her understand

---

[1] It appears to have been written several months after the incident.

the difference between operating upon a live body and a dead one. And the Empire, though by no means a healthy body, is very much alive. A few months ago I read a book on *The French Revolution*, by an Englishman,[1] and one passage struck me as particularly pertinent to the present state of affairs. 'Meanwhile it is singular how long the rotten will hold together, provided you do not handle it roughly.' I am afraid those twenty-three newly-elected deputies, five of whom have sat in the Chamber for the last six years, are going to handle the Empire roughly, and the mistake of the Emperor lies in his having given them a chance. He ought to have prevented their return by hook or by crook. The man who made a clean sweep of at least ten times their number twelve years ago ought not to have afforded any of them an opportunity now of making a clean sweep of him, for that, assuredly, is what they will endeavour to do.

"How long they will have to wait for such an opportunity it would be difficult to determine, but when that opportunity comes they will be ready for it. In fairness to them it should be said that they do not disguise their intentions; the noise they make in preparing their brooms—by stamping the handles on the ground in the orthodox fashion—is loud enough to awaken any one who is not wilfully deaf; but they are either that at

[1] Carlyle's.

the Tuileries, or else their own buffooning prevents them from hearing as well as seeing what is going on around them. From what I gather it is not easy to decide whether the latest *travesties* of Meilhac and Halévy and Offenbach are the pure outcome of these gentlemen's imaginations, or simply a faithful picture of some of the scenes enacted now and then at the Château—unless the scenes at the Château are a deliberate attempt to imitate, nay, to surpass, Mdlle. Schneider, Léonce, and their fellow-artists. The gods, demi-gods, heroes and heroines of Homer, as portrayed by the authors of *Orphée aux Enfers* and *La Belle Hélène*, and set in motion by that truly magic music of Maitre Jacques, are assuredly not more astounding to the unsophisticated, and for that matter to the sophisticated, than a great many of the warriors, clericals, grandes dames and grands seigneurs constituting the innermost circle at the Court. What after all is the high priest Calchas to that astonishing Abbé Bauer, the latest fad, I am told, in the way of ascetic, but at the same time, elegant Christianity. He is a convert, he was educated for the Jewish ministry, and if everything people state be true, Judaism is well rid of him. It appears that a little while ago the abbé tried to convert Adolphe Crémieux, for Crémieux, though baptized when quite an infant, is distinctly a Jew and not a Catholic; a Jew, moreover, of whom Judaism throughout the world may well feel proud.[1] Of course the conversion of such a man as Crémieux, if at all feasible, could not be accomplished by an Abbé Bauer who was more than roughly handled in the encounter. Bauer, however, in spite of his quasi-refined exterior, is a vulgarian to his fingers' ends, and thick-skinned besides. Crémieux's hard hitting did not make him wince, and at the end of the interview he said, 'I am very much surprised at your views about the founder of our religion, for I really believe that you are so liberal a Jew as to have legally defended Christ if you had lived in His time.' 'That I certainly should have done,' replied Crémieux, 'and, what is more, I should have got Him acquitted—unless—unless I had been obliged to put the like of you in the witness-box for the defence.' More scathing than even this is Monseigneur Dupanloup's criticism on Abbé Bauer's first sermon before the Court. The preacher, in spite of the warnings of his superiors, had given too much prominence to the Virgin in his address. 'Place aux dames,' said the Bishop of Orleans. 'According to Abbé Bauer there is no God, and the Virgin Mary is His mother.'

"I may be permitted to doubt, though, whether this treatment à l'ancien régime of sacred subjects, or rather the reintroduction of the perfumed,

[1] Adolphe Crémieux, one of the most eminent Frenchmen of his times, both as a lawyer and as a political authority.

theatrical, and too worldly abbé into Court circles, by which the Empress wishes to emphasise her admiration for Marie-Antoinette, her surroundings and legitimacy in general, is calculated to give the nation a very exalted opinion of their rulers. One does not want a John Knox thundering against everything, nor does one want an Abbé Bauer 'under-studying' the role of a Cardinal de Rohan. Monseigneur Dupanloup notwithstanding the sally just quoted, is a highly gifted, worthy, and absolutely disinterested prelate. He is thoroughly imbued with the dignity of his sacred office, and although very militant at all times, and often abrupt and the reverse of amiable, he would not condescend to enact the buffoon or instruct his clergy to this effect for no matter how good a cause. He would not do evil that good might come. But a great many of his fellow-prelates do not possess the same tact and discrimination. They fulminate, or allow their clergy to fulminate, against the vices and foibles of the hour in a manner which is apt to breed as much contempt for the would-be physician as for the patient. Not long ago a parish priest inveighing against the *can-can*, actually held up the two sides of his cassock and performed some steps in the pulpit to show his flock how the Holy Virgin danced and how they, his flock, should dance. 'This priest decidedly beats Calchas in *La Belle Hélène*, but there is a warrior at the Court who beats both the curé and the Calchas and the Agamemnon of the opéra-bouffe. This is no other than Count Tascher de la Pagerie, who imitates barn-yard fowls, the sun and the moon—by making idiotic grimaces—at the command of his Imperial mistress, and who is 'trotted out' on all occasions for the amusement of visitors. Count Tascher does not think it incompatible with his rank in the army, his relationship to the Emperor, and his position of chamberlain to the Empress to oblige in that way. He is prouder of these accomplishments than of his birth, the brave deeds of his father, and of everything else besides. After that people need not wonder at Gustave Doré's performing somersaults and standing on his head for his own amusement, and at his announced intention of abandoning his own career, in which he has already won much fame, for that of Auriol, the clown.

"And it is more than probable that in the intervals of his clowning, this same Count Tascher pretends to lend a hand in the steering of the 'Ship of State,' for the Tuileries is fast becoming a 'cour du roi Pétaud et chacun y parle haut.'[1]

"The worst of it is that those whose very existence as a body depends upon their unques-

---

[1] In olden times the mendicants, in imitation of the guilds, corporations, and communities in France, annually elected a king, who took the title of King Pétaud, from the Latin *peto*. In *Tartuffe*, Orgon's mother compares her son's house to the court of King Pétaud. "On n'y respecte rien, chacun y parle haut," she says.

tioning obedience and abstention from comment until such comment is invited are becoming infected with the prevailing mania for laying down the law on every conceivable subject. When I say 'becoming infected' I put it mildly; in reality they have set the example—I mean the army. I have seen enough of soldiering to know the inestimable value of silent obedience to the orders of one's superiors. The order may be wrong, and tantamount to a death sentence to its recipient; he is bound to carry it out to the letter. And yet, with the examples of Lords Lucan and Cardigan at Balaclava before them, French officers will go on discussing orders not only from a military point of view, but from a political.

"One instance in point will suffice. The delinquent is gone, and peace be to his ashes! for he was a brave and honourable soldier. But his well-known bravery and uprightness, and above all his position near the Emperor as *aide-de-camp*, called for more circumspection on General de Cotte's part than he exercised on the occasion alluded to. The thing happened a few evenings before the Emperor's departure for the Franco-Austrian War. General de Cotte was on duty at the time, and after dinner went down to the smoking-room set apart for the military and civil household. 'The thing is settled,' he said aloud, lighting a cigarette; 'in a day or two we shall be on our way to Italy, unless Providence or the Lunacy Commissioners stop us at the first stage, at Charenton.'[1] Half-an hour later the General went up stairs to the Empress's drawing-room. He had scarcely entered the apartment when the Emperor came up to him with a smile. 'My dear General,' he remarked quietly, 'I have too much respect for the opinion of others, even when they are diametrically opposed to mine, to ask people to fight battles the motives for which they do not approve. You will remain in Paris with the Empress.'

"That did not suit the General's book at all; but he did not utter a word in defence, he only bowed. He was, in fact, too astonished at his comment having reached the ears of the Emperor so soon. As far as he was aware, no servant had entered the room while he was there. He was, then, reluctantly compelled to conclude that an equal had played the part of tell-tale; and that alone would convey a fair idea of the code of honour that prevails among the immediate *entourage* of the sovereigns. Nevertheless he was not going to be left out of the fighting, therefore on the 14th of May he simply had his horses

---

[1] Charenton is the well-known madhouse just outside Paris. At the news of the declaration of war in 1870 Prince Napoleon made a similar remark. He was on his way to Norway with Ernest Renan. "Reverse your engines," he said to the master of the yacht; "we are going back." "Where to, Monseigneur?" was the question. "To Charenton." The reply was quoted as something spitefully witty and original. It was spiteful but not original

and baggage taken to the Imperial train, selected a seat in an empty compartment, and only showed his face at Marseilles. The Emperor merely smiled and held out his hand. This is a sample of the Emperor's amiability, of his willingness to let bygones be bygones."

My notes contain a hundred similar anecdotes, all tending to show that the Emperor was *too good-natured*; and I shall have no difficulty in proving, when the time comes, that this excessive *laissez-faire* finally caused his ruin.

As yet, however, the cloud on the horizon is not bigger than a hand, and certainly not visible to the naked eye. And France is too busy enjoying herself to scan the sky with a spyglass. She does not even enact the fable of the hare with the telescope; she remains profoundly ignorant of the approach of her enemy. France resounds with laughter, and above it all rings that modern version of Rabelais' "Fay ce que vouldras," viz. the chorus of Thérésa's song, "Rien n'est sacré pour un sapeur," which chorus paints the moral atmosphere in one line.

For the sapper stood not alone in his irreverence for any and every thing. He simply took his cue from those above him, from educated and talented men who deliberately mocked at "the whole world and his wife," including the sovereign and his consort, the former of whom they not only slighted in his private capacity, but as the chief of the State.¹ Rochefort, at a later period, had at any rate the courage to attack openly ; the partisans of the d'Orléans régime lacked that courage. They sailed as close to the wind as they dared without risking penalties. Strange to say though, the worst blows to the Emperor's dignity came from the Emperor's friends and protégés, and were dealt in fun—"histoire de s'amuser et d'amuser les autres." They came in the shape of practical jokes at which Society roared and the victim himself, who was rarely seen to smile, laughed outright.

On the face of it, the jokes perpetrated by "Napoleon III.'s double," as Eugène Vivier was called, may appear trivial. But the startling likeness of the famous cornet-player to the Emperor which made those jokes possible had its influence nevertheless on the Emperor personally, and gave rise to the most absurd stories during the heyday of the Empire, and above all at its fall ; all of which stories only tended to diminish the Emperor's prestige. People were too apt to remember Louis Napoleon's erratic habits before his accession to the Imperial throne, and albeit that, as we have seen already, those habits did not entirely cease until the end of his reign, they were both consciously and unconsciously exagger-

[1] I remember the *Journal de Paris* devoting one paragraph to the speech of the Emperor at the opening of the Chambers. The paragraph was inserted in the column headed "Faits Divers (*Anglicé*, "General News")."

to 1 by friends and foes, mainly through the unpardonable vanity—or worse, of Vivier—who took delight in impersonating the sovereign in and out of season and in all sorts of company, creditable or not as the case might be.

"Paris is ringing again with another exploit of Vivier," says my note. "This time he has impersonated the Emperor at a supper at Mme. de Païva's, and to such good purpose that several of her guests who frequently see and talk to his Majesty were completely taken in. It would appear that about a week ago the Emperor and the Empress were at the Italian opera, where Mme. de Païva's box faces that of their Majesties, and that the glare of the footlights hurt her Majesty's eyes. There was no screen in the Imperial box, and the Empress had only her fan to keep off the heat.[1] The Emperor remarked quite casually on the inconvenience to one of his aides-de-camp, saying, 'Mme. de Païva is better off than we are; look, what a beautiful Japanese screen she has!' The aide-de-camp in question happened to be on friendly terms with Mme. de Païva, and paid her a visit between the acts. Quite as casually as the Emperor, he remarked upon the beauty of the screen, adding that the Emperor would be pleased to have a similar one for the Empress. Thereupon Mme. de Païva

[1] Fans were very small in those days; the large ones date from much later.

unfastens the screen in question, hands it to her visitor, and bids him offer it to the Emperor with her respectful compliments for the use of the Empress. The aide-de-camp, though considerably embarrassed, dare not refuse the offer, and makes his way to the Imperial box with the screen, which he quietly adjusts in front of the Empress, who, however, sweeps it contemptuously out of her way. The Empress has not got her temper under sufficient control, and often allows it to get the better of her in public; under such circumstances the Emperor invariably pours oil upon the troubled waters, and he did so in this instance. He picked up the screen, and with a smile placed it in front of himself; and inasmuch as Mme. de Païva had narrowly watched the scene from the other side of the house, he considered himself bound to go and thank her personally the next day or the day after. For that part of the story I will, however, not vouch. I am under the impression that it is a pure fabrication, whether of Mme. de Païva herself or of some of her familiars I am unable to say. Both are equally inventive, and the rumour was evidently set afloat in order to find a basis for the next scene in which Vivier was to play his part. For even if one admits that the Emperor paid the alleged visit, his Majesty would certainly not have followed it up by inviting himself or accepting an invitation to a supper at Mme. de Païva's at any rate not to a supper in company with a half score of guests, not one of whom is particularly famed for the art of holding his tongue.

"Be this as it may, the supper with the carefully 'prepared' entrance of Vivier, took place and has furnished fresh gossip for at least a week. Practically, the Emperor is powerless to prevent these things; he can neither send Vivier into exile nor condemn him to wear a mask, but there was no necessity to invite Vivier to the Tuileries and to have the performance repeated for the delectation of all and sundry as the Emperor has done.

"The fact is, Vivier is *persona grata* with Louis Napoleon for a far different reason than people suspect. To begin with, Vivier is a Corsican; secondly, many years ago Vivier gave unsolicited testimony of Louis Napoleon's legitimacy, which has been so often called into question, and on the subject of which the Emperor is so exceedingly sensitive. It happened in 1844, while Vivier was giving some performances in London. One day he met a countryman of his named Ceccaldi, who told him that Prince Louis was in London, and that he (Vivier) ought to pay his respects to him. 'Come to the French Theatre to-night and I will present you,' said Ceccaldi. At that time Vivier had never set eyes on the Prince, but the moment he entered the Theatre he pointed him out to his companion. 'How do you know?' asked Ceccaldi; 'you have never seen him before?' 'No,' was the reply, 'but

I recognised him at once by the likeness to his father, to whom I was presented at Pisa.' Then there is the truly startling likeness between the Emperor and Vivier himself. Although it has already led to much mischief, *and may lead to further mischief*,[1] the Emperor, with his 'big heart,' his somewhat too-active imagination, and his fatalism, is almost convinced that Vivier's existence is more or less bound up with his own.

"Thus we have the Jester in Ordinary to the Court, *i.e.* Count Tascher; the Jester who performs 'by command,' namely Eugène Vivier; and we have also the *corps de ballet* and the *corps dramatique*, for now and again there are choregraphic and other entertainments, generally arranged by the Princesse von Metternich, who enjoys herself at the Tuileries as she probably would not be allowed to enjoy herself at the Hofburg. The daughter of the famous Count Szandor who, by the by, was as mad as a March hare does not think it incumbent on herself to observe the same strict rules of etiquette towards the grandson of a Corsican lawyer and his wife as she would be bound to

[1] I feel convinced that there was no prophetic intent to the words I have underlined in the above note. Nevertheless, after the fall of Sedan there were hundreds of people in France, and above all in Paris, who said that the Emperor was not at Wilhelmshöhe at all, that Vivier had been sent for in hot haste and had taken his place. Absurd as was the story, it was encouraged by the Republicans who saw in it a means of still further damaging the Emperor's prestige.

observe towards a Hapsburg and his spouse, herself a Princesse des Deux-Ponts-Birkenfeld. And to make the resemblance to the ordinary theatre complete, the noble and aristocratic ballerinas quarrel among themselves just like *rats de l'Opéra*, born of concierges and cabmen, and would come to blows now and then like the humbler born dancers, but for the timely intervention of the Empress.[1]

"Is it a wonder then that the Païvas, the Skittles, the Cora Pearls, and the rest shrug their shoulders and smile, nay, laugh outright, at the mention of some of those *grandes dames de par le monde*. I doubt whether many of those *déclassées* be very witty; nevertheless, they are credited now and then with saying things which are worthy of Ninon de l'Enclos or Rochefoucauld—although I strongly suspect that some of the clever literary men and journalists among their familiars are mainly responsible for the epigrammatic form of these remarks. This is perhaps another instance of 'Nemesis at work again,' for if in the beginning of the Empire the

[1] This is an allusion to a story, well known at the time, of a quarrel between Princesse von Metternich and Mme. de Persigny on the subject of the latter's dress in one of the entertainments. "Let her do as he likes," said the Empress to the Princesse, who would not give way. "Let her do as she likes; you know that her mother was more or less mad." "If that is a justification for letting her have her way, I am sure I shall not admit it," replied the Princesse; "for my father was downright mad." And the granddaughter of Michel Ney had to give in, and the Empress too. The Emperor told the story all round with great glee.

papers had been allowed a certain latitude in their comments upon matters political, the writers would not have been obliged to make themselves the assiduous chroniclers of the *faits et gestes* of the least creditable section of society, in order to live. As it is, these records have become a permanent feature and will probably not disappear, however much the stringent rules with regard to political comment be relaxed in the future. At present there appears to be a tendency in the other direction, and the Emperor—who I feel persuaded is liberally inclined—does not know which course to adopt in consequence of the multiplicity of his counsellors, not two of whom appear to be agreed as to the degree of liberty to be granted, and all of whom—not to mince words—are making fools of themselves."[1]

"Of course, the Cora Pearls, the Skittles, the Païvas, and the rest are only too delighted at all this, and, confident of the support of their friends the journalists, have entered into open rivalry with

[1] Strong as the latter words may seem, they do not exaggerate. M. Charles Boissière, a well-known literary man and a member of the Philotechnic Society, having applied for leave to hold courses on dramatic literature, the leave was granted by the Department of Arts at the Ministry of Public Education on the express condition that the name of Victor Hugo should not be mentioned. This same Department of Arts offered later on to buy Lazerge's picture "A Première at the Odéon," on condition that the artist should paint out the name of Rochefort. Barrias' "Exiles of Tiberius" was skyed at the Luxembourg; Eugène Delacroix's "Liberté guidant le peuple sur les barricades" was cut out of its frame, rolled up, and relegated to one of the attics.

the Court beauties—again, of course, on the only ground where such rivalry was possible, namely, Longchamps, the Bois de Boulogne, the Champs-Élysées, and the theatres. Mdme. de Païva's boxes at the Opéra and at the Italiens are more luxuriously appointed than those of the Emperor and Empress, her diamonds are more costly than the latter's; Skittles' pony chaise, with its pair of black cobs, and its two grooms on coal-black cattle behind, beats anything and everything from the Imperial stables; Cora Pearl's turn-out throws everything into the shade except Skittles', the two latter cut a better figure on horseback than either the Comtesse de Pourtalès, Mdme. de Gallifet, Mdme. de Contades, or Mdme. de Persigny; they have only two equals in that respect—the Empress and Mdme. de Metternich. Their carriage-horses, hacks, and hunters look better, are better bred and broken in than the best elsewhere, and need not fear comparison with those provided by General Fleury for the use of her Majesty. As may be readily imagined, her Majesty is not particularly pleased. Fleury admits that there is cause for displeasure, but professes himself unable to alter the state of things. 'In order to bring about the desired distinction between *les femmes comme il faut* and *les femmes comme il en faut* on horseback and on wheels, the former would have to revert to the condition of shabbiness that prevailed during the reign of Louis Philippe,' he said the other day. 'The Court would have to have the courage of the Comte de Lambertye, who, I should add, did not act from motives of disappointed pride.' And then he told me a story which, even in the annals of shady horse-dealing and horse-coping, it would be difficult to beat.

"When about two years ago at Lord Pembroke's death part of his stables was sold, few dared to venture on the purchase because they were under the impression that without the head groom and the head coachman the whole would come to grief, and both these worthies—but especially the latter—demanded terms which were absolutely prohibitory. Both, moreover, required special agreements for two or three years and specifying their duties beyond which they were not bound to perform any. More plucky than the rest the Comte de Lambertye submitted to every one of their demands—and to his cost, for he soon discovered that neither the head groom nor the head coachman, nor the two combined, had brought Lord Pembroke's establishment to the pitch of perfection it had enjoyed; but that this perfection had been due to the active surveillance of his lordship himself, and also, perhaps, to the intelligent care of his lordship's kinsman, M. de Montgomery who, out of the twenty-two horses constituting the stable, bought in two thirds.

"Comte de Lambertye, who is very young and

looks very innocent, is not a fool by any means. To ask those two Englishmen to rescind their engagement would have been so much waste of time. So he sold all his new purchases and bought the two vilest crocks imaginable, with which he showed himself every day in the Bois, to the great disgust of the head coachman, who had to drive them. At night the head groom had to take the latter's place. In a few weeks both the groom and the coachman offered to tear up their contracts. That was exactly what the Comte wanted."

But, as Fleury remarked, it required a good deal of courage on the part of a man to do this, still more on the part of women, the majority of whom were young, many exceedingly handsome, all very elegant, and whose great ambition it seemed to be to outvie each other in the beauty and costliness of their carriages and horses. By that time I was a young man of over twenty, and had paid several visits to London in the season, which enabled me to appreciate the difference—of course from a merely amateurish point of view—between the two capitals in the matter of horse-flesh and conveyances. Well, the trained and severely critical eye of the real connoisseur would have unquestionably awarded the palm for merit to the simple elegance of the Row and the Ladies' Mile; to the uninitiated the spectacle in the Avenue de l'Impératrice (at present the Avenue du Bois de Boulogne) would have appealed with greater effect. It was more showy; nevertheless, it was very beautiful, and the Parisians of that and the preceding generations had, from what I was told, never seen anything like it. The aristocracy drove in the Champs-Elysées and went to the races at Longchamps before the advent of the Second Empire, but as my informant observed, "their turn-outs as a rule looked as if they had come out of a circus, or else had been borrowed from a second-hand coach-dealer's; there was a great deal of brass and metal about the harnesses, and yellow predominated in the colour of the carriages, but what with the untidiness of the coachmen and footmen, who, in spite or because of their gorgeous liveries, were untidy, and the defective grooming of the horses, it was but a poor show." During the Restoration only a fifteenth part of the royal stables was "drafted" annually; in Louis Philippe's time the same, or nearly the same, system prevailed. The accident which caused the death of the late Comte de Paris' father was owing to a mistake of one of the grooms; the horse that was "put to" his carriage that day had been "drafted" on account of his hard mouth. During the Second Empire a third of the Imperial stables was annually "drafted," but the money thus spent would have simply made Louis Philippe's hair stand on end, if the hair had been real. Nevertheless the result was very beautiful.

So beautiful that the recollection in the shape of mental pictures has remained bright and vivid throughout these many, many years. I have no need to refer to notes to reconstruct the scenes; in fact, I have no notes bearing on that subject. I have simply to sit still and let the pictures uprise before me. The backgrounds are almost invariably the same; it is either the Arc de Triomphe standing like a grey pawn against a deep blue sky or the masses of dark green of the Bois apparently forming an impenetrable barrier at the end of the Avenue de l'Impératrice. That was where "fashionable Paris" foregathered during the spring and summer afternoons in the sixties, to see and to be seen. And verily, all had their reward, whether they played active or merely passive parts, even unto the two magnificent gendarmes on horseback, with their tall bearskins, who got their due share of admiration while they regulated the traffic.

The first in the field was generally Mdme. Feuillant with her two charming daughters, mere girls at that period. The whole of the turn-out was absolutely perfect, from an artistic point of view —I am not quite so sure about the other point—from the small heads of the two big black steppers, with large tufts of Parma violets at their headstalls, to the hood which appeared to do duty as a storehouse for similar bouquets large and small. Violets predominated in the whole of the arrangement; they were conspicuous in the bonnet of Mdme. Feuillant herself—a bonnet with a vallance and which enframed the face like a portrait; the footman and coachman had huge nosegays of violets, the tint of which harmonised admirably with the collars and cuffs of their dark green liveries. And the spectator who was not overburdened with worldly goods silently tried to calculate the probable amount of the florist's bill, who supplied them every day of the week.

More conspicuous, though not by reason of its floral adornment, was the carriage of Mdme. de Metternich. It was yellow, and yellow had almost entirely disappeared in those days, to be revived, however, later on. But in the early sixties only Mdmes. de Gallifet, de Jaucourt, and the Austrian Ambassadress patronised that colour.

Then came Rothschilds' turn-outs, always more remarkable for their magnificent horses than for the beauty of their carriages, and hard upon them the landau of Mdlle. Schneider, who as yet was not the Duchesse de Gérolstein, but simply La Belle Hélène.[1]

[1] During the Exhibition of 1867, Mdle. Schneider made a bet that she would pass through the gates exclusively reserved for the sovereigns and royal princes then visiting Paris. One day she appeared with the panels of her landau adorned with a fancy coat-of-arms. The gatekeeper challenging the footman, the latter replied—"The Duchesse de Gérolstein." The bet was won.

Between half past four and five there was generally a slight stir of expectation among the occupants of "la Plage," better known to-day as le Cercle des Décavés."[1] In a little while there appeared on the horizon four troopers of some crack regiment of the Imperial Guards, flanked by a corporal, and immediately afterwards came the carriage of the little Prince Imperial followed by a captain's escort of the same regiment. To the left of the carriage rode the officer in charge, with a trumpeter by his side; to the right M. Bachon, the Prince's riding-master and equerry, in a gold-embroidered green tunic, cocked hat with black feathers, white breeches and jack-boots. About that period, however, M. Bachon's office was an absolute sinecure, the Prince having met with an accident which disabled him for many, many months from mounting his ponies and the cause of which accident subsequently became also the cause of his premature and sad death in Zululand, although the effects of the accident itself had entirely disappeared.[2]

The Cercle des Décavés is the left side of the beginning of the Avenue du Bois de Boulogne on coming from the Champs-Élysées. It is set with chairs.

[2] I quote a note I made on the day the particulars of the Prince's accident came to hand. The note was written entirely from memory, but I feel certain that all my facts are correct. "Several of the Prince's little playfellows had a foreign (English?) riding-master who knew nothing of the classical traditions of the French school, or who taught his pupils things which M. Bachon, the Prince's riding-master, was probably unable and certainly unwilling to teach him. M. Bachon had been second master to the celebrated

Shortly afterwards came the Emperor in his phaeton without an escort of any kind and only his aide-de-camp by his side. The pace of his Orloffs, which had cost 40,000 francs, was remarkable and somewhat dangerous to those who got in their way, for every now and then, and up to the last, the Imperial whip forgetting that he was in France and not in England mistook his nearside for his offside. Not once but a dozen

M. d'Aure in Paris, afterwards he had taught at Saumur. M. d'Aure, however, though a most brilliant horseman himself, had not founded a school of horsemanship. He was what I should call a brilliant equestrian improvisator rather than a sterling teacher. M. Bachon was an excellent riding-master and that was all. He had none of the flashes of genius of his chief. He taught the Prince to ride perfectly broken-in ponies, and tacitly discountenanced all showy riding and tricks. And the showy riding and tricks were exactly what the little lad seemed to like most. Fired by the example of his playmates who vaulted in the saddle while their tiny mounts were going at a gallop, jumped down again, and repeated the feat over and again in spite of their frequent tumbles, the Prince tried to do the same, and one summer evening at Saint-Cloud while the Emperor was looking on, his son came heavily to the ground. He was up again in a moment, and there was no sign that he was badly or even slightly hurt. Had there been such a sign, the Emperor would have been too seriously alarmed to countenance for a single moment the continuation of the game, for assuredly no man ever loved his child better than Louis Napoleon loved his. The boy returned that affection a hundredfold, and it was this sweet trait in his character that caused him to hide his pain, for he fancied his father was annoyed with him for his inferiority to his playfellows. Was his father annoyed, and did he show his annoyance? I cannot say. Certain is it that the little Prince went on vaulting; young as he was he would not be beaten.

"I know of a similar case of perseverance on his father's part. One severe winter while he was staying at Leamington there was a great deal of skating, and one of the favourite games was to jump over an upturned chair while going at a great pace. Prince times have I heard the indignant Jehu exclaim "Where is he going to, the brute? Where did he learn to drive?" Though no man looked better on horseback than Napoleon III., he left off riding almost immediately after he ascended the throne, except on special occasions such as reviews and at Compiègne while out hunting. Already at that time the Emperor had his horses broken in by M. Faverol de Kerbrech, just as he had his new boots worn by his barber. Then came the Empress in her elegant calèche drawn by four bays with postilions, outrider, and grooms in green and gold, the first-named wearing jockeys' caps half hidden by the golden fringe of the tassels.

He attempted the feat several times without success, coming down each time with a tremendous crash that made the lookers-on stare. He would not give in, though, and finally conquered the difficulty.

"To come back to the little Prince who, after that night went on taking his riding lessons, but so languidly that M. Bachon began to reproach him with laziness. Instead of jumping into the saddle as he was wont to do, he had to be assisted, and in a little while barely lifted on to his pony. M. Bachon, as yet ignorant of what had happened, peremptorily bade him one day to place his foot into the stirrup, and then it all came out. Intensely frightened, the riding-master immediately communicated with the Emperor, who only remembered his son's fall in connection with his pluck. For months and months the child suffered and never mounted his pony. He recovered gradually, but the habit he had contracted of hoisting himself into the saddle by means of his hands clung to him. Many of his friends in England could bear testimony to it. It was the cause of his death in Zululand. Trusting to his skill, he attempted to jump on to his horse which was already in motion; the holster, of which he caught hold for the purpose, gave way, and he was left to face the foe by himself."

Amidst all this splendour the elegant simplicity of Lord and Lady Cowley's carriage, returning from the "Folly Saint-James" to the Embassy in the Faubourg Saint-Honoré, passed almost unperceived, just as later on the turn-out of Lord Cowley's successor (Lord Lyons), which was equally elegant, though a trifle less simple, would have attracted little or no notice but for one of its occupants—a fat black and tan terrier, gravely seated by the side of his lordship and the property, I believe, of the then Mr. (now Sir) Edward Malet, her Majesty's late Ambassador at Berlin. In those days, Lord Lyons was not the familiar figure to the Parisians he became subsequently. They had seen his immediate predecessor for over a decade and a half, and during the fifty years that had elapsed since Wellington bought the former mansion of the Ducs de Charost from Napoleon's favourite sister for £24,000, to convert it into the English Embassy, there had been in reality only about half a dozen chief tenants, including the purchaser and the latest comer, both Lord Granville and Lord Cowley having filled the office twice during that time.[1]

Wellington's bargain was a good one; at present the property is worth eight times the amount he paid for it. It was the only bargain he had

---

[1] During the century and five years that have elapsed since the First Revolution there have been twelve English ambassadors to France, forty French ambassadors to England.

during that stay, for on his own account he spent £120,000 in six weeks. But we must not forget that Wellington came to teach the Parisians to live decently and cleanly like gentlemen, to repair the mischief done by that libertine of a Napoleon. That was probably the reason why he provided so liberally for la Grassini, one of Napoleon's mistresses, for Wellington was such a saint.

CHAPTER IX

Joshua, the Son of Nun, was either a very clever man himself, or else the two emissaries he sent to spy the land, even Jericho, were thorough worldlings. Instead of applying for information to the "respectability that drives a gig" they went straight to Rahab, who was the reverse of respectable, because they knew that she would be able to tell them better where the shoe pinched in that prosperous country than ninety-nine per cent. of the ordinary inhabitants. For Rahab, wherever and whenever we meet her, whether it be in the West or in the East, whether it be in ancient or modern times, is sure to be possessed of more secrets than all the family doctors and lawyers of the locality put together. The stories of Holofernes and of Samson might have been left unwritten for the good they have done in teaching captains or statesmen reticence about their own and the public's affairs while they are under the spell of Dalila. As a consequence,

Dalila becomes not only sceptical with regard to the strength of mind of Holofernes and Samson themselves, but somewhat incredulous with regard to the virtues of Samson's and Holofernes' womankind. Ages before Byron had formulated the results of a husband's neglect of his wife in one line, Rahab knew that "what one man neglects another picks up."

The Rahab of the Second Empire—as distinct from la demi-mondaine[1] was probably neither

[1] In order to make this distinction clear to the reader, I must refer him to the inventor of the term itself. "But just as they gave to the land discovered by Columbus the name of a navigator who only came after him, so they have given to this word 'Demi-Monde' another meaning to what it really has; and this neologism which I was so proud to introduce into the French language, hospitable as it is in the nineteenth century, serves to designate, through the error or carelessness of those who use the word, the class of women from which I wished to separate the others; or at any rate serves to confound into one category two categories, not only very distinct from each other, but even very inimical to each other.

"In the interest of the dictionaries of the future let me lay down the principle that the 'Demi-Monde,' contrary to the common belief and in spite of what is printed, does not represent the ruck of courtesans, but the class of women that have lost caste. It is not given to every one to belong to the 'Demi-Monde.' It requires certain credentials to be admitted to it. Madame d'Ange says it in the second Act. 'That world represents a fall for those who start life at the top of the ladder, but it is a rise to those who begin at the bottom.' That world, in fact, is composed of women, all of honourable origin, who either as young girls, wives, or mothers were admitted by right into and warmly welcomed by the best families and who have deserted. The names they bear are simultaneously borne in the real society which has ostracised them, by men, women, and children for whom you and I profess the most deserved esteem and to whom, by a tacit convention, we never mention their wives, daughter, or mothers. Nevertheless, as it will not do to be too severe, especially when one is bent on amusing one's self always, the 'Demi-Monde' also admits young girls whose *début* in life was marked by a false step, women who merely live with a man better bred nor better educated than the majority of her predecessors and successors. Now and then one met with a replica of Alphonsine Plessis (the original of *La Dame aux Camélias*) who in spite of her neglected childhood, humble birth and profligate associations was naturally refined; but as a rule the Lola Montès type predominated. There was neither a Ninon de l'Enclos nor an Esther Guimont, still less an Aspasia among the cour-

whose name they bear, elegant and pretty foreign women recommended and vouched for by one of the familiars of that circle under her personal responsibility—in short, all the women who originally belonged to a more regularly constituted society and whose fall was caused by love, but by love only; *nudus, sed pauper*.

"That world begins where the lawful wife finishes; it finishes where the venal wife begins. It is divided from the world of honest women by the public scandal it provokes; it is divided from the world of courtesans by money. On the one side its boundary is determined by an article of the Code, on the other by a roll of gold pieces. The last argument it clings to is this: 'We give ourselves, we do not sell ourselves;' and a member of that world is ostracised for having sold herself, as she was ostracised from the regularly constituted society for having given herself. In that world the man always remains the debtor of the woman, and the latter may flatter herself that she is respected as of yore on seeing her debtor treat her in the street as if she were still his equal. On those women who have recovered their freedom of action one cannot bestow one's name, but one may offer her one's arm at any time. They give themselves to those who please them, not to those whom they happen to please. Nevertheless, everything in that world is still strictly conducted in accordance with the love of pleasure and the pleasure of love; and that very same world might easily be mistaken now-a-days for that of the women 'who want none of him' rather than for that of the men 'who want none of her.' In spite of all this, there is no denying that during the latter-day oscillations of the social planet these different worlds have become so often intermixed as to have engendered by contact some pernicious inoculations."—Alex. Dumas, Preface to *Le Demi-Monde*.

courts of that period. Various causes combined, however, to give them a different standing from that which their sisters had occupied during the preceding reigns. Though no saint, Napoleon I. detested the courtesan under no matter what guise she plied her trade. Neither La Grassini nor Mdlle. Georges would have found favour in his sight if she had used her talents as a singer or as an actress for a bait. "Many women have fallen because they were on the stage;" he said one day: "no woman should be on the stage for the sole reason that she has fallen, and she should not make the stage a pedestal for the exhibition of her charms to be sold to the highest bidder." For having done this before her marriage with the coachbuilder Simon, the notorious Mlle. Lange was one night shown the door of the Tuileries, after she had been made "an honest" woman. During the Restoration all mention of the courtesan was distinctly avoided in polite society, and she was certainly not made the subject of newspaper articles. Although there were five young princes in Louis Philippe's time, all five were exceedingly circumspect in their intercourse with this class of women. The princes had, if not the fear of God, the fear of their father before them, and the latter dreaded the censure of the "austere and respectable M. Guizot" who nevertheless was on one occasion drawn into a correspondence with Esther Guimont.

Justice compels one to state, though, that there was no epistolary interchange of sweet nothings but simply a very practical and hard-headed attempt on the part of the Minister to win over to his cause Emile de Girardin, who was an intimate, albeit platonic, friend of Esther. But at no time during the period just reviewed did the courtesan claim moral and social equality with the *grande dame de par le monde;* it was reserved for the Second Empire to see that claim preferred on the former's part, and to have the claim admitted by society at large.

There is no doubt that the Emperor himself was largely responsible from beginning to end for this demoralising condition of things. The Païvas, Skittles, Cora Pearls, and others originally belonged to the same class whence had sprung Marguerite Bellanger, and there was no reason in the minds of the former why they should not hold their heads as high as the latter ; for let there be no mistake about it, the discovery of Marguerite's love epistles (?) after the fall of the Empire taught the people nothing that they did not already know, and the compeers of Marguerite were even better informed than the world at large. There was no reason why the courtesans who had not attracted the sovereign's attention as yet should not hold their heads as high—in anticipation of what might happen—as the one who had ; inasmuch as the next day might bring the desired distinction.

Even if that distinction were denied to them, they were amply justified in considering themselves as good as the majority of the *grandes dames de par le monde*, the doings of the latter differing but little from their own. The barrack-room stories that enlivened the soirées and dinner parties of a De Païva came straight from the Tuileries, unless they went straight thither from De Païva's drawing room. When in the early morning of the 16th August of every year, the Bal Morel disgorged its revellers, there was not a pin to choose between the appearance and behaviour of the Court beauties in their quasi-disguise of grisettes and that of the *filles de joie au naturel*. The women knew one another's names and biographies as if they had been playmates and schoolfellows; the men who escorted the two sections had probably left their clubs together the night before, and would most likely meet there again in a few hours to discuss the merits (?) of their respective partners. Several among those proud and aristocratic cavaliers had been on one or two occasions the more or less successful peacemakers, or, at any rate, the ambassadors, between the two contending factions when one of its members found themselves on ground more exclusive than Morel's *al fresco* ball, and would not leave the coast clear to one another. The most notable mission of that kind was the one undertaken by the Duc de Gramont-Caderousse

—" notre duc," as the counterjumpers and clerks of that period who aped him in everything, called him. Skittles made her appearance at a meet where her presence was objected to by a foreign princess. The Duc was despatched to Skittles, and knowing the temper of the *lady*, thought he would proceed diplomatically. "You who are at the head of your profession," he said, most insinuatingly, "how dare you run the risk of being asked to leave?" "That's where you are mistaken," was the answer, " I am not at the head of my profession, it's the princess. That's why I am here; you may tell her I say so."

History does not relate how the Duc got out of the dilemma; and my only reason for telling the anecdote was to show by something more than mere assertion the attitude of the courtesan towards the *grande dame* in those days. And let it not be thought that Skittles was the only one to censure by comparison. With her terrible French, which was that of an illiterate stable boy, and which Alphonse Daudet faithfully reproduced in *Sapho*, where she figures under the name of " Wilkie Cob," Cora Pearl was even more brutal than Skittles. She not only lashed the women of the Imperial *entourage*, but poured the vials of her contempt on the men who flung fabulous sums at her feet. "Your princes and kings," she said, in her gibberish, " your princes and kings, I have trampled upon them; and then they went for

consolation to the *Tuileries*; why, the *Tuileries*
my lumber room."

The Vicomtesse de Païva, afterwards Gräfin Henckel von Donnersmarck, was even more brutal, more vicious than Skittles and Cora Pearl together. She had the advantage over both, though, in the possession of more brain. The daughter of a German-Jewish pedlar named Lachman, her childhood had been spent in the Ghetto of Moscow, which she left to marry a poor French tailor whose name was Villoing. A few years later she became the inseparable companion of the famous pianist, Henri Herz, with whom she visited the principal cities of Europe, until, frightened at her extravagance, he was compelled to part from her. With the natural aptitude of most Germans and Russians for picking up languages, Pauline Lachman soon mastered French, which she afterwards spoke fluently. With the natural intelligence of her race, she profited by her association with Herz, which brought her into contact with some of the foremost artists and writers of those days to get a layer of veneer which both Skittles and Cora Pearl lacked, which they would not have taken the trouble to acquire if they could have done so, and at which with the insular conceit of the English cad—whether male or female—they jeered. Nevertheless, Pauline Lachman, as I have said, was more brutal and more vicious than either of these. There was no attempt on their part to enact the *grande dame*, to ape the Aspasia of ancient Greece, or the grand courtesan of the Renaissance; they professed no admiration for journalists and authors nor did they seek to entertain them; at the same time, their hospitality, on the rare occasions it was exercised, had no *arrière pensée* in it; it was not gratitude for a favour to come in the shape of an advertisement. They were not devoured with envy of the court beauties; they looked upon them frankly as competitors, and hated them accordingly. They only defended themselves when attacked directly or indirectly.

Pauline Lachman attacked both court beauties and others without the smallest provocation. Unlike Esther Guimont, Anna Deslions, Skittles, and Cora Pearl themselves, she never admitted another woman to her parties; and one evening when a guest, who was probably somewhat weary of that everlasting "one woman arrangement," casually remarked upon her solitude as regarded female companionship, she flew at him like a tigress. "If you would like me to send for some of the Faubourg St. Germain beauties, you have only to say so," she snarled. "I am sufficiently rich to treat you to a few duchesses; their fees do not run higher than some of ours, at any rate, not higher than mine." The reader will agree with me that Pauline Lachman was more brutal, were disgustingly coarse in her strictures than was of the others.

To ascertain the exact proportions of truth and falsehood contained in those accusations is impossible, or, if not impossible, at variance with my personal inclinations. If the *chronique scandaleuse* of the Second Empire were not so inextricably mixed up with its political history, I would fain have kept my pen clean of the former altogether; as it is, I cannot do so except at the risk of becoming unintelligible. When one stands confronted with a *régime* which, during its eighteen years' existence waged four formidable wars, not one of which on careful examination seems to have been necessitated by the nation's welfare, the natural impulse is to look for the causes of such wars below the surface.

And a glance below the surface reveals, behind that glittering Court which every one knows, with its ambassadors, chamberlains, generals, ministers, and ladies of honour, a seething mass of intrigue and corruption to find the like of which we must revert to the reigns of Charles II. in England and of Louis XV. in France. True, there is no titular mistress of the Emperor, either in the shape of a Lady Castlemaine, a Duchess of Portsmouth or a Marquise de Pompadour, but it is doubtful whether erstwhile Mrs. Palmer, Louise de Kerouailles and Madame d'Étioles were more fatal to the Stuart and the Bourbon than the women who surrounded the nephew of the great Bonaparte. Not one, save Princesse Clotilde inspired the public with that respect which is the first and foremost condition of the prestige of a dynasty, whether that dynasty be hereditary, founded by the sword or by intrigue as were the dynasties of Louis Philippe and Louis Napoleon. Of one thing we may be sure, in spite of the cheers that greeted the Empress in public; the French spoke of her and the ultra-fashionable throng that surrounded her as the English of the latter end of the seventeenth century spoke of the court beauties of Charles II., as the French of the middle of the eighteenth century spoke of the *grandes dames* of Louis XV.'s Court. And the gossip, an attractive dish of truth and fiction, especially where the Empress herself was concerned, spread over the borders of the land; and, as in the days of Charles II. and Louis XV., found its way to the Courts of Europe. Smart attachés, if not their chiefs themselves, sent amusing accounts of the *faits et gestes* of the women and men that foregathered at Compiègne, Fontainebleau, and the Tuileries; accounts which vitiated beforehand all the serious documents emanating from the Quai d'Orsay; the recipients of the latter refusing to take *au sérieux* the political aspirations of a sovereign who tolerated around him a society fully as profligate and corrupt as that which had danced and disported itself in the *salons* and gardens of Ver-

…under the *ancien régime*, a society led by a [...] "hallowed by marriage," it is true, in[asmuch] as she had successfully angled for an Im[perial] husband, where the other had only angled [for a] Royal lover, but a Pompadour for all that, and [who] only differed from Jeanne Antoinette Poisson [in] the possession of fewer brains, and if it were possible of more vanity and misdirected ambition.

The comparison between the mistress of Louis XV. and the lawful wife of Napoleon III. was not of my seeking. It was practically forced upon me by several notes the source of which I have already indicated at the beginning of the [4th?] part of these papers and for which I could find no room in *An Englishman in Paris*. There is no indication as to the exact date of these notes, nor were they all written at the same time, but several events to which they refer incidentally show them to belong to the first half of the sixties, I have given most of them *in extenso*, for the writer, not content with pointing out casually the likeness between Madame Lenormand d'Etioles and the ex-Empress of the French, takes up each moral and mental trait of their characters and provides a semi-historical, semi-social background for each of his portraits, thereby allowing us to judge for ourselves as well.

" I have just returned from Compiègne, where I had not been for three years, and was irresistibly reminded of a conversation with Vély Pasha at a dinner party at the Tuileries shortly after the Emperor's marriage. The haunted look we noticed then on the faces of the courtiers and even on those of the Sovereigns has altogether disappeared. *On s'amuse ferme*,[1] and I am not at all certain whether they are not enjoying themselves a little too much, and in a fashion not altogether calculated to enhance the prestige of the dynasty with the other courts of Europe. I must confess that my foresight, or let me say my expectations, in that respect have been woefully disappointed, although at the outset they bade fair to be realised. I did not for a moment imagine that the Tuileries would become dowdy, dull and respectable the greater part of the year and ridiculously *bourgeois* on so-called grand occasions as it was in the days of Louis Philippe; but I fancied that the golden mean would be observed; I fancied that the company there would become a cross between that of Versailles, in the most brilliant days of Louis XIV. and that of the First Empire at its most prosperous period; in other words, I fancied that part of the Faubourg St. Germain would gradually rally to the Second Empire, and neutralise by its grand air and unimpeachable manners the too obviously soldatesque *sans-façon*, from which even the best of Napoleon III.'s marshals and generals —with the exception of Macmahon—are not wholly

---

[1] A paraphrase of a French commercial term "acheter ferme," that is, buying outright without any restrictions.

for the somewhat too conquering attitude of the male civilian element towards the women, and the rather challenging tactics of the latter in response. This blending of two sections of society no doubt commended itself to the Emperor, especially when, after his accession to the throne, he cast a look around him and found himself deserted by the '*vraie compagnie*,' and notably by the female part of it, that had graced the Salon of the Elysée during the presidency. With this end in view he would have willingly made many sacrifices to concentrate the old *noblesse*, and even gone a step further than his uncle under similar circumstances. Napoleon III. would have put the old *noblesse* into places short of the very highest, by which I mean that he would have entrusted the men with diplomatic missions as he eventually did with a few that came to him, although at that time he would not have conferred a ministry on a known partisan of Legitimacy.[1] 'These people

[1] Napoleon I.'s policy with regard to the Faubourg Saint-Germain may be judged by the following scene which is scarcely known. In 1811, at the death of M. J. Chenier, Chateaubriand was elected to fill his vacant chair at the Académie. As a matter of course, the opening speech of the author of *Le Génie du Christianisme* was looked forward to with considerable interest. The Emperor was equally anxious to see what the great writer would have to say on the events of the Revolution, the trial, condemnation, and execution of Louis XVI., and subsequent transformations. The proofs were submitted to Napoleon, who was the reverse of pleased with them. He began by venting his bad humour on the members of the Académie, who would have quietly allowed these things to go forth to the world without considering the harm they might do. He never ceased talking about it to his

understand nothing of politics, and I did not want them for that. I only required them for decorative purposes, for they are eminently fitted to wear gold lace. I would have willingly gilded them on all their edges,' he said afterwards.

entourage; in fact, for several days it was the only subject of his conversation. M. d'Haussonville (the grandfather of the present count), who was one of Napoleon's first chamberlains, has preserved for us the exact words with which the Tuileries rang at the time. "This surpasses everything! I am killing myself body and soul to make this country forget her divisions in the past; I cured her of her revolutionary fever by intoxicating her with military glory. All my efforts have been directed to making old and new France live in peace under my sceptre. I have gathered in unison around me men who formerly detested one another. I have succeeded in causing to live in amity at my court and near me, erstwhile *émigrés*, members of the Committee of Public Safety and regicides, for you Cambacérès, you also voted for the death of Louis XVI., albeit that you deny having done so, but I know very well what to believe and what not to believe. Having done all this, am I tamely to submit to a vainglorious man of letters compromising the happy results of my policy, simply in order to afford him the chance of elegantly rounding off his periods. They are a lot of ungrateful idiots indeed. They have no idea what they are doing; they have not the least comprehension of the part I am playing. The royalists have always their mouths full of Henri IV. But I am Henri IV. My situation is absolutely similar to his; I am simply recasting his work and in much more difficult times. Nay, I am, perhaps, doing his work better than he did it, although he was a very able prince. He was placed between the champions of the League and the Protestants, just as I am placed between the revolutionaries and the partisans of the *ancien régime*. When he attempted to do something for his former co-religionists, the Leaguers shouted that he had remained a Huguenot. When he granted a favour to the Catholics, Duplessis-Mornay and the companions of his first campaigns shouted that he had forgotten his old and true friends. I am labouring under similar difficulties. People hold their tongues or else they recriminate with closed doors because I do not allow them to adopt a loud tone. But for all that, I can hear with half an ear; I know exactly how the land

And some of them have consented to be gilt in that fashion, but, unlike their predecessors under the First Empire, they consider that the obligation is entirely on the side of the dispenser of the favours, and the nephew has not the strength of character of the uncle to tell them to leave the Court, if not France, unless their presence confers credit and not discredit on the dynasty. In fact, I doubt whether any except the most drastic measures in that respect would be of the least avail now: the thing has gone on too long, and instead of the Versailles society of Louis XIV., blended with some of the virtues of the military and civil *parvenus* of the Napoleonic era, we have a glittering, but utterly dissolute and ethically worthless society, which is simply a startling reproduction of the Pompadour era, *plus* the swagger and barrack-language of the *beau sabreur* at his worst whom, in spite of that swagger and his late successes in the field I suspect to be lacking in the sterling soldierly qualities and unquestionable warlike talents of his *devanciers*. The Court, as I

le , and if I did not impose my own laws, these people would devour one another, for the passions that are at the bottom of our hearts nowadays are a bit more intense than those of the Vert Galant's time, and all these beauteous ladies who hold their heads so high and refuse to appear at my court would be in a sad plight if I let my lions loose. It is I who protect them all, and after having done all this, I shall not be fool enough to be defied openly by a paladin who does not understand in the least degree the work I am accomplishing. M. de Chateaubriand is not pleased with the France such as I have made it for him. Very well, let him go and live elsewhere."

saw it at Compiègne a day or two ago, presents the most heterogeneous gathering of humanity it has ever been my lot to behold away from the gaming-rooms at Baden-Baden, with which it has also one trait in common besides its outward elegance, namely, its absolute egoism, the unscrupulous hostility of each of its members towards his neighbour, like himself in pursuit of a favour, a possibly profitable transaction, or an intrigue. Like the gathering at Baden-Baden it is, as I have said, composed of utterly dissimilar elements. There is the semi-ruined old *noblesse* side by side with the prosperous Jewish financial fraternity; there is the *bourgeoisie* with all the greed of the French *bourgeoisie* of olden as well as modern times thick upon it and sorely perplexed at its inability to keep its hoard; there are Harpagons emulating with wry faces the lavishness of the Gramont-Caderousses and the Demidoffs and the rapacious would-be Massenas and spendthrift would-be Lasalles but lacking the military genius that distinguished the Duc de Rivoli and the hero of Prentzlau.

"Do what one will, it is impossible to close one's eyes to these facts forced upon one's notice the moment one sets one's foot within the court circle, and the mental cataract which evidently prevents the Emperor from seeing them will, I am afraid, have to be removed one day, remote or near, with danger to himself and to his dynasty. The gambling stories alone are sufficient to make one's hair stand on end, and the culprits, whether they figure as hawks or pigeons, invariably belong to the army. Those convicted of cheating, albeit not publicly—not merely suspected— are not only allowed to retain their commissions but are received at Court as if nothing had happened. The Comte d'Andlau was caught red-handed at Chantilly a twelvemonth or so before the revolution that cost Louis Philippe his throne. He was compelled to lie low during the remainder of the Citizen Monarchy, and during the whole of the Second Republic, but at present he holds his head as high as ever.[1] A lieutenant in the Guards, a victim this one, lost 20,000 frs. at one sitting. He had not a red cent towards the money, but he did not worry himself in the least, and in the morning he simply applied to the Emperor. The move was a masterly one, apart from the young fellow's knowledge that the Emperor never refused an appeal for money as long as he had any to give. He wound up his request by saying that there were only three courses open to him, viz., the appeal

---

[1] This is the same Comte d'Andlau who was implicated in the "Caffarel Scandal" in 1887 and had to fly the country. He died about three years ago, very poor, in one of the South American Republics, the Argentine, I believe. When in 1870 he started for the seat of war, one of his trunks got lost. On its recovery it was found to contain nothing but woman's underclothing, the property of the companion who had joined him at Metz.

he ventured on, dishonour, or suicide. Of course under the circumstances the Emperor could not very well refuse if he had felt inclined to do so, which, truth to tell, he did not. He could not very well have had it said of him that he had driven a promising young officer to suicide for the sake of a few thousand francs. I know well enough, though, what would have happened if a similar request had been preferred to Wilhelm of Prussia or Francis-Joseph of Austria who, I have not the least doubt, are as tenacious of the honour of their officers as is the Emperor of the French. The honour of the officer would have remained safe, but he would have had to pay for it with the loss of his commission.[1]

[1] The laws on gambling in the army were and are very strict both in Austria and Germany proper. I do not know enough of Austria to be able to say what would have happened there under similar circumstances, but I fancy the author of the note is correct in his surmise that King Wilhelm would not have been quite so lenient as was Napoleon III. At any rate I knew two Prussian officers who lost their commissions for having gambled away more than they could pay. In the one case the gambling debt was paid; the gambler was, however, cashiered. During my stay in Paris I used to meet him frequently; he had become a correspondent for several German papers. In the other case the debt was not paid; the dishonoured gambler was obliged to leave the country. He took service in the French foreign legion. The last time I saw him, about four years ago, he was doing well as a military coach in London, for by that time he was close upon sixty. The late Emperor Wilhelm, though, did not always punish so severely, especially when the offender happened to be the gainer instead of the loser. For some time after the revolution of 1849 the Duchy of Baden was occupied by the Prussian troops that had helped to quell the insurrection. The officers quartered at Rastadt had been especially cautioned against playing at Baden Baden. One summer

The Emperor scarcely reprimanded the young fellow. Opening a bundle of notes, he handed him the money. 'The life of one of my soldiers is worth more than the sum of which you stand in need;' he said, with that peculiar smile which constitutes his greatest charm. 'But I am not at all rich and I might not be able at all times to redeem it at such a price. Go and sin no more.'

"Of Napoleon III.'s goodness of heart there cannot be the smallest doubt, but I am afraid it is being taken advantage of on all sides; and, what is worse, he knows it, and half of his sadness is due to his knowledge. The sentence, 'The

current King (then Prince) Wilhelm strolled into the gaming rooms and noticed an officer in mufti at play. The officer was winning, not much, but a good deal for a Prussian lieutenant, for there were four Friedrichs d'or on the red. He had begun with one and the colour had turned up twice. Just as he was about to pick up the money he caught sight of the Prince watching him. Terror-stricken, he stood as if rooted to the spot. The red turned up a third, then a fourth time, still the officer did not move. At last the maximum was reached, and the croupier asked—"Combien à la masse?" No answer. "Combien à la masse?" shouted the croupier once more. Thereupon the Prince walked round to the officer's side, tapped him on the shoulder and said gently—"Take up your money and go, lest one of your chiefs should catch you here." As a matter of course, the lieutenant did not want telling twice. A couple of days later there happened to be a review at Rastadt. Prince Wilhelm caught sight of the lieutenant and sent for him. "Lieutenant * * * *," he said, "after you went away, the red turned up four times more. I prevented you from winning four times the maximum which you would have been sensible enough to stake. You can draw upon me for that amount. But take my advice: do not gamble again. M. Benazet is not the enemy to attack twice under similar conditions."

life of one of my soldiers is worth more than the sum of which you stand in need,' is very pretty, but utterly untrue. I doubt whether Napoleon III. uttered it for effect, I do not think so ; but take his army from whatever point of view you will—from the military, the moral, or the social—there are not many officers in it the redemption of whose life is worth 20,000 francs.

"This does not mean that there are no competent and honourable men in that army to the efficiency of which France will eventually have to trust for her political supremacy in Europe ; but these men are systematically snubbed, discouraged, and thrust into the shade by the military Court party, which is distinctly a creation of the Empress, to whom the barrack-room manners of a Pélissier, for instance, are naturally distasteful. She seems to be entirely ignorant of the fact that between the fall of the First Empire and the rise of the Second there has sprung up a race of soldiers as far removed from the very wonderful but nevertheless very ignorant and rough-hewn generals of the great Napoleon as the latter were removed from the highly-educated and highly-polished but nevertheless the reverse of wonderful generals of the *ancien régime*, who, like the Duc de Saint-Simon, grumbled and threw up their commissions because at the age of twenty-seven they had got no farther than their colonelcy which, like that of the immortal author of the *Memoirs*, their

parents had bought for them when they were
  ...dless lads. That military court *coterie* dare
  ...t ignore the claims of a Pélissier, but it pooh-
p...hs the claims of a Stoffel, a Trochu, and a
score of others who are their superiors in every way
except in the art of bowing and scraping, leading
the cotillon, and coining smart epigrams. These
men, the Stoffels and Trochus, are of opinion
that if promotion cannot always be gained on the
battle-field face to face with the enemy, it should
at any rate not be sought for in the drawing-room,
but be won in the barrack's schoolroom, on the drill-
ground, and in the camp. They are gentlemen in
the best acceptation of the term, somewhat Puri-
tanical as far as their profession is concerned and
consequently as averse to the introduction of the
barrack-room into the boudoir—which is the
Pélissier way—as they are to the introduction of
the boudoir element and influence into the army—
which is the way of the court *coterie*. The Stoffels
and Trochus are the lives which are worth more
than 20,000 francs a-piece, or would be if their
owners did not allow their tempers to be soured
by the others and did not keep sulking in their
tents.

"But if the court *coterie* objects to barrack-yard
manners à la Pélissier¹ in the drawing-room, they

This repeated harping on the Duc de Malakoff's name is prob-
... e to a well-known story of the Duc's behaviour on his
... day. I am neither strait-laced nor squeamish, but I
... print it.

do not appear to entertain a similar objection to introducing *boudoir*-influence into the army. Of course the *coterie* would fain preserve a monopoly in this respect, but the courtesan claims in this, as in all other things, equality with the aristocratic *intrigante*. Here is a story to that effect which was running the round of Paris only the other day, and a story running the round of Paris soon spreads to the provinces and across the frontier provided it be scandalous enough.

"Anna Deslions, whose real name is Deschiens and who a few years ago was taken under the wing of the famous Esther Guimont, lost her father. I suppose he was neither worse nor better than a great many French fathers of the lower classes; he was perfectly aware of his daughter's doings, which knowledge did not prevent him from living very comfortably on the allowance she made him. Anna, it appears, was never tired of extolling his virtues, and insisted on his having a magnificent funeral, for the funds for which she applied to her 'protector-in-chief' who happens to be a general of brigade and a curmudgeon of the first water. He simply applied to the Military Governor of Paris for a battalion and the band of the regiment quartered in the Faubourg Poissonnière *for the obsequies of a veteran of the First Empire*, which request was granted most graciously. The funeral service was held at St. Laurent, and the female friends of the bereaved daughter mustered in great force. The papers gave a minute account of the affair, but somehow the story of the deception leaked out. The general was reprimanded, but the Emperor, always anxious to avoid scandals, ordered the thing to be hushed up. He, however, stopped the general from inviting private tenders for the celebration of the yearly mass for the repose of old Deschiens's soul, which that delectable warrior wanted to do in imitation of his fellow-soldier, General Fabvier, who died in '55.[1]

"When Esther Guimont, who intellectually, at any rate, is a cut above the rest of *ces dames*, was told of the Emperor's displeasure at the indignity put upon the army, she had her answer ready, and truth compels one to admit that from her point of view it was unassailable. 'If the Emperor is so tenacious about the honour of his army,' she said, 'he should not allow his wife to bully one of his Cent Gardes for fun, and to slap his face—still for fun—because the bullying failed to make him abandon his statue-like attitude.'"

Thus far the note, the absolute accuracy of

[1] The author of the note is perfectly right, but he should also have stated that General Fabvier, who fought with Byron in Greece, was comparatively poor and very religious. Fabvier signed the contract about eighteen months before his death, and paid a lump sum down. It was the curé of St. Germain l'Auxerrois who was the successful competitor "for the life-insurance hereafter," as an irreverent wag described the arrangement.

which I could prove by others in my possession
and from entirely different sources. A careful study
of these leads me to one conclusion, which I will
endeavour to state as briefly as possible. Of all
those who " had the ear" of Napoleon III., there
were not more than four—certainly not more than
half-a-dozen counsellors—who were loyally devoted to him and to his dynasty. The others
merely looked upon the dynasty as a stepping-
stone to the acquisition of enormous wealth, as
an instrument for the gratification of their vanity,
and the realisation of ambitious schemes more
guilty still. If the latter were unfolded here in
their naked truth, the revelation would raise a
storm of invective such as a man endowed with
far greater courage than mine might well wish to
avoid. This much I will say, come what may :
with the exception of Persigny, Fleury, Rouher,
Mocquard, Princesse Mathilde, Princesse Anna
Murat (Duchesse de Mouchy), and to a certain
extent Walewski, every man and woman at the Tuileries worked for his or her own hand, and by their
matchless selfishness, utter absence of scruple, and
overweening conceit, incurred the withering contempt and scathing, but nevertheless deserved, criticism of a section of society, the existence of which
is tacitly ignored in every well-ordered community,
in spite of its presence being as plain as the sun
on a bright summer's day.

The male counterpart of this section, consisting

of *chevaliers d'industrie*, company promoters of a kind, shady financiers, and the like, were more practical. They neither indulged in profitless sneers and recriminations against the *manieurs d'argent* at court, nor instituted comparisons between the latter and themselves. They knew that such comparisons would have been simply ridiculous. From the time that Mouvillon de Glimes had started his "limited company" entitled Société Anonyme de Produits Chimiques, and without as much as showing a printed share or prospectus, had swooped in a million and a half of francs, with which he decamped across the Pyrénées to join the Empress's mother, unmolested then or afterwards; from that time the swindlers not affiliated to the court knew the futility of competing with those who were. The former might be just as clever as the others—in many instances they were as clever and cleverer—but the law when it overtook them had to show itself doubly severe to dispel the suspicion attached to it of having been utterly apathetic on former occasions. No one was ever deceived by this except Napoleon III. himself, who fondly imagined that the nation could be hoodwinked by the system of making the less guilty pay for the more guilty, for it finally became a system. And thus it came to pass that the sovereign, who, during the whole of his reign had been contantly engaged in shielding the most unscrupulous, and at the same time most cowardly, freebooter of his time, lent himself to the persecution—for prosecution is too mild a term—of a comparatively innocent man. I am alluding to Mirès, who was to Morny as John Law to the fraudulent son of a banker. The latter goes on using his father's name and influence to make dupes, knowing full well that when the crash comes the father will step in and hush the matter up at the risk of being reduced to beggary himself.

That the Emperor had to do this frequently, the papers found at the Tuileries after the fall of the Empire leave not the smallest doubt; that he finally got tired of this incessant and enormous strain on his purse there is equally no doubt. One instance among many will suffice. One morning there came—by appointment of course—to the Emperor's private room an individual a mere glance at whom revealed the prosperous, irrepressible, loud-voiced and loud-mannered *brasseur d'affaires*.[1] His fingers and shirt-front blazing with diamonds, the formidable gold chain across his chest, the ample cut of his brand new clothes, everything in short proclaimed the prosperity to be of recent standing. He came to submit to His Majesty the project of some new works to be constructed in the heart of the capital. The Emperor, though rarely surprised at anything, was surprised this time, and could not help showing

[1] Literally "a brewer of business"; the French equivalent for the still more modern and more euphemistic English term "promoter."

surprise. The scheme, though a vast one, had nothing to recommend itself or to distinguish it from a hundred others; it was on the face of it a gigantic building speculation, and nothing more. The Emperor as good as said so, and added that in any case it was a matter for his Minister of Public Works and not for himself to decide, at which remark the applicant opened his eyes very wide. "That would be true, Sire, under ordinary circumstances," he began somewhat timidly, "but in this instance your Majesty has been informed of the whole affair beforehand." This time it was the Emperor who opened his eyes very wide. "I have been informed of nothing, Monsieur," he said. "I beg your Majesty's pardon," stammered the applicant, "but——" "I beg your pardon, Monsieur," replied the Emperor, "but——" "M. de Morny has told your Majesty nothing?" "M. de Morny has told me nothing."

Thereupon the applicant, unable to contain himself any longer, burst out, "The cheat, the cheat! And I who gave him a hundred thousand francs but two days ago, because he told me that your Majesty had promised to support my project!" The Emperor calmly dismissed his visitor, but a few hours later there was a stormy scene between him and Morny, or, to be absolutely correct, he enacted a stormy scene with Morny as a spectator, for the latter remained perfectly unmoved and simply smiled. "For two twos he would have applauded as one applauds a mummer at whom one laughs inwardly for overdoing the thing," said the Emperor bitterly, when he told the affair to Fleury. "Instead of which, when I left off abusing him for sheer want of breath, he quietly remarked: 'Your Majesty is really too kind to worry yourself about such an idiot as that. As for myself, I wash my hands of him.'"

This is the synopsis of one of the innumerable one-act pieces that preceded the big tragedy entitled "The Campaign in Mexico," the inception of which must have been due to some such scene as the one I described just now between the Emperor and Morny's dupe—though with a difference. Jecker, the Swiss money-monger, who had lent Miramon 7,425,000 francs—or at any rate nearly half that sum in bare money—was a somewhat more important personage than the Frenchman whom the Emperor had been obliged to dismiss so unceremoniously; especially after he, Jecker, had done France the honour to become naturalised and had begun to press his claim of 75,000,000 francs against Mexico. Morny himself, though daring enough, would not have dared to wash his hands of him, and instead of the play ending with the exit of Jecker from the private room of Napoleon III., whither he may have gone not unknown to Morny, the play had

T

only reached the end of its prologue. I do not state this to be an absolute fact; I merely surmise, for everything connected with the initial business of the War in Mexico is so enwrapped in mystery that one must not speak with certainty. Consequently an attempt to let in light on that subject as well as on the subsequent events becomes impossible at the end of a chapter, but I will endeavour to do so in the next.

CHAPTER X

There is no doubt in my own mind that the corruption of the Second Empire to which I referred in the preceding chapters has led some writers astray in their appreciation of the first cause—or may be causes—whence sprang the war in Mexico. Amidst the haze which unquestionably enwraps these causes the figure of the Swiss banker Jecker, with his claim for 75,000,000 francs against the Government of Benito Juarez, seems to loom inordinately large; but a few moments of serious consideration must inevitably lead to the conclusion that the huge outline is due to the peculiar disposition of a light behind a comparatively small substance; in other words, that the shadow is out of all proportion to the object reflected. For not the most "slap-dash" leader-writer, not the most theorising and dogmatic essayist, still less the more evenly-balanced student of human nor could for an instant imagine that at the period at which we have arrived, Louis Napoleon would have embarked on the Mexican campaign for any other reason than a prospective lion's share of those 75,000,000 francs. Louis Napoleon was not a Louis Philippe, constantly haunted by the dread of poverty, grudging every penny he spent and always anxious to increase his hoard. The man who during his eighteen years' reign distributed two millions and a half sterling in private charity would assuredly not have gone to war for the sake of securing, let us say, a million and a half sterling (60 per cent. of the Jecker claim) even on the assumption that the war would be a relatively easy one.

And yet, the note, the substance of which I quoted at the end of the foregoing chapter when describing the interview between the Emperor and one of Morny's dupes, seems to point to such an illogical step. It says: "This is the synopsis of one of the innumerable one-act pieces that preceded the big tragedy entitled 'The Campaign in Mexico,' the inception of which must have been due to some such a scene as the one I described just now." The note belongs to the collection given to me by M. de Maupas, and I have every reason to regard the author of them as one of the best-informed men on the Undercurrents of the Second Empire, my grand-uncles included.

How did a man of that stamp make a mistake of this kind? I cannot say. When I wrote that everything connected with the initial business of the war in Mexico was so enwrapped in mystery as to prevent one from speaking with any amount of certainty, I did not purposely exaggerate the difficulties in order to make my attempt at elucidation more valuable. I wrote what I conceived to be the truth, for in fact, I feel by no means confident of the slightest amount of success. Of one thing I feel, however, sure; the idea that prompted the whole affair in Napoleon's mind was not the wish to participate in the spoil of the "Jecker swindle." I have a note in my grand-uncle's handwriting which vaguely hints at an interview between the Emperor and Jecker, which note will find its due place presently. A careful perusal of its contents made me write the lines at the end of the ninth chapter. "Jecker, the Swiss moneymonger, was a somewhat more important personage than the Frenchman (Morny's dupe) whom the Emperor had been obliged to dismiss so unceremoniously. Morny himself, though daring enough, would not have dared to wash his hands of him, and instead of the play ending with the exit of Jecker from the private room of the Emperor whither he may have gone not unknown to Morny, the play had only reached the end of its prologue."

As far as I am aware there does not exist in
the history of the drama a single instance of an
author having conceived a play necessitating a
prologue without having constructed that prologue first, and to suspect Napoleon III. of
having done the former would decidedly expose
one's self to the laughter of many people; yet
at the risk of incurring that laughter I maintain
that Napoleon had thought out his play on the
subject of Mexico long before the interview with
Jecker (if it did take place) provided him with
the material for his prologue. Nay, more;
I maintain that he had selected his principal interpreter of that play long before the name of
Maximilian of Austria announced the result of
that selection to the world at large; and that both
the conception of the play and the selection of
the interpreter had nothing whatsoever to do
with the money transactions between the banking
firm of Jecker and Co. and the insurgent president of Mexico, Miramon.

Those who lived in France during the late
fifties and early sixties, and took an intelligent
interest in her home and foreign policy, could
not but have been aware of the conflicting
feelings aroused in the nation itself by the
preparations for and the termination of the
Franco-Austrian war. The deep-seated dynastic
opinions which even up to the present day
have never ceased to divide the French were

then much stronger and consequently made the chasm between the opposing parties wider than it is now, and that, notwithstanding the military glory and prosperity of the Second Empire.

We must remember what the heirs to the overtoppled thrones and the leaders of the strangled Second Republic were thirty-five years ago, and what they are at this moment; such recollection renders all further comment on my part unnecessary. In spite of these divisions, there was however one sentiment or a professed sentiment, common to the majority of Frenchmen, viz. that the temporal power of the Papacy should remain intact, that a *liberated* Italy should not lay hands on Rome, and every one felt that a *free* Italy would do this as soon as she had the chance. No one understood this sentiment of the nation better than Napoleon III. himself, whether he shared it is a question which, after consulting many documents on the subject, I dare not decide for myself, although I am inclined to think that from motives of policy, he felt disposed to act upon it; from motives of policy alone; religious convictions had absolutely nothing to do with it. Madame de Staël said of Louis Napoleon's uncle that he felt the need of a clergy around him just as he felt the need of chamberlains, to enhance the splendour of his court. It was a gratuitous libel. Napoleon wanted a clergy not to adorn his court but to serve his policy. If how and pomp had been his main objects, he might have taken example from Henry VIII. and furthermore made his new Church and her clergy as ornamental as he pleased. By so doing he would, at any rate, have reduced some of the hostility the Concordat provoked. Perhaps I may be permitted to explain.

The old *noblesse* would have remained irreconcilable under any circumstances, and Napoleon knew it. If he had delivered France bound hand and foot to the Papacy, the attitude of the Legitimists towards himself would not have changed one jot, unless he had, at the same time, consented to surrender himself to their mercy. Hence he dismissed them at once from his calculations. The hatred of the priest was the sole bond between his soldiers and what he termed "his enemies, the *idéologues*." The latter were powerless by reason of their small number and the very nature of their ideas. The opposition of the army was vanquished beforehand by reason of its absolute devotion to the person of its general. The bulk of the *bourgeoisie* was scarcely less hostile than the army to the clergy and the project of their reinstatement; the *bourgeois Voltairien* was, in spite of everything that has been written to the contrary since, a real and not an imaginary personage at that period; nevertheless, he had already begun to look upon the First Consul as the sole breakwater against another deluge in which there being no longer an aristocracy to submerge, he might be swept away—and he submitted. The rural populations were divided between the desire to return to the Church and the fear of having to restore the confiscated lands of the clergy which they had bought for a song. The Church which Bonaparte would in all probability have grafted on the ineradicable roots of the Roman one, if as Mme. de Staël said, mere courtly display had been his object, would not have differed sufficiently in dogma, tenets, and ritual from the latter, to have aroused the objections of the agrarian populations, among whom delicate discrimination in matters theological does not exist and whose greed, moreover, would have caused them to acquiesce in many things. With regard to the dispossessed Romish priesthood, formidable as they might have proved, Bonaparte would have dealt with them as Henry VIII. did in his time.

Or if not inclined to found a new Church, Bonaparte might have let things right themselves without a new Concordat, there being still 40,000 parishes in the enjoyment of spiritual guidance of a kind, nay, having in many cases too much spiritual guidance, for there were often two priests to one parish; the Constitutional one in possession of the church, and the Non-juror who was watching to get possession and was meanwhile celebrating mass in private. The latter had let alone] after Thermidor; Fructidor was more or less fatal to the former; at any rate at the advent of Bonaparte to the First Consulate, there were many priests of both categories in prison. He unlocked the prison doors to all. He might have been satisfied with this, and if he wanted to be still more generous, might have added a subsidy which in order to wound as few susceptibilities as possible, he could have disguised as the just payment of a debt by the State,¹ and thus created liberty of worship, which at no period of the history of France would have been so easy to create as then. Personally it would have made no difference to Bonaparte what kind of form religion took in France or how many forms of it sprang into existence. One might, perhaps, go still further, and say that from purely conscientious motives, Bonaparte might have been content to let France do without religion at all. But he was of opinion that *a religion* was absolutely necessary to a nation in order to complete and supplement the effects of the penal laws. He had two maxims in this respect; that it is impossible to suppress religion; that unless religion becomes an auxiliary of the State, it becomes a peril to it. And he who had spoken as a great Mussulman chief might have

---

The refractory clergy had been despoiled; those who submitted to the oath were never regularly paid the ludicrous stipend promised to them, which a decree of 1794 suppressed altogether. As the former said of the latter: "they never enjoyed the benefits of their defection and only preserved the opprobrium of it."

spoken to the Egyptians ; who had addressed the priesthood of Milan with the knowledge and confidence of a theologian, was quite ready, should the opportunity present itself, to enact the part of a thoroughly Christian Emperor.

I have already mentioned some of the obstacles which met him at the very outset. Nevertheless, the official return of France to the bosom of the Papacy was soon decided in his mind, for, let there be no error about it, the decision was practically his and his alone, as was the Concordat embodying that decision. Neither Pius VII., nor his court, nor Cardinal Gonzalvi, nor the Council of State, nor any French statesman had a share in the making of it. Bonaparte enforced its acceptance by the Holy See as he imposed it on the French nation, without giving either time to formulate objections, for he would not and could not wait, apart from the fact that his character chafed at delay of any kind. "You will sign this in three days ;" ran his message to Rome, just as the besieger says to the besieged—"I will give you four-and-twenty hours." Why did Bonaparte at that early period of his power, and consequently not sated with it, consent to part, nay insist upon parting, with some of this power ? Why was he so anxious to constitute the Church of France a fraction of the Universal Church when the real Gallican Church would have been so easy of foundation at that moment ? There were many reasons, some of which I will endeavour to show, for I cannot enumerate them all. The necessity for this incursion into the domain of pure history will become apparent by-and-by; as it is, abridgment is absolutely imperative. Why then did Bonaparte make the organisation of the clergy the subject of a Concordat with the Pope when he might have made it integrally a law of the Empire, the possibility, nay, the probability of which, was then already haunting his ambition.

In the first place, Bonaparte felt that a religion to be truly powerful in every sense must have stood the test of ages. It was an analogous feeling with regard to the potentiality of a dynasty that made him exclaim, "Why am I not my grandson?" Secondly, he considered that a nation shaken by the scepticism of the XVIIIth century, as the French had been, was only likely to believe in a prophet on the condition of not being able to see him. His compounding with Rome was to a certain extent a concession to the mysticism of the majority, against which even scepticism beats in vain, and of which mysticism he intended to make practical use. Thirdly, he found himself confronted with two Churches inveterately hostile to one another. Pacification by purely human means would have required time, a great deal of time, and the result would have been very uncertain then, apart from the difficulties attending such pacification. His temper was opposed to delay, even if his policy in this instance had not imposed immediate action, for while waiting he would have had an implacable enemy in the Papacy, which enemy, moreover, he considered it impossible to grapple with. Had it been an army, the thing would have been different, but the two hundred thousand disaffected priests, scattered all over France—I am taking his own expressed estimate of their number, which computation was below the reality, as he subsequently hinted—were not an army, but a moral force each component part of which his legions would have pursued in vain, and a victory over which, had they chosen to gather, stand, and deliver battle, would have been worse than a defeat. It was a moral force whose grandeur and power increase in direct proportion to the sufferings inflicted on it. Bonaparte wanted no such implacable enemy within, he wanted a sacred ally without. That was his main reason for making the Concordat.

I need not do more than remind the reader that Napoleon III., being the professed heir to his uncle's universal ideas, stood particularly committed to the latter's policy of conciliation towards Rome. As in the case of his predecessor, the friendly attitude of Napoleon III. was due, however, to policy alone, and not to religious belief, and least of all to admiration for the tactics of the Roman clergy. The following story will plainly show this.

I have used it once, but it will bear repeating. "I have been wasting my breath," said the Emperor one morning to my elder grand-uncle; "I have been wasting my breath trying to prove to Sibour" (the then Archbishop of Paris, who was stabbed at St. Etienne-du-Mont) "that I cannot remove the tombs of, or rather the monuments to, Jean-Jacques and Voltaire from the Panthéon just in order to please some of his flock. Truly, these monuments do not contain a pinch of Rousseau's or Voltaire's ashes;" this in answer to my grand-uncle's remark; "and like you asked me, I asked Sibour why his flock should wish the monuments to be removed. But to that question I could get no answer. He simply kept repeating that 'his flock felt uncomfortable in the presence of the two atheists.'"

"How did you pacify him, Sire?" asked my uncle.

"I did not pacify him at all. I got out of temper myself in the end, and then I exclaimed: 'Look you here, Monseigneur, how do you think these two atheists feel in the presence of your believers?' That settled him, and he did not say another word."

It is more than probable that Pius IX. himself would have relished the Emperor's clever retort. But between the pithy epigrammatic and antithetical rebuke of an archbishop—even an Archbishop of Paris—for having lent himself to the bigotry of his flock and the abetting of Italy to deprive the Holy See of its temporality, there was a wide gulf. That Cavour, Garibaldi, and Victor Emmanuel were contemplating that spoliation, and that Napoleon III. was going to furnish them with the first means, there was already as early as the beginning of 1859 not the faintest doubt in the minds of the Catholic hierarchy, from Pius and Antonelli down to the humblest parish priest all the world over. The "eldest daughter of the Church"— the title France had assumed for centuries—was openly accused as an accessory before the fact of the intended robbery. What was worse, both Napoleon III. and his nearest advisers were conscious of the justness of the charge; although, as will be seen directly, the sovereign, with that fatalism of his, trusted to unforeseen events, also to his astuteness, to prevent the actual commission of the deed. Meanwhile, to prove his unalterable attachment to the Church of Rome, he let his officials bungle, by proving too much.

One instance of misplaced zeal on the latter's part must suffice here. It is a companion picture to the gagging of M. Charles Boissière, the ostracism of Barrias' picture, "The Exiles of Tiberius," and the attempted bribing of Lazerges to efface Rochefort's portrait from his "Première at the Odéon."

I remember as if it were to-day the 1st January 1859. My elder grand-uncle was confined to his

... y and I had to stop at home to keep him company, while his brother paid the calls prescribed by French society on such occasions. At the latter's return his elder brother almost mechanically put the stereotyped question to him. "Any news?" he asked. The other stroked his chin reflectively for a moment or so. "Practically none," he answered, "for the news is no news to us: it is what we expected all along; it is war." He then told him what had occurred at the Tuileries between the Emperor and the Austrian Ambassador.

It is no exaggeration to say that from that moment the whole of the French Catholic clergy were up in arms, and that the relations between the Vatican and the Tuileries became very strained. During the eleven years that went by between that day and the occupation of Rome by the troops of Victor Emmanuel these relations never resumed their former cordial footing, and I am not speaking without authority in saying that throughout these eleven years Napoleon III. felt the burden of this condition of things all the more acutely by reason of his powerlessness to alter *France's foreign policy towards Europe* which he had inaugurated as part of his uncle's behest, and especially his policy towards Italy, which the concern for his own safety had practically forced upon him, and from which, he knew full well, the rancour of the Holy See had sprung and would further spring. The reason for my having italicised the five words above will soon become apparent. Throughout, however, there was the wish on his part not to wound the susceptibilities of the Holy See in smaller matters, not to add actual insult to impending injury, while trying to delay the latter as long as possible. How that wish was generally interpreted by his *bureaucracy* it would take too long for me to tell, but I promised one story; here it is.

About the middle of January, 1859, while Europe was settling down to the idea of a war between France and Austria in the plains of Italy during the forthcoming spring, the masterpiece of the greatest modern French composer was being put in rehearsal at the Théâtre Lyrique by Léon Carvalho, the husband of the original Marguerite, Caroline Miolan-Carvalho whose ashes are barely cold as I write this. In spite of the many changes and cuttings that had to be effected, everything was proceeding satisfactorily when the fiat came that the whole of "Cathedral Scene" had to be suppressed. The reasons for the "order" were not officially stated, but M. Plancé, who was entrusted with the transmission of it to the manager, condescended to explain that the representation of such a scene might give umbrage to the Holy See. The governmental thunderbolt came in the midst of a rehearsal, and it so happened that while M. Plancé was talking to M. Carvalho on the stage, Mgr. Gaston de Ségur, Arch-Canon of St. Denis (and Papal Nuncio *ad interim*, I believe) who has been incidentally mentioned already in these pages in connection with the Carbonaria, was sitting in a stage-box listening to the music. The prelate had been a school-fellow of Gounod, and being passionately fond of music had expressed a wish to attend the last rehearsals, though he was stone-blind. M. Carvalho took M. Plancé to him at once. " Monseigneur," he said, " the order has just come from the Government to suppress the cathedral scene as being calculated to wound people's religious feelings and give umbrage to the Holy See. Can your 'grandeur' formulate any objection to it?" "I?" exclaimed Mgr. de Ségur, " I formulate objections? Would to Heaven there were many scenes like that represented on the Paris stage!" And to mark the sincerity of his words, on the morning of the *première*, he sent to Mme. Miolan-Carvalho the missal which Marguerite carries in her hand at her first meeting with Faust. Mme. Carvalho looked upon it as a precious relic, nay, as something like a talisman, and would no more have appeared without it, in her famous impersonation, than Frédéric Lemaitre would have assumed a new part without first attending mass.

This story is a sample of the apprehensions with which the official *entourage* of the Emperor looked upon the forthcoming war as likely to affect the relations between the Papacy and France. When the eventual liberation and unification of Italy could no longer be a matter of doubt, after the treaty of Villafranca, the apprehensions became intensified a hundredfold in French political and diplomatic circles, and the Emperor himself was literally frightened at the consequences of the fast-gathering hostility of the Catholics over the civilised globe. The knowledge that practically there had been only one course open to him in defence of his own life and of the direct succession to his throne proved no comfort to him. He felt that the whole of the Catholic world would uprise against him if it had not already done so, and to avert this danger, provided it was not too late, to divert the already threatening flood of animosity, he humbled himself before the Pope as no modern ruler had done before him, as no modern ruler has done after him. Allowing for time, circumstances, and the absence of all religious dread of excommunication on Napoleon III.'s part, his avowal of guilt to Pius IX. reminds one of Henry IV.'s (of Germany) penitential attitude before Gregory VII. at Canossa. "Besides," he writes to the Holy Father in January 1861,[1] "after having made common cause with Piedmont in a war for the deliverance of Italy, it became absolutely

[1] See the whole letter in the appendix to this chapter.

impossible that I should turn my arms against it the next day, no matter how severely I may blame its resolutions."

The letter was so much ink and paper wasted. The Papal Court continued to be a hotbed of conspiracy against the Emperor and his dynasty. Cardinal Morlot, Archbishop of Paris, was invited to tender his resignation as Grand-Almoner of France. In spite of the laws on foreign enlistment, the bishops and lower clergy openly recruited men and collected money for the defence of the Papal States. In spite of the occupation of Rome by French troops, the representations of France on the abduction of the Mortara child were treated with the same haughty indifference, not to say scorn, as the representations of the other Powers who had not the means ready to hand for enforcing respectful attention to, if not compliance with their wishes. And yet Napoleon III. almost tamely submitted to these insults when with one stroke of his pen—*i.e.* by the withdrawal of his troops from Rome—he could have put an end to the temporal sovereignty of the Holy See. That is exactly what Bonaparte would have done in the case of Pius VII. if the latter had proved deaf to his remonstrances and refused to comply with his wishes within the term he himself had fixed. Truly, the position of the uncle with regard to the Papacy was different from that of the nephew.

The former owed the Papacy nothing, and shortly after his advent to the Consulate, the Papacy became his debtor, inasmuch as he not only delivered the orthodox—as distinguished from the constitutional—priest from prison, but, in spite of the strenuous opposition of those around him, made the Concordat, virtually reinstating this priest in his former standing, which without the Concordat he might not have recovered for another decade and a half, if then. For it is extremely doubtful whether the Bourbons, albeit this they had forgotten nothing and learnt nothing, would have dared to inaugurate their Restoration by such a measure. On the other hand, Napoleon III. owed the Papacy a good deal. It is certain that, at his first appearance in the arena of politics in 1848, the French priesthood—taking its cue from Rome, which at the time chose to ignore the revolutionary beginnings of Hortense's son, or considered those beginnings as buried for ever—hailed him as the restorer of order, and influenced the elections that gave him, first, the Presidency, secondly, the imperial throne.

Nevertheless, even under such conditions of indebtedness, Napoleon I. would have made short work of the temporality of the Holy See and of her priesthood, if either or both had systematically tried to undermine his authority, though he would not have been blind to the danger at home of such summary proceedings. For a careful study of the French temperament with regard to religious matters had made him—not a Frenchman—aware of this one important fact, i.e., that the spirit of contradiction inherent in the French is apt to sever them from religion when they are driven to it—to make them rally to it at the least attempt to detach them from it. Imperious considerations of space prevent my insisting on the subject as I should like ; but I feel certain that Napoleon I., if placed in the position of his nephew towards the Papacy, would have either cut the knot that bound France towards Pontifical Rome, or would have drawn that knot tighter ; he would not have allowed the ends of that knot to hang down for the priesthood to make a rope of, wherewith to belabour his own back.

That spirit of decision was lacking in the nephew, who, in fact, was the incarnation of the spirit of indecision. It shows itself already in the beginning of his real career—I mean from 1848—when having made up his mind as to the necessity of a *coup d'état*, in order not to relapse into obscurity, he postponed the execution of his design twice, and would have postponed it a third time but for the strenuous opposition of Persigny. It is the dominant trait of his character, nearly every act of his private life, the whole of his policy, is marked with it. He reminds one throughout of those gamblers at Monte-Carlo who after the most careful calculations suddenly fling all calculation to the winds, and fling their stakes haphazard on the first number that comes into their heads. His marriage with Mlle. Eugénie de Montijo was to a great extent the upshot of this lack of mental thoroughness. With the strength of mind to remain single for another year or two there is little doubt that Napoleon III. would have secured an alliance with one of the princely houses of Europe, and that the Second Empire would not have come to such an abrupt and ignominious end. There is no doubt that with the strength of mind to deal promptly and firmly with the caballing of the Papacy, the idea of a Mexican Empire would have never reached the experimental stage, for it may be conceded at once that the idea was there some considerable time before its execution received a justifying sanction—in the Emperor's own mind— from external causes.

Cæsarism, of which Napoleon III. was the heir, is fatally bound to do something. Prince Albert wrote that "by depriving France of her political freedom, Napoleon III. had made the French the spectators of their own government." Curiously enough, the French, though very critical when seated in the ordinary theatre, are not quite so critical at the political playhouse. Provided the piece proceeds in a spirited manner, and stirring incidents follow hard upon one another, they do not trouble themselves much about the logical and psychological truth of the scenes, especially if their progress be marked by spectacular display—by preference, military spectacular display. What the stage-managers must avoid above all, is long waits between the acts. The nation which insists upon an interval of twenty minutes between every act at the ordinary theatre in order to repair to the adjacent café, will not accord a proportionately long interval to the stage-manager of the political theatre. Nor must the house ever be shut up or the stage business allowed to flag; there must be an uninterrupted succession of novelties. The virtual suppression of the parliamentary *régime* compelled Napoleon III. to look for that succession of novelties outside France; he knew that the sensation pieces he was bound to produce would have to be constructed on the lines of his foreign policy. After all, Cæsarism was not altogether to blame for that state of things. It had prevailed to a greater or lesser extent during the last seventy years. It was the Revolution, treading hard upon the American War of Independence which had made foreign politics the handmaiden of home politics, which had made war the overflow tank for the uneasy spirit of the French nation. Napoleon I.

only continued what General Bonaparte had begun in the service of the Republic. "Le pli était pris," as the French themselves would say. The Restoration, finding the necessity to divert the public mind from home affairs as strong as ever, provided that diversion in the shape of three expeditions, viz., to Spain, Greece, and Algeria. The Citizen Monarchy, though, perhaps less inclined to military adventures than its predecessors, followed suit with the conquest of the whole of Algeria, its naval expeditions, its intervention in the affairs of Belgium, the East, and Spain. The continuance of that showy and militant foreign policy became, however, more and more difficult under the Second Empire for many reasons. To begin with, the want of political freedom at home imposed the necessity of more frequent and more brilliant diversions than those under the two preceding monarchies. Secondly, the unprecedented glory attached to these diversions under the First Empire had to be matched if it could not be surpassed by the Second Empire, which was the acknowledged heir of the first. "Sire, faites grand" (*Anglicè*, "Sire, you must do grandiose things"), exclaimed Clement Duvernois, when the Empire already seemed to want to rest on its military laurels in order to foster liberty at home. He was but echoing the words of About, which Louis Jourdan, in his "Frontières du Rhin," and Prévost-Paradol in various pamphlets, had echoed before him. Nearly the whole of Napoleon III.'s *entourage* whispered or loudly cried the same words. But France at that time was also beginning to be practical. Though military glory was always nearest to her heart—or at any rate shared that place with greed—the prospect of annexing territories which might prove profitable outlets for her industries on the protective system was assuming considerable importance in her mind, for France considered her industries seriously threatened by the policy of Free Trade inaugurated by Cobden and Bright on the one hand, and by the Emperor and Michel Chevalier on the other. The Emperor himself knew well enough that *for the moment* a militant foreign policy in Europe could give him no more than it had already given in the way of territorial aggrandisement, that Nice and Savoy had to constitute *for the time being* the whole extent of his acquisitions; hence, the Mexican policy.

The following notes, emanating from the two different sources I have so often had occasion to indicate, will throw a better light on the causes that led to the Mexican campaign than any attempt of mine could. Their authors had not only the privilege of being frequently behind the scenes at the Tuileries and the enviable and instinctive talent of deduction, but one of them the late M. de Maupas' friend—was unquestionably, as I have already shown, on intimate terms with some of the foremost members of the Corps Diplomatique. There are but two drawbacks to the mass of information these notes supply; first, it is very fragmentary, consequently, it lacks sequence; secondly, the dates are wanting in nine cases of every ten. This latter defect probably arose from the authors' utter indifference as to the ultimate fate of their jottings; I have endeavoured to remedy it by classification and condension, in which, however, I was guided by the wish to give a succinct account of events rather than by considerations of chronology. I may be permitted to remark that this obvious indifference of the authors lends additional value to their evidence, for it renders their good faith above suspicion. They may have erred in their appreciation; the authenticity of the facts themselves is beyond dispute. The uniformity of style—some people might say the want of style—of these notes is due to me. As usual I have had to abbreviate and correct many of those that were in English, the French ones I have had to translate.

"There is to be more military glory and more marching at the head of civilisation." Thus runs one of my English notes, evidently written at the very outset of the affair. "There is to be more military glory and more marching," it says a second time. "The military glory is almost a foregone conclusion, and there will be plenty of room for marching and even for countermarching a country as vast as Mexico; it remains to be seen whether it may not prove a bit too vast to be furrowed by the wheels of gun-carriages instead of the plough for the reception of the seed of that civilisation; it is questionable whether bayonets are the most efficient implements to 'set' seed with, even the seed of civilisation. I have got an idea that one of the causes for this anxiety to march at the head of civilisation through the erstwhile Empire of Montezuma is jealousy of the growing influence of the United States in that quarter and the probable consolidation of republican principles which would result from that influence. In spite of the sympathy with those principles supposed to lie dormant in Louis Napoleon's breast, he does not like them practically any more than his uncle, albeit that some of the coins of the latter's reign bear the words 'Empire et République.' Moreover, if there be jealousy in the mind of the Emperor with regard to the United States, the United States do not appear to be altogether free from an analogous sentiment with regard to him. Her public men have had, as it were, a prophetic feeling of antagonism against him for years, in fact, almost since his very accession to the throne which feeling, perhaps, showed itself against their wish in such matters, for instance, in their lukewarm participation in the Exposition of 1855. This lukewarmness was, if not resented, at least regretted by the new Emperor, who especially at

THE SECOND EMPIRE 301

that period was never tired of proclaiming his admiration of, and his cordial friendship for, the United States, and who expected, perhaps, a return of the compliment. He not only did not get that, but President Buchanan sounded a distinct warning against him and his probable policy with regard to Mexico as early as two years ago.[1] The feeling of displeasure on the Emperor's part was probably heightened by the curious coincidence that President Buchanan had given umbrage to Napoleon III. before.[2] The disturbed condition of the Union's home affairs is not the absolute reason for Napoleon's taking action in the matter just now, but it is one of them. He knows perfectly well that in 1857 the United States did not send their representative to Zuluaga but to Juarez, because the erstwhile Oaxaka lawyer is a man after their own heart. And it would appear that President Lincoln thinks as much of him as did his predecessor. I have all this on very good authority, not from one source but from at least half-a-dozen. President Lincoln has, however, his hands very full, and the Emperor thinks that Lincoln's poison may prove Napoleon's meat; for from all I hear,

---

[1] Buchanan's speech in Congress, 1859.

[2] Then follows the story of Mr. Buchanan's conversation with the Emperor at the French Embassy in London in 1855, related in a previous note by the same author, both which note and story I used in Chapter V. The repetition is, to my mind, another proof that the notes were never intended for publication.

the Emperor is absolutely working for his own hand, and if all I hear be true, for his own hand is, &c."

The note does not end here, but I am obliged to interrupt its transcription to make room for one in my younger grand-uncle's handwriting, which note affords, as it were, a kind of explanation of the last sentence of the other. The italics of that sentence are not mine, and I may also be allowed to state that if my surmises with regard to the identity of the writer of the notes given to me by M. de Maupas be correct, as I have every reason to believe they are, the two men whose information I print, that is, my younger grand-uncle on the one side and the English nobleman on the other, were never even on speaking terms with one another. Their social standing and their tastes were too wide apart. They may have met in society, and the name of the Englishman was a household word among the Parisians of that day, in the sense that the name of the Duc de Gramont-Caderousse was a little later on, but I feel certain that they never held any communication. The similarity of opinion expressed in these notes is therefore apparently all the more striking, not in reality though, when we remember that both writers were behind the same scenes. The note of my uncle, I should say, is of a somewhat later date.

"The English are really not showing their

usual and admirable common sense in their criticisms on the Campaign in Mexico. A few weeks ago Lord Montagu" (Lord Montague?) "gave a statesmanlike account of the 'Jecker claim' in the House of Commons. He told his listeners how Jecker had sold an enormous portion of the shares of his loan to the then French Minister in Mexico, M. de Gabriac, how the latter had sold them to others until they finally came into the hands of Morny, who, according to his Lordship, bought still more from various holders, and also induced a still higher placed personage—by which, of course, he meant the Empress—to participate in the purchase. The English nobleman is unquestionably a capital speaker, and marshals his real or supposed facts with great ability, but his absolute ignorance of the character of the Emperor, Empress, Morny, and the rest of the foremost personages at Court, has led him into one or two most amusing blunders, besides deluding him and his countrymen into the belief that the recovery of the Jecker claim was the main object of the expedition to Mexico in the Emperor's mind. The idea of Morny's disbursing money for such things as the Jecker bonds is too ridiculous for words, and the thought of the Empress acting upon any suggestion from Morny in that or any other matter is if anything still more ridiculous. These bonds were never sold by Jecker to Gabriac;

they are probably in Jecker's possession now, though there is certainly an understanding between him and Morny that the latter shall have a considerable number of them the moment they look capable of being realised even at a tremendous discount. Why, when Jecker became bankrupt about two years ago over 68 millions of francs of these bonds, out of 75 millions issued, were found among his assets. I have this on excellent authority, namely, on that of Baron James de Rothschild, who told me at the time. It is pretty well known here that Mr. Mathews, the English Consul in Mexico, sent word to Lord Russell that Benito Juarez had not even the comparatively small sum wherewith to send La Fuente to Europe, though it is equally well known that Abraham Lincoln, notwithstanding his own difficult position just now, has fulfilled his secret promise to the real defender of Mexico's independence to send him money, arms, and, if possible, volunteers. But Juarez is scrupulously honest, and with the subsidies received he no doubt discharged his most pressing liabilities, and left himself almost penniless. Not only are the personal resources of Juarez and his adherents practically exhausted, but the country itself is in a similar sad plight. The report has just reached here that the capital had not even sufficient funds for the decorations and triumphal arches on the occasion of the entry of the French troops, and that M. Martin Daran, a banker in that city advanced 40,000 francs for the purpose. One can scarcely imagine the Emperor to be ignorant of these reports, and yet it is assumed by a prominent member of the English parliament, and probably by others also, that in order to press the Jecker claim more forcibly, the Emperor continues his occupation, for there is scarcely any contention about the purely French claim, though the Emperor for reasons of his own would scarcely admit this.

"The English Government informed Lord Cowley about five months ago that in a conversation with the French Ambassador Lord Russell had given the latter to understand that if the French would completely abandon the Jecker claim, her Majesty's Minister would support the purely French claim, though not for the amount claimed. I wonder whether Lord Russell is aware that the Comte de Flahaut, the French Ambassador in question, is the father of Morny, that Morny has been mainly instrumental in procuring the appointment of Dubois de Saligny as French Ambassador in Mexico in succession to the Comte de Gabriac, and that Dubois de Saligny who aroused all the ill-feeling of the Mexicans or rather of the Juarists—although the terms seem almost to be synonymous—against the French in order to report that ill-feeling to his Government, has boasted to one of the Civil Commissioners of the army of occupation that his (Saligny's) sole merit consisted in having foreseen the intention of the Emperor to intervene in the affairs of Mexico, and to have rendered such intervention absolutely necessary.' All these doings and sayings are recorded in private letters from Mexico, private letters which would be useful indeed to some of the European statesmen who seem to be stone-blind with regard to the real motives and intentions of the Emperor.

"For the support thus generously offered by England is the very thing the Emperor does not want. It would smooth the money difficulties between Juarez and himself, and would at once destroy the pretext for a protracted occupation. Jecker's claim, as being less likely of settlement, affords a pretext more difficult to destroy, and that is where Jecker will probably score and Morny pocket his ill-gotten gains. Let it not be thought for one moment that the Emperor has the faintest sympathy with Jecker as the creditor of the Mexican Government or erstwhile Government. He is as firmly convinced of the iniquity of the claim, and that apart from the amount, as all those must be who have given the matter the slightest attention. But he saw in it at once the opportunity for which he had been looking at least three years, that is, ever since it became patent to him that the war with Austria for the liberation of Italy, now that it had been successful, would inevitably lead to complications with the Holy See. For the wish to regain, if possible, the good graces of the Vatican is another factor in the Mexican Campaign, and a much more powerful one than the recovery of the money Mexico owes to France. It must be remembered that the Liberals, the partisans of Juarez, have confiscated the lands and property of the clergy, which property, if realised, would assume almost fabulous proportions. Unfortunately for the real independence of Mexico this realisation is at present impossible. In the disturbed state of the country no foreigner would invest, and the Mexican higher clergy have already threatened the Mexicans born with major excommunication if they bought the tiniest plot of this property or paid rent for it. General La Forey has already had to interfere in this respect.

"At the first blush nothing seemed easier for the Emperor than to have made France's claim against Mexico the basis for an intervention, although—and I am absolutely certain of what I say—the whole debt with regard to money lent at the beginning of the intervention scarcely exceded a million of francs. The rest had been incorporated into the Jecker loan which 'giving new bonds for old ones' had nominally made Jecker and Company, the chief creditor of Mexico. The whole of the French claims other than for money lent, even if every claim had been justified, would not have exceeded another million. The latter is the claim which in the first clause of the ultimatum at Soledad has been magnified into sixty millions francs for damages and losses sustained by French subjects up to July 1862. The ultimatum did well to insist that the claim had to be acknowledged by Mexico, without discussion on her part and without France furnishing particulars. Monstrous as this may appear in the light of the comity of nations, it is still more monstrous in view of the following fact, for the authenticity of which I can vouch. After the bombardment of Sant-Jean d'Ulloa (1838), the French had their claims settled to the amount of three millions of francs, a million of which remained after a careful examination of the claims by the French Government itself. That million was afterwards divided by the French Government among the necessitous Frenchmen in Mexico.

"France, therefore, has not fared badly either at the hands of Juarez or at those of his predecessors. Nevertheless, as I said just now inasmuch as a claim, which upon conscientious examination would not have amounted to two millions (including money lent), was magnified into one of sixty, the Emperor might as well have taken that one as the redemption of the Jecker bonds for the basis of his intervention, with the additional prospect of having a more ungrudging material support from England, and a moral one from the rest of the powers.

"But this would have been altogether at variance with his temper. That spirit of indecision of his, that tendency to have any number of strings to his bow, in reference to various and often conflicting ends, that spirit and tendency which to a great extent, though not wholly, had remained in abeyance in the beginning of his reign, has recently assumed the upper hand. The Emperor likes to suspend his decision about any and everything until the last moment, and after having weighed the *for* and *against* of a scheme for ever so long, he ends up by taking a sudden but entirely unforeseen resolution. The resolution to make the Jecker bonds the pretext for the expedition was of this kind, and surprised no one so much as Jecker himself who had certainly no such hopes when he applied to the Emperor, as so many dupes of Morny had done before him, as many are likely to do after him. Far from disbursing money for Jecker bonds, which at that time were practically worthless, Morny must have had a pretty lump sum from Jecker on the promise of interesting the Emperor on his behalf. There was, moreover, a correspondence very compromising to the natural brother of the Emperor. The sum Morny had received was too considerable to be refunded by the Emperor—

people say it was a million and a half of francs—and Morny had not taken a step towards redeeming his promise. Jecker on the other hand, positively refused to part with the correspondence, nay, threatened to publish it unless that sum was refunded; and as Jecker was not naturalized then, consequently not a Frenchman, the usual means for gagging him, or for that matter, for suppressing him altogether, resorted to by the Prefecture of Police were not available.

"It is doubtful whether the Emperor would have resorted to them if they had been available. He jumped at the redemption of the Jecker bonds as a valid pretext for intervention, though he had for some time quite as valid a pretext in his own hands, but that one absolved him from the necessity of disbursing a million and a half of francs in order to avoid a fearful scandal in connection with his half-brother and the President of the Corps Législatif. For I repeat again and again, the redemption of the Jecker bonds is a pretext, just as the offer of the crown of Mexico to Maximilian of Austria is a sham. I may not live to see this, but if the expedition be successful and Maximilian elevated to the throne, he may remain there for his lifetime, if for so long, but the succession will devolve upon Napoleon's heirs; for what the Emperor has really in his mind is a great empire in America for the French, just as there is a great empire in India for the

English. If the thought had been seriously entertained to found a stable empire for any one but Napoleon III. and his heirs, Napoleon III. would not have selected a childless prince and that after five years of marriage. There is another end the Emperor has in view by this selection, the reconciliation with the Holy See. Maximilian is a staunch Catholic, and the Mexican higher clergy, the most corrupt in the world, will regain their influence under him. It will be a set-off against the probable loss by Pius IX. of his temporal sovereignty. If that fails, Napoleon III. will think out something else to conciliate the Vatican."[1]

[1] My uncle was right, the Convention of 1864 between Italy and France was "the other thing."

APPENDIX TO PART X

LETTER FROM NAPOLEON III. TO PIUS IX

January, 1861.

VERY HOLY FATHER,

The letter of your Holiness, dated December 25, affords me the opportunity of making known the whole of my thoughts. I have always considered the good understanding between sovereigns and the head of religion as indispensable to the happiness of peoples, for when that understanding is there, everything may be smoothed, and the questions of self-love and strict right vanish before an amicable *entente* and reciprocal concessions. But when unfortunate circumstances have bred defiance and almost hostility between powers created by the Almighty to live in concord, everything becomes difficult. The slightest divergences are apt to degenerate into serious embarrassments and into incessant causes of antagonism. The signal proof of this may be found in the occurrences of the last eighteen months.

The moment that events, discounted eagerly by various parties in their own interests, have made a doubt possible in your Holiness's mind with regard to my sentiments, the former harmony had to make room for a spirit of defiance, and in Rome as in Paris everything that comes from one of these two countries is viewed with suspicion in the other.

Nevertheless amidst the embarrassment created by

grave conjunctures, my conduct has always been clear in its acts, pure in its intentions.

When, nearly two years ago, I started for the Italian War, I declared to your Holiness that I undertook that war with two sentiments deeply rooted in my heart ; the independence of Italy and the maintenance of the temporal authority of the Holy Father; that I cherished no illusions as to the difficulty of reconciling the interests of those causes ; that I would use my utmost endeavours to succeed in that task. I have remained faithful to this promise as far as the interests of France did allow me. The facts speak for themselves.

At the Peace of Villafranca I wished the Pope to be at the head of the Italian Confederation, in order to enhance the Holy Father's power and moral influence. When the revolution began to develop itself contrary to my desires, I proposed to the Catholic Powers to guarantee to the Holy Father the remainder of his states. Though Rome became the centre where all the enemies of my government foregathered, I nevertheless maintained my troops in Rome. When the personal safety of your Holiness became more and more precarious, I increased the strength of the army of occupation.

I may well ask how my conduct has been appreciated ? I have been pointed at as the adversary of the Holy See; the minds of the most exalted members of the French clergy have been poisoned against me ; they have gone as far as to solicit the Archbishop of Paris to tender his resignation as Grand-Almoner of France ; there was an attempt to convert the bishops and their subordinates into a foreign administration, recruiting men and collecting money in contravention of the laws of the land. In short, Rome has been made a hot-bed of conspiracy against my government and yet I have authorised the man who had most openly enacted the partisan of the Republic to become the head of the Holy Father's Army (Lamoricière).

Even all these many hostile demonstrations have not been able to change my line of conduct. I have done everything I could to maintain the authority of the Pope without compromising the interests of France. Nevertheless, it appears that I have not done enough. I can well understand this, but I can only make answer as follows. In spite of my just veneration for the head of the Church, my troops, unless the honour of France herself be at stake, will never become instruments of oppression of foreign nations. And besides, after having fought by the side of Piedmont for the deliverance of Italy, it became absolutely impossible for me the next day, as it were, to turn my arms against it, no matter how severely I may blame its resolutions.

In the actual condition of things I regret deeply that our relations are no longer animated by that spirit of conciliation which would have enabled me to accept the proposals of your Holiness. If your Holiness will recommend the Archbishop of Paris to continue his functions, I have no doubt that this prelate so praiseworthy in many other things, will submit to your Holiness's will. If, however, he insists on retiring, I will look among the bishops for the one who appears to me most fit to fulfil the religious requirements and the political conventions.

I sincerely trust that the feelings of uneasiness and uncertainty in which we move will soon come to an end, so that by their cessation I may enjoy once more the whole of your Holiness's confidence and friendship.

NAPOLÉON.

CHAPTER XI

"A FEW nights ago there was a scene at the Tuileries more dramatic, perhaps, than any scene in that most powerful of Alexandre Dumas' melodramas, *Henri III. et sa Cour.* The château was wrapt in silence, for the Empress is away in England or Scotland, and the Emperor was sitting in his own room deeply engrossed with the second volume of *L'Histoire de Jules César*, which is just out. Suddenly, one of the gentlemen-in-waiting, the Marquis de Caux, I believe, enters the Emperor's room; but the Emperor pays no attention, he scarcely looks up. 'What is it?' he asks almost impatiently. 'The Prince de Metternich, sire,' is the answer. The Emperor half rises from his chair and turns very pale as if with a presentiment of disaster, and before the Ambassador is fairly in the room, the presentiment is verified. 'I am sorry to inform your Majesty

that the battle of Sadowa, which was fought
to-day, has been lost by us,' he says, remaining more calm than the Emperor himself. In
another moment several horses, which are always
kept ready harnessed at night, were put in, and
Rouher, Fleury, Drouyn de Lhuys, and Randon
sent for. The Master of the Horse and the
Minister for War reached the Tuileries within
a second of each other. The Emperor, who is
phlegmatic enough at ordinary times, invariably
loses that phlegm in Fleury's presence. 'We
have gained Venice for others, we have lost
the Rhine for ourselves!' he exclaimed, before
the door had been fairly closely behind his most
trusty adviser, handing him at the same time the
telegram announcing the Austrian defeat. 'We
have lost nothing yet, sire,' remarked Fleury
glancing at the paper. 'On the contrary; now
or never is your chance to reconstruct the map
of Europe.' The sentence had barely left his
lips when the door opened once more to admit
Randon. He had heard what Fleury said.
'We are not ready,' he remarked, addressing
Fleury directly and summarily saluting the
Emperor. Then turning to his sovereign, 'Your
Majesty is well aware that I have not got
thirty thousand troops fit to take the field at such
a short notice.' 'Thirty thousand troops!' repeated Fleury with his usual dash; 'thirty
thousand troops! That's more than sufficient to

mask the absence of those that are not ready.' The Emperor shook his head. His eternal want of decision at the critical moment came strong upon him. 'Ah,' he sighed, 'if the Empress were but here.' For once in a way I agree with him; if the Empress had been there, she would have counselled a headlong war with Prussia there and then, and I fancy it would have been the right thing to do. In three months, in six months, in a year, or a couple of years—for that struggle must inevitably come now—it will be too late. Nay, the longer it is delayed the worse it will be for France in the end, for those who know best aver that Prussia is gaining strength every day. Sadowa has effaced the glory of Solferino, Prussia has proved her single-handed superiority over Austria in Bohemia, just as France proved it seven years ago in Lombardy. If anything, the proof is in favour of King Wilhelm's legions, for Victor Emmanuel's troops did, after all, count for something. Practically, though, the two nations stand confessed equal on the battlefield with regard to one adversary, and that one, the military power hitherto deemed too strong for attack by her latest victor who for years submitted to great humiliations at her hands.

" Unless I am greatly mistaken in the temper of the French, they will not relish that real or supposed equality ; it will rankle in their minds and they will hold Napoleon III. directly responsible for it. There, I feel, lies the rock ahead. The French will not be satisfied until they have proved to the world at large that Jena and not Leipzig or Waterloo was the test of their military supremacy over Prussia. They will not rest until they have tried conclusions with the descendants of the armies of Frederic the Great once more, and that rather than the prospect of the acquisition of territory on the banks of the Rhine will be the real cause of the next contest between them and the Teuton. I feel convinced that no diplomatic skill will avert this contest, unless Prussia would submit to the most extravagant demands on the part of France. Sadowa, to my mind, has put an end to the probability of such concessions, if ever they were seriously entertained by King Wilhelm, since he has had two such men as Helmuth von Moltke and Otto von Bismarck by his side.

"I like and admire Napoleon III. as much as any man, but I am not blind to the fact that it would want a Richelieu and a Jomini to co-operate with him in order to withstand successfully the combination arrayed against him. There is not a Metternich or a Talleyrand in the whole of France, still less a Richelieu ; if there be a Jomini, he is carefully kept away from the Court by the dancing and swaggering clique who maintain that *le courage fait tout*. And worse than all, Bazaine is in Mexico. I am told by those who are competent to express an opinion, that he and Niel are the only two among the marshals who can lay claim to the name of strategists in the serious acceptation of the term; although those same informants do not hesitate to aver that there are at least half-a-dozen officers of lesser grades that are superior to both. The competent ones are, however, systematically ostracised by the Court party, which though devoured by jealousy of one another does not even condescend to be jealous of these. They are simply ignored. The jealousy, intriguing, and caballing are reserved for those who cannot be ignored; the result of all this is an all-pervading spirit of meanness which it would be impossible to describe and still more impossible to impress upon the outsider but for some startling proofs in individual instances. A lawyer would call them *pièces de conviction morales*.

"Here is one among many. When Bazaine was raised to the marshalship a little less than two years ago, not one of the marshals of France (with the exception of Randon, the Minister for War) sent him his congratulations.

"Some time after the fall of Sebastopol, its eminent defender paid a visit to France and met with a distinguished welcome at the Tuileries. When taking leave of the Emperor, he mentioned casually that on his way home he was going to spend a day at the camp of Châlons to see

General Raoult, the chief of the staff. Noticing the look of surprise on the Emperor's face, Todtleben explained, 'During the late war, sire, General Raoult was my most formidable adversary.' It wanted a foreign general to draw the Emperor's attention to an officer of his army whose attainments were common talk in every war-office of Europe except that of France herself, an officer whom Queen Victoria had delighted to honour by conferring upon him the Order of the Bath, who bore the insignia of the Medidjé, of Saint Maurice and Saint Lazare, the military medals of Sardinia and England, who during the siege itself was made a Knight-Commander of the Legion of Honour. Just, nay, generous to a fault, the Emperor repaired his oversight in a little while by naming General Raoult chief of the staff of the Imperial Guards.[1]

"Did the Emperor point out afterwards to his Minister for War that it is his most sacred duty to enlighten him on the merits of his officers? It is more than doubtful, for there is nothing Napoleon III. dislikes so much as being compelled to reprimand. He generally errs the other way. He endeavours as far as lies in his power, to remove ignorance and incompetence from their

---

[1] General Raoult was mortally wounded at Reichshofen, and died three weeks later at the castle of that name. His surrender on the battle-field to von der Tann, who had been his comrade-in-arms in Africa, would, if fully narrated, make one of the most dramatic stories of the Franco-German War.

active spheres, but his method is, to say the least, curious. General Forey, who wasted many months in Mexico, and showed a lamentable want of decision and an utter absence of military skill before Puebla, had to be recalled. The merest sub-lieutenant could have pointed out the flagrant mistakes he had committed. The Emperor could think of no better way of removing him from his command than by making him a marshal. Here is an extract from the Emperor's letter dated exactly three years ago, which Forey has been showing everywhere. 'It has afforded me much happiness to hear of the entry of my troops into Mexico; and now I think that all serious resistance will be at an end. By the time my letter reaches you, Mexico will have been in our power for three months, and the military expedition may be considered as terminated. Under these circumstances, I think it useless to prolong your stay in Mexico. A marshal of France is too big a personage to be allowed to worry about intrigues and administrative details. Hence you have my authority to delegate your powers to General Bazaine the moment you think fit, and to return to France to enjoy your success and the legitimate glory you have won.'

"Of course, the non-recall of Bazaine when he was raised to the dignity of marshal is explained by Forey's friends on the plausible theory that since then, affairs in Mexico have gone from bad

to worse, but I and many like me who are neither
Bazaine's friends nor Forey's enemies know the
difference of calibre between these two.

"And then that magnificent sentence – 'A
marshal of France is too big a personage to be
allowed to worry about intrigues and administrative details.' Ye shades of Davoust and Ney,
who worried themselves, without being asked,
about the soldiers' tin kettles and the washing of
their feet. And Bismarck, as big a personage as
any marshal of France, and who, Körner[1] told
me yesterday, worried himself in the thick of the
campaign about his soldiers' cigars, and made his
wife worry too, while he, Bismarck, was sleeping
on the flagstones. The present marshals are too
big for that sort of thing, they do not care a single
jot about the soldier's camp kettle, or about his
cleanliness. The general of division takes his
cue from the marshal, the general of brigade
takes his cue from the general of division, and so
on, until in the end the barrack-room becomes an
unspeakable thing, and the soldier, in spite of his
outward smartness, a far from pleasant being to
come into close contact with. Of course, as to
the soldier himself, there are exceptions, and
notably among the older ones; but of the younger
the least said the better. Cleanliness is not the
besetting sin of the urban and rural lower-middle

---

[1] Körner was an old German gentleman to whom I have already referred to in the first of these papers.

classes, from which the bulk of the army is recruited, 'In barracks cleanliness is simply a shifting of dirt from one corner to another,' said a meritorious young officer to me when discussing the subject. 'One may have as many inspections as there are days in the year,' he went on; 'but one will never succeed in teaching cleanliness—I mean real cleanliness—to a peasant lad who has no desire to be cleanly. What he will do is this: He will call to his aid all his astuteness, which is great, to *shift* the evil whenever the surveillance of his chiefs shall compel such shifting. That is the utmost one can accomplish under conditions of the strictest supervision. The evil is dear to him. A liking for and the habit of cleanliness are easily acquired, seeing that sailors and old soldiers are almost faultless in this respect; but this material transformation requires time for its accomplishment, inasmuch as it corresponds in reality to a moral transformation. It is just as difficult to compel a young soldier to be spick and span from top to toe as to compel an old soldier not to be. And by spick and span, I mean wholesome throughout. This, under conditions of the strictest supervision; I leave you to imagine what the result will be if these conditions are relaxed in the slightest degree. You are aware that the Cent Gardes before going on duty are compelled to take a bath, in case of accidents. This will give you an idea of the state of affairs in the other regiments where no such regulations prevail.'

Practically, my young informant told me nothing new, but it is as well to have one's own opinions confirmed now and again by those whose knowledge is derived from daily experience. These, then, are the hygienic conditions of an army which, unless a miraculous change in the temper of the nation be wrought, will be called upon sooner or later to confront the Prussians, whose marvellous military progress is best shown in the bitter defeat they have just inflicted on those whom sixteen years ago they dared not meet in battle. As for the intellectual régime, one little story will suffice to show that it is still more deplorable than the hygienic. The thing happened at Saumur, the admission to which is at any rate hedged round by a preliminary examination. On the face of it, therefore, the cadets would seem entitled to a wider latitude in the interpretation of their manuals than a mere schoolboy or lad from the plough. Not at all, unless they can repeat word for word the contents of their theoretical handbooks, they are considered so many failures. Absolute literalness is required of them. As long as they can stand this test, their fitness for a sub-lieutenancy at the end of their two years' term is not questioned. Lately an inspector-general (read an examiner) asked a young fellow at his final 'go' if he knew his 'theory.' The latter modestly answered in the affirmative. 'Then please to tell me which is the word that occurs only once in the Cavalry Manual.' As a matter of course the cadet was at a loss. 'Well, you see, you do not know your theory. The word that occurs only once in the whole of the manual is *nonobstant.*'"[1]

The above note or notes—for from internal evidence I came to the conclusion long ago that the whole was not written at one sitting—belong to the collection from which I have so often drawn in these chapters. But the impartiality of the mere chronicler of facts, which is an essential feature of the majority of the others, appears to be gone. The writer—my younger granduncle in this instance—was evidently yielding to a bitter feeling of resentment against the army, and from personal experience I can state that that feeling was shared by hundreds among the higher educated classes. They instinctively felt the error that had been committed by Napoleon III. allowing Prussia to make good her claim to hegemony in Germany at the expense of Austria. Even those whose political acumen was of the slightest became alive to the fact that the events

[1] The word "nonobstant," the absolute English equivalent for which is "notwithstanding," has almost entirely disappeared from the French language, and been replaced by "malgré," "néanmoins," &c., &c. Nowadays it is only used by the comic writers who interlard it freely in the speeches of a martinet officer or an ignorant and would-be pedantic non-com.

of the last month had suddenly created a most
formidable neighbour on the very flank of the
country. Few suspected, however, that the
Emperor had made the supposed mistake through
a want of confidence in his army. That, I repeat,
was farthest from their thoughts. When the truth
about the inferiority of the army partially leaked
out, as it did less than three months afterwards,
the effect upon the nation was complex, as we shall
see directly. Meanwhile, I may be permitted to
quote the finish to this particular series of notes.

"It was Fleury who who told me of the scene
at the Tuileries. I own that I fostered few illusions with regard to the state of the army. No
man who is constantly being told the stories I
hear could foster such illusions; but whatever the
quality, I thought at any rate that there was a
sufficient quantity. The sentence of Randon—
'Your Majesty is well aware that I have not got
thirty thousand troops fit to take the field at such
a short notice'—was a kind of revelation, and not
of a pleasant nature. 'What did his Majesty say?'
I asked. 'What could he say?' was the answer.
'In view of Randon's words, "Your Majesty is
well aware," there was not even the loophole of
a denial of the knowledge. His Majesty simply
bowed his head. The Emperor's knowledge of
the thing is not the worst feature of the affair.
By this time Austria knows of France's weakness
also, for Randon has not even the sense *de ne pas*

découvrir le pot aux roses (not to let the cat out of the bag). He blurted it all out in front of Metternich, who was still there when we came in. This has virtually shut the door against any future alliance with Austria, for, mark my words, such an alliance will be attempted sooner or later. Austria with her usual duplicity will pretend to entertain the thought; at the last moment, whenever that be, she will fail us. The next thing we shall hear of will be a scheme for the thorough reorganisation of the army. What the fate of such a bill will be, I dare not say; but I have not much trust in it. But ready or not ready, my advice was the right one. It would have been followed but for one consideration, and that consideration is not the non-readiness of the army; it is that damnable exhibition (*cette exposition damnée*). France has been sacrificed once more to Paris, for Paris could not have her preparations for the orgies that will put money in her pockets interfered with by a war.'"

I was not in Paris when these notes were written; in fact, I never saw these or any other until three years later. By that time both my relatives were dead. But by the end of July 1866 I was back in the capital and I recollect perfectly well that a few days after my arrival I took a walk with the younger one to the Champ de Mars to look "at the preparations for the orgies that would put money into the Parisians' pockets"; to use the words of Fleury. My uncle who was generally most sympathetic with regard to everything likely to affect the prosperity of the Empire, was not only apathetic but could scarcely conceal his impatience. He knew English and English literature fairly well, though he spoke English very indifferently. Suddenly he turned round and said in French. "They are building up the scenery for the third act of *Sardanapalus*. Do you remember Byron's stage directions?" And there and then he quoted them with a strong French accent, but the text was nevertheless very intelligible to me. "'The hall of the Palace illuminated—Sardanapalus and his Guests at Table—A storm without, and Thunder occasionally heard during the Banquet.' And when the thunder growls and the lightning flashes there will be hundreds of people ready to explain to his Majesty that there was no tempest at all; that the noise he heard was simply the roll of the drums of his massed regiments which had turned out to do him and his guests honour; that the lightning he saw was fireworks. In sober words, my dear nephew, the danger comes as much from within as from without. Napoleon III. has his Arbaces and Belesis too; they are, perhaps, not such hypocrites as the minister and the grand-priest of the Assyrian king; but they are not the less formidable enemies for all that. Their names are Adolphe Thiers and Jules Simon. The latter is honest, swayed by no personal ambition, and absolutely and blindly yielding to his political convictions, which, however much one may disagree with them, are entitled to respect. The former is the incarnation of selfishness and of political intrigue. Neither of them has any need of hypocrisy; they are not Napoleon's ministers; they are, I repeat, the one the inveterate enemy of the Emperor and the Empire, the other the sworn foe of the Empire alone. They have openly stated their intention to overthrow the existing régime at the first opportunity, and if the first opportunity does not come quickly enough they will make it. You know what Ferrari said in his latest book—'The parliamentary opposition of a country is always working into the hands of the alien." Read in this instance the alien who is watching the most vulnerable spot of France in order to attack it, and you will gain a pretty correct idea that my contention about the danger being as much within as without is justified. Why, when the news of Sadowa came, not one, but half-a-dozen, French papers were rejoicing at it. There was quite a scene at the offices of *Le Temps*, where some Republicans, right for once, protested with all their might against the short-sightedness of such rejoicings."

In less than three months from that day my relative's and Fleury's words were verified, and opposition—of all shades, be it said began to play into the hands of the alien. The stupefaction produced on the Emperor by the unexpected revelation of Prussia's military supremacy over Austria—I could, if required, prove that it was altogether unexpected—was not of long duration In October, 1866, he instituted a grand commission to examine the question of reorganising the French army. Only they who lived in Paris in those days can conceive an idea of the formidable opposition, of the blind antagonism the project met with from the very outset; and to be fair, that antagonism was not confined to the *irréconciliables*, as the twenty-two parliamentary guerillas under the leadership of Thiers were called. The most devoted supporters of the Empire rallied to that group almost uninvited. "There will be an end of lucky numbers," was the universal cry; and it is more than probable that those whose seats had hitherto been deemed the most secure, namely, the majority, shouted loudest.

"Give a dog a bad name and it will stick to him." During the last few years I have been so persistently accused of systematic hostility against France both by the English and the French themselves that I have grown absolutely callous to the accusation. Nevertheless, I should be sorry to write one line of unfavourable comment on a matter of such importance as the patriotism of a nation on insufficient proof. The opposition to Napoleon III.'s scheme of army reform was, however, prompted by such mean and personal motives on the part of some deputies that silence on the subject would, to my mind, be more blameable than outspokenness.

The sayings and doings of the Peace Society generally inspire me with an irrepressible desire to throw politeness to the winds and to call its members names; yet there is no one more alive to the hardships of conscription than I. If the opposition to Napoleon's contemplated army bill had sprung from a sincere wish to diminish these hardships no one would or could have withheld his sympathy, though even then the "Salus Patriæ suprema lex" would have acted as a damper to one's admiration. But neither the *conscrit* himself, nor his mother, sisters, nor sweethearts, all of whom suffer most from his enforced absence in times of peace, from his non-return in times of war, occupied the thoughts of the deputy. The relatives for whose feelings the deputy showed the deepest concern were those who suffered least, namely the father and uncle of the ploughboy or young workman. And for a very good reason: the father and uncle could mar or make the deputy at the next general election; that is, could deprive him of his snug stipend of at least £500 per annum, or secure him the undisturbed possession of it for so many years.[1]

---

[1] The members of the first French Parliament (1798) received 18 livres per day, the livre representing to within a fraction the

I shall probably return to the subject in the next chapter; for the present suffice it to say that this hostility of the majority even while the bill was only in incubation produced the most disastrous effect outside France with regard to her hitherto preponderant influence in European affairs. To restore that preponderance, a second *Coup d'État* was necessary in order to show the world at large that the Louis Napoleon of 1851 had not altogether ceased to be; but the frequent want of decision that marked the latter years of the Emperor's reign, and had already produced two formidable errors as far as France's prestige was concerned, was fast developing into a chronic disease, which the approaching opening of that "damnable exhibition" was not calculated to remove even temporarily.

For by this time "the invitations to the feast" were out, and had been eagerly accepted by the crowned heads of Europe. Joshua would have been equally glad to get such an invitation from the kings

fran of the present day. The members of the Council of the Five Hundred overthrown by Bonaparte on the 18-19 Brumaire, year VIII. (9 10 November, 1799) received 28 francs per day. During the Consulate and First Empire the deputies had 10,000 francs per annum. The Restoration and the Citizen Monarchy gave them no stipend. The Second Republic allowed them 25 francs per day, about the same amount they receive at present. Napoleon III. did things on a more liberal scale. The members of the Corps Législatif had 12,500 francs per annum, provided the session did not extend over six months, and 2,500 francs for every additional month. It is not surprising they did not wish to relinquish their "mandat" as it is grandiloquently called.

of the land of Canaan. Twelve years before this, Marshal Vaillant had expressed his opinion on the futility of trying to promote international friendships and conciliating rival sovereigns by such means. "When the other one [Napoleon I.] gave them entertainments and theatrical performances, it was on their ground and not in France; they paid the expenses, and not he."

Napoleon III., I fancy, knew the Parisians better in one respect than did either his uncle or any sovereign before him (the nephew). He had probably come to the conclusion that in default of incessant victories, the Parisians' good-will to their rulers was largely dependent on the latter's ability and efforts to provide them with magnificent public shows and court pageants. I doubt if Napoleon III. had he decided to be crowned or to crown himself, would have gone to Rheims like Charles X. and some of his ancestors, or, like Napoleon I., hesitated between the capital and a provincial city as the scene for such coronation. Instead of taking the Comédie-Française to Erfurth to act before a *parterre* of kings, Napoleon III. invited the *parterre* of kings to the Rue Le Peletier, knowing that he would please his metropolitan subjects and still trusting that he might dazzle his royal and imperial visitors. The experiment of twelve years previously had been so eminently successful in this respect, and the exhibition of 1867 was to eclipse that of 1855 as well as the twelve others which had opened their portals during the nearly seven decades that had gone by since the "Temple of Industry" had been inaugurated on that same Champ de Mars.

And truly, results seemed to justify the Emperor's expectations. At no period of modern history had any capital of Europe offered its hospitality to so many exalted personages within so short a period. Three emperors (for the Sultan of Turkey is styled an Imperial ruler, I believe); seven reigning kings, three of whom were officially accompanied by their consorts; nine grand-dukes; two archdukes; two dozen princes of the blood, among whom there were at least a half-dozen heirs apparent; princesses, grand-duchesses, dukes and duchesses by the score; all these were calculated to give Paris in particular, and France in general, an intoxicating idea of their Emperor's power. Did France dream at that moment that among those visitors some had come to spy the martial nakedness of the land, however carefully hidden behind a gorgeous array—an almost too gorgeous array—of glinting cuirass and resplendent gold lace? Did one visitor in particular, as the French maintain to this day, have his cupidity aroused by the unmistakable evidences of material prosperity, in such curious contrast to the lack of power to guard this prosperity by force of arms, suspected, however, by those who had eyes to

see? I cannot say. But here is a story for
the authenticity of which I will vouch, although
the source from which it is drawn is not the usual
one.

The King of Prussia, accompanied by Bismarck,
Moltke, and others, arrived in Paris on June 5th,
1866. The Elysée being occupied by his nephew,
the Czar of Russia, King Wilhelm took up his
quarters at the Prussian Embassy in the Rue de
Lille, the history of which building I intend to
write some day, as well as that of the mansion in
the Faubourg St. Honoré, which at present
shelters the English Ambassador.

On June 8th the Municipality gave a ball at
the Hôtel de Ville in honour of the Imperial and
Royal visitors, who as a matter of course were
received by M. Haussmann, the Prefect of the
Seine—for in those days there was no Mayor of
Paris, nor is there now.[1] There is a maire for
each of the twenty arrondissements of the capital,
but there is no Maire de Paris. In shaking
hands with Haussmann, King Wilhelm is reported to have said: "Monsieur le Préfet,
I have not been in Paris since 1814. I find it
very changed indeed." Next morning, Haussmann accompanied the King, Bismarck, and Moltke
to the heights of Montmartre, where the whole

---

[1] There was a Mayor of Paris from the 4th September, 1870, up
till the outbreak of the Commune. The post was filled first by M.
Arago; then by Jules Ferry.

of the city of Paris lies practically at one's feet. "That's where I was encamped in 1814, M. le Prefet," said the King, pointing in the direction of Romainville. "Yes, sire, but there's a fort there now," replied Haussmann.

This is the story in full. That those two sentences of the King would have been better left unsaid under the circumstances, it would be idle to deny; but to build upon them a theory of sudden, invincible cupidity or ambition which nothing would satisfy but the possession, if for ever so short a time, of the magnificent city that lay outspread at his feet would be too extravagant. And yet, if such invincible cupidity or ambition had suddenly obtruded itself, where would have been the wonder? For years Napoleon III. had striven and plotted about that Rhine frontier, the inordinate desire for which on the part of the French had nearly led to a war twenty-seven years before Wilhelm of Prussia stood on the heights of Montmartre. Do the French imagine that Wilhelm's head was a sieve, that Jena, the humiliation of his father and mother by Napoleon I. had simply run through his head without leaving traces there? Do they imagine that Nicholas Becker wrote his *Hymne am Rhein* and Max Schneckenburger his *Wacht am Rhein* without provocation? And if it was permissible for Alfred de Musset to reply to the former:—

> Nous l'avons eu, vôtre Rhin allemand ;
> * * * * * * * *
> Où le père a passé, passera bien l'enfant,

it was assuredly permissible for Wilhelm to think, if not to say, perhaps : " We have had your Paris ; where the father passed, the children can also pass."

I myself am inclined to agree with the author who said, " The journey to France of Moltke and his royal master in 1867 was not a pleasure trip, but a downright military reconnaissance." This in itself would prove that the idea of a possible, nay, a probable, war with France had suggested itself to the minds of the three men who were mainly responsible for the issue of the struggle. I am confirmed in my belief by a scene I witnessed some seventy-two hours before King Wilhelm, Moltke, Bismarck, and Haussmann stood on the heights of Montmartre. It was at the review held in honour of the sovereigns at Longchamps on the 6th June. Thanks to my uncles' numerous friends in the army, we had two tickets; one had been given us by General Fleury, the other by the Emperor himself. We were placed in the enclosure right in front of the imperial stand, where the Empress, with her son by her side and surrounded by a brilliant suite, was seated. At two o'clock the Emperor, the Czar, and the King of Prussia, followed by their respective staffs, appeared on the ground. It would want a great word-painter to describe the

spectacle, and I shall not attempt it. The
Austrian and English officers in their white and
scarlet uniforms closed the procession, and then
about a score of yards behind them came a solitary
figure, also in white and on horseback. He was
riding very slowly, much slower than the rest, and
seemed to scan every regiment as he passed it, as
if to impress deeply on his memory its number,
its numerical strength, its probable potentiality.
"That's not an Austrian," said my uncle, who in
spite of his strong field-glass was not able to distinguish very clearly. "I wonder who it is?"
He had to repeat the latter part of his sentence,
for I, too, was watching the figure closely. It
was the second time I had seen it within a
twelvemonth. The first time was on the evening
of Friday, the 29th June, 1866, at a window in
the Wilhelmstrasse in Berlin. At the very moment
it appeared at the window, a clap of thunder rent
the air and a flash of lightning made the sky lurid.
"This is Heaven's salvo in honour of our victory,
boys," it exclaimed, its voice being distinctly
heard above the roar of the crowd.

"I wonder who it is?" repeated my uncle,
nudging me in the side with his elbow. "That,"
I answered; "that's Bismarck."

"Ah!" remarked my uncle, lowering his glass
for a second. He did not say another word for
at least an hour, but I noticed that he kept
watching the white figure.

"I wonder," he said very slowly on our way home, "whether the sixty thousand troops assembled to day have hidden the nakedness behind them. Fleury averred that it only wanted half that number. I wonder whether that white figure is to be hoodwinked in this way."

He scarcely spoke for the remainder of the day, but seemed lost in deep thought. The reader may remember that on his return from this review, Alexander II. was fired at by Berezowski, in the Bois de Boulogne. The bullet only struck the mouth of the horse of M. Raimbaux, the Empress's equerry, who was riding by the side of the Imperial carriage. The jury of the Seine made the would-be assassin a present of his life. It has been stated, not once, but a hundred times, in print that this act of clemency, perhaps, deprived France of Russia's alliance in 1870.

To those who knew Alexander II. best, the statement constitutes not only an insult to his memory, but is ridiculous besides. It marks the same train of thought that credited Wilhelm of Prussia with nothing but cupidity at the sight of Paris in all her glory.

But on that June 6th, and for two months afterwards, such thoughts found no crevice in the minds of the majority of Frenchmen. The intoxicating idea of their power as attested by the presence of all these exalted guests left no room for any other. I said the majority. My uncles were not French, and if they had been they would not have belonged to the majority.

On the evening of that day, when the papers came out with their glowing accounts, my younger grand-uncle who, as I said, had scarcely opened his lips since our return home, quietly got up and walked to a bookcase, from which he took a Shakespeare. He slowly turned the leaves until he came to *Macbeth*. "That's the future quotation for the King of Prussia, Bismarck, and Moltke," he said. Then in an impressive voice he read the first line of the second scene of Act II.—"That which hath made them drunk hath made me bold."

He spoke no more that evening until he bade us "good night."

CHAPTER XII

" Thus far the scene on the Boulevards a few hours ago.[1] Be the upshot of this war what it may, one thing is certain; the prologue to it does not redound to the credit of French diplomacy. Before the first shot has been fired, the moral opinion of Europe, or to be correct, the diplomatic opinion of Europe in as far as it influences the moral opinion, will be on the side

[1] The following is the continuation of a note, the whole of which was apparently written in the early morning of Saturday, 16th July, 1870. The first part I published in *An Englishman in Paris*, Vol. 2, pp. 201, 202, and 203. The present part I omitted, firstly, for want of room; secondly, because though highly interesting, I did not consider it consistent with the original plan of the book. I have, moreover, a doubt with regard to this particular note. Though it is absolutely in the same handwriting as all the others from the same source, there is a slight alteration in the style, which is maintained throughout the short sequels relating to the siege of Paris and the Commune. If I had to pronounce an opinion I should say this : the whole of the notes in my possession were unquestionably written by the same man, who in the beginning acted as a kind of amanuensis and afterwards continued them on his own account, modelling his phrases on those of the original dictator.

of the King of Prussia, and I fancy it is bad diplomacy to set opinion against you at the outset. For we may be sure that Europe will not be hoodwinked by France's pretext for the quarrel. Nay, it is doubtful whether, among the French themselves, those who think are deceived by it. This does not exactly mean that they are averse to the struggle, but they would have preferred to let the provocation come more directly from Prussia, of whose growing military power they are intensely jealous and have been ever since that power was revealed to them just four years ago. That, in fact, is the sole foundation of their grievance, as far as the bulk of the nation herself is concerned. I question whether any cessation of territory on the part of Germany or her assent to the annexation of Luxemburg by France would have wholly removed this grievance; but it might have proved some balm to their wounded military pride, inasmuch as this assent would have implied Prussia's fear of France. I am not at all certain that Prussia is not afraid, but if so she is not going to show it.[1] Besides, she knows that if she were to

[1] When the Crown Prince of Prussia (afterwards Frederick III.), who was in Silesia at the time, heard of the scene in the Corps Législatif on the 6th July, he exclaimed: "That means war, and we are not prepared." He almost burst into tears. Moltke did not say that Prussia was not prepared, but he felt nevertheless very uneasy. "My agents have either misinformed me," he said to Baron Nothomb, the Belgian statesman, "or else France has suddenly gone mad to challenge us in this way with her feeble resources and lack of preparation."

shirk a war now, she would have to engage in one a few years hence, for with a Bonaparte on the throne of France, the question of remodelling the map of Europe is never killed, only scotched. This is the fault of the first, not of the third, Napoleon; the latter stands almost irrevocably committed to his uncle's policy. And the remodelling of the map of Europe as at present interpreted by the Emperor means only one thing, viz., the possession of some of the Rhenish provinces, the partial or whole reconstruction of the French frontier on that side on the basis of 1814. Prussia might as well cut her throat at once as concede such demands. The resentment caused by compliance with that would practically reduce her to her status of the pre-Bismarckian days—in other words, to her former vassalage to Austria, for neither South nor North Germany would forgive her for having nipped German unity in the bud, and Austria's humiliation of four years ago is too fresh in her mind for her not to risk reprisals by having another throw for the hegemony of the Fatherland proper. I am virtually repeating what my friend S—— of the English Embassy said to me last Tuesday; I am not clever enough to have thought this out for myself.[1] 'If every one of Napoleon III.'s Ministers for Foreign Affairs

---

[1] I have an idea, but it is no more, that "my friend S—— of the English Embassy" was Mr. Sheffield.

had been a Richelieu and every one of his
ambassadors a Talleyrand and a Metternich in
one, the whole combined would not have succeeded in bringing this consummation about,'
he added.

" But though no diplomatist, I am sufficiently
observant to know that there is neither a Richelieu
nor a Talleyrand at the Quai d'Orsay, and that
there has not been one ever since M. Drouyn de
Lhuys signed his first despatch there nearly
seventeen years ago. The first tenant of the new
Hôtel des Affaires Etrangères was probably far
superior to any of his successors as a scholar and
a student of history, and he had a kind of prophetic insight into the future when he wished to
prevent a war between Prussia and Austria, or in
default of this advised the Emperor to cast in
his lot with Francis Joseph. Unfortunately for
France he was too honest, and Napoleon III. is
not honest enough in his diplomacy. Conspiracy
appears to be in the latter's blood, and it leads
him to conspire even against his own ministers
and ambassadors, so that they never know what
mine is going to be sprung under their very feet.

" A couple of instances of this duplicity will
suffice. While in 1866 he instructed Drouyn de
Lhuys to treat with Austria in the sense of his
(the minister's) recommendation, he himself endeavoured to negotiate a secret treaty with Prussia,
always in pursuance of that greatest of his ambi-

tions, the possession of German territories on the left bank of the Rhine. In spite of his many mistakes with regard to Bismarck's real value as a diplomatist, the Emperor assuredly cannot imagine for one instant that his adversary has kept the contents of the draft of that and of other treaties—precedent and subsequent—from the intended victims of the spoliation ; for I am told that there were at least a half-dozen, all aiming at the same object. I do not flatter myself that I was specially singled out for the confidence of the English attaché who told me all this, although I may boast of being an intimate friend. Nay, the attaché himself must have got his information from somewhere. And what about the informant of the attaché? Let us take it, however, that the channel through which the secret (?) has filtered down to me is as yet an extremely narrow one and only been opened within a comparatively short time. What in the name of all that is sensible can induce the Emperor to be so certain as he seems to be of the armed support o those identical South German States, some of which he has for years been trying to despoil ? That there is not the slightest doubt in the Emperor's mind about this support, if not at the beginning of the hostilities, at any rate after a few signal victories of his troops, the following will show. I happen to know two or three bandmasters of infantry regiments—the bands of the cavalry have been almost entirely suppressed since 1867. Having had occasion to go to Escudier's, the music publishers, twice within one week, I on each occasion met one of my acquaintances there. Both gave the same orders—the national hymns of the South German States, scored for regimental bands. The coincidence struck me, and I inquired of the second after we had left the shop. 'I do not know the reason,' he answered; 'all I know is that all the foot regiments of the Guard have the same instructions, which therefore, I fancy, must come from higher quarters.'

"His answer only whetted my curiosity and I inquired of some one connected with higher quarters. 'Oh!' he said; 'I thought you would have guessed the reason at once, seeing that you are aware of Lebrun's departure for Vienna. We are also trying to negotiate some South-German alliances, and the Emperor considered it would be polite to hail their junction with us by the performance of their national hymns.' This was about the middle of last month. Talk about selling the bear's skin before it has been caught, it is nothing to it. It is like buying a currycomb for a wild steed on the Pampas. If there were a Richelieu at the Quai d'Orsay, he could not under such conditions, initiate, let alone carry out, a consistent foreign policy, and Duc Agénor de Gramont, Duc de Guiche, is not a Richelieu. He is one of the old *noblesse* whom, twenty years ago, the Prince-President, in prevision of the Empire, succeeded in attracting to the Elysée 'for decorative purposes'—to use the words of Louis Napoleon himself. The Duc de Guiche's secession from the Faubourg St. Germain caused no great stir then, the Legitimists flattering themselves that he was working for the Comte de Chambord, with whom he had been brought up. There was no other apparent reason for his defection, the Duchessed'Angoulême having left him close upon £40,000 a year.

"But the Duc soon showed that he intended to be something more than merely decorative. Being *very* noble, he claimed to be endowed with the gift which, according to Molière, was vouchsafed to noblemen *only* in the poet's time; namely, that of knowing everything without having learnt anything. 'Nature intended me to be a diplomatist,' says one of the elder Dumas' characters. 'If that be the case,' replies his interlocutor, 'we had better get you an opening in the diplomatic career as soon as possible. I was under the impression that diplomatic skill is to a certain extent a matter of hard study and experience You say it is a matter of instinct, and that it cannot be taught. You ought to know, seeing that by your own admission you are a born diplomatist so I must needs believe you.'

"One cannot help thinking that some such conversation must have taken place between the

Prince-President and the erstwhile playfellow of *l'enfant du miracle*, for without the slightest preliminary training as a diplomatist, the latter was sent to Cassel, then to Stuttgard, then to Turin and Rome, and finally to Vienna. Of course, when the Faubourg St. Germain discovered, after the *Coup d'État*, that Guiche had been working for his own hand, and not for the Comte de Chambord's, there was a great outcry, but I am not concerned with that, I am looking at his diplomatic career, though I feel convinced that the Embassy of Turin was the reward for Guiche's final rallying to the Empire. Nor do I say that he had learned nothing during his two previous missions. What I do wish to say is this: that he never served a diplomatic apprenticeship, part of which consists in the study of the archives, in getting the substances of past treaties at one's fingers' ends upon which to base future treaties. I am well aware that a life-long study of such documents will not make up for the want of diplomatic genius, any more than a thorough mastery of harmony and counterpoint will compensate for the absence of musical genius in a composer. Nevertheless, as I heard Lord Granville—who speaks French like a native—say one day while discussing the subject: 'Un ministre des affaires étrangères ou un ambassadeur qui n'a jamais mis le nez dans les archives, finira tôt ou tard de se mettre le doigt dans l'œil" (*Anglicè* : a Secretary for Foreign Affairs or an Ambassador who has never put his nose into the archives will sooner or later "put his foot into it"). That is exactly what Gramont has done at present. If, as it is alleged, the complications arising from the withdrawal of Prince Leopold von Hohenzollern's candidature are but so many pretexts of Bismarck to force France into a war and to shift the moral responsibility of it on to France's shoulders, Gramont might have easily checkmated him. That is, if he, Gramont, had been more or less cognisant of the documents existing on the subject: or if cognisant of this existence, had cared to consult them, seeing that this candidature is no new thing. Nearly sixteen months ago the question presented itself for the first time. Bismarck seemed quite willing then to admit the objections of France to such a candidature. The Prussian Minister for Foreign Affairs (Herr von Thile, I believe) went farther still, and pledged his personal word several times that there had not been and that there could not be such a question as the candidature of the Prince von Hohenzollern for the crown of Spain. Of course, neither I nor my informant have seen the despatches of Benedetti to the Marquis de la Valette, but he (my informant) is positive that these despatches exist, and as in the course of our long friendship I have never known him to make an important mistake, either in dates or in the substance of his information, I accept his word in this instance as I would in all others, confident that in the main he is correct. Therefore, nothing would have been easier than to refer to these despatches. When Herr von Thile refused to discuss the matter on the plea that the Hohenzollern candidature was a family affair with which the Prussian Government had no right to meddle, he should have been confronted with Benedetti's reports, and the same ought to have been done in the case of Bismarck. If brought to book in this way, the Prussian Government would have been bound to face the question—unless it felt prepared to assume the position into which it has so skilfully beguiled France; the Duc de Gramont could not have averred, as he did, that practically he had no one in Berlin to interrogate; Benedetti would not have gone to Ems; the mischief would have been strangled in its birth, or if not, the blame for it would have been laid at Prussia's door instead of France's, and the latter could have gone to war with an innocent front, no matter how guilty the mind behind it might have been; for I repeat, the whole of this candidature is simply a stalking horse. That and that only would have been good diplomacy.

"But the practical application of such a policy would have required the loyal co-operation if not the mutual goodwill of at least four people ; namely, the Minister for Foreign Affairs himself, the permanent Secretary of the Foreign Office, the Ambassador, and the Minister's predecessor in office. As it happens, three of these four—Gramont, Benedetti, and Valette—are intensely jealous of one another, and Desprets, the Directeur Politique (read, permanent secretary), is afraid of all three, and, perhaps, afraid of himself. Desprets is the most deferential individual I ever saw outside a servants' hall ; this was why Drouyn de Lhuys, who, though honest, is a tyrant on a small scale, appointed him to the vacancy left by the appointment of the Marquis de Banneville to the Embassy at Vienna. But if Desprets ever dreamt at all, his wildest dreams never foreshadowed to him such a rise, and during the six years he has occupied the post he has not ceased to wonder at himself and at everything around him. Not the slightest spark of genius, not an ounce of initiative in his composition, he is, nevertheless, an able man and an absolutely trustworthy machine. At the faintest sign from Gramont, at the most casual hint, he would, no doubt, have produced all the documents relating to the Hohenzollern candidature of 1869, but it appears Gramont never said a word, and that, coupled with the silence of Benedetti, the author of the despatches, and of Valette, their recipient, may have induced Desprets into the belief that the mention of them would be inopportime. He may not have been altogether wrong. I myself am inclined to think that these documents were systematically kept back. Both Gramont and Benedetti wanted to score each off his own bat: a collective victory over Bismarck did not suit them. In fact, the latter's laurels of the last seven or eight years as a diplomatist have been so many thorns to them. Gramont, who fancied himself strong enough to cope with Antonelli, and who in private conversation willingly ascribes his recall from Rome (in 1861) to the Cardinal's fear and jealousy of him, thought himself a match for Bismarck, a presumption which his subsequent stay at Vienna has done not a little to increase, and which up to the last few days has been cleverly nursed both by Metternich and Nigra, who, for purposes of their own, have befooled him to the top of his bent. Of course, it is too early to foresee with any degree of certainty the consequences of all this, but of one thing I feel perfectly certain. In its utter lack of discipline, of preconcerted action, the French Foreign Office is not a whit better than the French Army; every one plays for his own hand.

"The Emperor is unquestionably to blame for all this in the past, though it seems hard to blame a man so seriously ill as he is. The outer world appears to be absolutely in the dark with regard to his condition, but I have my own reasons for knowing that it is even more critical than his most immediate *entourage* suspect.[1] But however charitably disposed, one cannot help doubting the wisdom that prompted the promotion of men like Benedetti to the foremost ranks of the diplomatic service and maintained them there after their incompetence had become apparent, or, to put it mildly, after their competence admitted of discussion. It is very certain that even as early as 1864 Bismarck had made too great a mark to admit of his being confronted with any but the best man the French Diplomatic Service could put forward. If Benedetti was that best man, then Napoleon III. ought to have resigned himself to abandon, at any rate, temporarily, his policy of France's aggrandisement at the expense of Germany, for he must have known that, with no more powerful instrument than the French Minister at Turin to carry out this policy, it was foredoomed to failure. When Gouvion Saint-Cyr was only second-in-command in Spain, he one day advised a retreat before the English troops. An hour or so afterwards his general-in-chief was severely wounded by the bursting of a shell during a reconnaissance. Saint-Cyr, compelled to take

---

[1] See *An Englishman in Paris*, Vol. 2, Chs. ix. and x. Since the publication of the book, and mainly in consequence of the denial given to the statements it contains, I have made my own inquiries, as my conclusion will show. Should this also be contradicted, I am determined to produce the whole of my documentary evidence with the names of the writers. I fancy, though, that I shall not be challenged to this extent.

the command, immediately countermands the retreat, gives battle, and wins the day. 'Why did you advise the general-in-chief this morning not to give battle?' asked one of his officers. 'Because he would have lost it,' was the answer.[1]

The moral of the story is obvious. Saint-Cyr knew his chief, and felt confident that an attack led by him would prove disastrous. Napoleon, when he appointed Benedetti to the Embassy at Berlin, may have fostered illusions with regard to his ambassador's ability to cope with Bismarck; after Sadowa these illusions must have vanished, and then he ought to have put a stop to these ceaseless demands for the Rhine provinces, although to do Benedetti justice, Sadowa itself was virtually foretold by him. After Sadowa, in fact, Benedetti lost his head and became the plaything of Bismarck, who appears to have exercised on him the fascination the snake exercises on the frog. One instance of this fascination will give an idea of the rest. It relates to the 'Luxemburg affair,' and I doubt whether with the exception of the Emperor, my friend S——, and myself, there is a living man in France who has heard of it. Benedetti did not describe the scene in his official reports, but

[1] Practically, the story is true, but it did not happen in Spain, it happened at Polotzk, and the Commander-in-Chief was Marshal Oudinot, who was wounded in the arm.

the Marquis de Moustier,[1] who had many sources of private information in Berlin, where he had been ambassador himself, came to hear of it and told it to Napoleon. Moustier, in spite of his love of gossip and epigram, was too indolent to tell many stories; he was a better listener than a talker, and could never shake off the sybaritism and the habits of *dolce far niente* contracted during his stay at Constantinople. S——, who probably had it from the same source (Berlin), told me, but quite casually; and curiously enough, exactly two years after the affair had happened, namely, on the 1st April of this year. We were talking of the time-honoured custom of trying to make a fool of some one on that day, when the evening papers came in. They contained an account of the deputations that had waited upon Bismarck that morning to wish him 'many happy returns.' 'Well,' said I, ' Bismarck's mother did not make a fool of her fellow-beings when she ushered him into the world on that day.' 'No,' replied S——, 'but the son takes a delight in making fools of others on that or any other day, but by preference on that one. Ask Benedetti." And noticing that I did not catch the drift of his remark, he told me the following :—

---

[1] The successor of Drouyn de Lhuys and the predecessor of the Marquis de la Valette at the French Foreign Office (September 1866—August 1868).

"' As early as the 18th March, 1867, the Luxemburg question was made the subject of an interpellation in the Parliament of the North German Confederation. Bismarck walked cleverly round it. Meanwhile the negotiations between William III. and Napoleon III. proceeded apace, the French Government reminding the Dutch Government throughout that the official announcement of the concluded transaction should reach Berlin from Paris, and not from the Hague. No heed was paid to this recommendation, and when on the 28th March the Emperor was informed by telegraph that William III. was willing to transfer the Grand-Duchy to France, and requested the latter to arrange with Prussia to that effect, Benedetti found that the information had been forestalled, and by no less a personage than the Dutch Minister in Berlin. As a matter of course, Moustier was wild, and his rage did not abate when two days later—on the 30th—Benedetti apprised him that the news had created the greatest excitement in Berlin, and that Bennigsen had given notice of an interpellation on the subject for the next day. It was said at the time that Moustier's answer sent early in the morning of the 1st April was couched in the most defiant spirit, that he was thoroughly aroused and paced his room at the Quai d'Orsay like a wild panther in his cage, that his habitual *insouciance* suddenly disappeared and that his antagonism against Bismarck, pent-up for many years, found vent in an avalanche of epithets and curses and yells.[1] The exact wording of Moustier's answer is probably known to few people, perhaps not even to Bismarck, for he prevented its communication to him—at any rate, its official communication; although on its receipt Benedetti went immediately to the *Auswärtigen Angelegenheiten* (Foreign Office) for the purpose. Bismarck was just going to the Reichstag when Benedetti was shown in. After the usual exchange of courtesies, Benedetti was about to produce the telegraphic message, when Bismarck held up his hand. Benedetti said afterwards that Bismarck was visibly affected; he may have been, for one word too much on either side might have driven both countries headlong into a war; but I feel certain that Bismarck did not show his emotion. He merely told Benedetti that he was unable to take cognisance of the message officially at that moment inasmuch as he was expected at the Reichstag, and invited the Ambassador to walk as far with him. They took a short cut across the gardens of the Foreign Office to a passage leading to the Leipziger Strasse, talking

[1] This antagonism dated from at least a score of years. Here is a sample of it. In 1851 Moustier was discussing Prussia's attitude in the Eastern Question with Bismarck. "That policy may lead you to another Jena," remarked Moustier. "Why not to another Leipzig or Waterloo?" was Bismarck's reply.

as they went; Benedetti trying all the while to communicate the contents of the telegraphic message in his pocket, Bismarck equally determined to prevent his doing so. "I am going to the Reichstag," he said, "to answer an interpellation on the question of the eventual sale of the Grand-Duchy of Luxemburg, which question is causing a great deal of excitement in the papers." "I am aware of it," replied Benedetti, "and that is why I am so anxious to communicate my telegraphic message to you. It appears to me most urgent." "One moment," interrupted Bismarck, waving off the telegraphic message for the fourth or fifth time, "one moment. I am going to tell you my answer to the interpellation. I am going to say that the Government has no knowledge of the real condition of the question; consequently, that I cannot make a public statement of what it intends to do. I am going to add that I feel assured that there is no intention on the part of any Power to encroach on the unquestionable rights of the Germanic countries, and that the Government trusts to have these rights respected by means of a pacific policy. This is what I am going to reply to the interpellation, because it is the truth, and because this declaration will enable me to open negotiations in a friendly way and to get, perhaps, to an understanding. But I could not give a similar answer *if I knew that the convention for the sale of the Grand Duchy has been concluded.*" The last words were spoken with great emphasis: then Bismarck went on, "In this case I should be obliged to hold quite different language, and a conflict between France and ourselves would be the inevitable result." By that time the two had emerged into the Leipziger Strasse where Bismarck stopped Benedetti. "And now," he concluded pointedly, "I ask you whether you have a telegraphic message to hand to me or not?" Benedetti did not answer, he simply bowed his head, put the paper into his pocket, and walked away.'

"Others may judge the direct and indirect political consequences of this scene; I am mainly concerned with the absolute lack of discipline at the Quai d'Orsay as implied by it. Here is an ambassador who deliberately disregards the instructions of his chief and yet he is not recalled. On the contrary the Emperor virtually pats him on the back and says, 'Well done, thou good and faithful servant; thou hast prevented a bloody strife between two great countries.' For that is what the sequel to the episode practically means; the contemplated purchase of Luxemburg was allowed to drop, the telegraphic message was never shown, and was annulled in spite of those who, when they heard what had happened, insisted that it was not too late to show it then. But the Emperor, it was said at the time, did not want to go to war, he was not prepared. And yet his foreign policy which, we must remember, was not imposed upon him by his parliament as late as two years and a half ago when he did not profess to be a constitutional sovereign, this foreign policy is always bringing him within an ace of war; in fact, to use an Americanism, "he is always 'spelling' for it.¹ If he did not wish to make the Luxemburg question a *casus belli*, he ought to have begun by doing what he did in the end; submit the matter to the Powers that signed the Convention of 1839. If he does not wish to go to war, Moustier ought to have been relieved of his functions there and then, inasmuch as his

---

[1] I have by me a short note in the handwriting of my younger grand-uncle which practically says the same thing, but illustrates it with an anecdote. "The Emperor in his foreign policy always reminds me of Franz Hals and his aspirations 'to be translated to Heaven shortly.' Whether from personal inclination or in order to keep the 'pot of military glory' of which the French are so fond 'on the boil,' the Emperor seems to be ever within a hair's breadth, but at the critical moment recoils from it. Our worthy of the brush was for ever praying to be taken to the Almighty's bosom. One night, when, as usual, he was 'half seas over' and had been fetched in that condition from the tavern by two of his pupils who were to become famous, namely, Adriaan Brouwer and Adriaan van Ostade, he uttered his nightly prayer, 'Good Lord, take me to thy bosom soon,' and got into bed. Immediately afterwards, he found himself slowing rising in the air, 'Not yet, good Lord, not yet, thy humble servant is not prepared.' And to his great satisfaction, the bedding with himself in it, assumed its original position. The two Adriaans with a fellow pupil, Dirk van Deelen, had slung ropes under their master's mattress and given him a foretaste of the ascent he was always praying for. It is said that Franz never prayed again. If the Emperor could only be made to take warning in some such manner! But all lessons appear to be lost upon him."

telegraphic message, if delivered by Benedetti, would have made war almost inevitable. All this brings me back to my original contention, viz. that if there happened to be a Richelieu or a Talleyrand at the Quai d'Orsay, he would practically be manacled under the present conditions, which not only admit of every man's working for his own hand, but put a premium on his doing so.

"Such a system or rather want of system is apt to influence all but the highest-minded. The others forget that they are only so many wheels in the machinery of their country's foreign policy, and that if they tamper with or clog the other wheels the machinery must necessarily come to grief. Benedetti, in order to obtain a personal victory over Bismarck which would obliterate the various defeats he has suffered at the latter's hand subsequently to Sadowa, systematically neglects to point out the existence of previous documents on the Hohenzollern candidature; Gramont, who owes his exalted position to a kind of favouritism, which would not for one moment be tolerated in a well-regulated mercantile office of second-rate importance—Gramont, the Minister for Foreign Affairs and sometime Ambassador at Rome and Vienna, not to mention the smaller capitals—either does not know of the existence of these documents or else is equally determined not to refer to them, lest reference should minimize the *éclat* of victory he confidently expected to obtain over Bismarck, and which he was bent upon having attributed only to his diplomatic skill. There has been 'bad blood' between these two for years. Bismarck has never curbed his tongue with regard to Gramont's over-weening conceit, his contemptible incompetence as a diplomatist, his dandy-like habits, and the rest; and Gramont hates him accordingly. In fact, I remember very well that exactly two months ago, at Gramont's advent to office, several German papers, strongly suspected of being inspired by Bismarck, expressed their fear lest this diplomatist (Gramont) who since Sadowa had been mixed up with all the attempts to establish an *entente cordiale* between the Court of Vienna and that of the Tuileries, should continue, as a minister, the policy he had pursued as an ambassador. 'Such an attitude,' they said, or words to that effect, 'would be fraught with the greatest danger to France from the side of Prussia.' This sentence, if properly analysed, was not only daring on Bismarck's part, but presumptuous besides; for it implied, firstly, a threat; secondly, a threat based upon the assumed military superiority of Prussia over France. No doubt, Bismarck felt and feels certain of this superiority, but that was no reason for him to fling the knowledge into France's face, knowing as he must that on no point are the French more susceptible than on that of their military prestige. This is but another proof that in Bismarck's mind war between Prussia and France had become inevitable, as long as the latter would persist in seeking an alliance with Austria, for he really could not have expected France to remain isolated at his bidding. The very fact of his opposition to France's *rapprochement* with a great European Power showed the necessity of such a *rapprochement* as far as France was concerned. The Emperor, however, should have chosen differently. Alexander II., and not Francis Joseph, was the logical ally of Napoleon III., and Napoleon III. himself would have probably cast his net in that direction but for two considerations. The first was the well-known affection of the Tzar for his uncle; the second, the invincible desire on the Emperor's part for those Rhine provinces, which desire would brook no delay in its satisfaction.

"There is a fourth man who, were he other than he is, might have saved the situation. I am thinking of la Valette. Although the whole of the *pourparlers* of the Hohenzollern candidature of '69 were kept a secret, he assuredly must have read the documents relating to it, for he was Minister for Foreign Affairs at the time. He could have easily reminded the Emperor of the existence of these documents. The Emperor, I repeat, is ill, in body and mind, so ill, in fact, as to be absolutely unfit for the slightest exertion of any kind. Did la Valette remind the Emperor?

Did the Emperor receive the reminder and in a moment of intense agony, such as he suffers frequently, put it aside and forget all about it afterwards? Was the letter suppressed by the Emperor's immediate *entourage* before it could reach its destination? All these surmises, but especially the last one, offer food for serious reflection. Justice, moreover, demands that one should give la Valette the benefit of the doubt. Unfortunately, those who know la Valette best are not disposed to give him that benefit. If all I hear from London be true, he created a worse impression there as an ambassador than Persigny. 'He is a badly executed copy of a not very sympathetic original,' writes one of my English friends. 'There is the same constant preoccupation to appear *le très grand seigneur* to which people objected so much in Morny. But Morny had brains, and could appreciate the brains of others ; la Valette has only conceit, impudence, and cunning. Nothing is more comical than to see him and Bernstorf together. It is a *tableau vivant* of the diplomatic ox and the frog. The ox, however, is very soothing, while the frog irritates one beyond endurance. He is intensely jealous of the reputation of others, and throughout wishes to convey that he and not the Minister for Foreign Affairs conducts the foreign policy of France.'

 " Thus far those who profess their allegiance

to the Emperor. Those who are the avowed enemies both of the sovereign, the dynasty he represents, and the Empire itself might have more effectually prevented this war, if instead of fanning the ever-smouldering embers of antagonism between the two countries into a blaze, they had thrown the cold water of their disapproval on it. The foremost of these offenders is Thiers, who by an interpellation he had not sufficient courage to make himself, positively goaded Gramont into his bellicose attitude, though truth compels one to say that Gramont wanted but little goading. Thiers chose Cochery as his mouthpiece. But for his illness the Emperor would have avoided the trap, for Thiers had warned him as late as six weeks ago of his intention to raise difficulties. Here is the whole of the story, as I have it on the most unimpeachable authority.

"One morning in the early part of June 1870, hence more than a month before the war-cloud appeared on the horizon, the Emperor, being then at St. Cloud, was strolling gently along that large avenue of sycamores situated opposite the windows of his private apartments on the ground floor of the palace. The disease from which he had been suffering for several years, and which was eventually to carry him to his grave, had reached an acute stage; nevertheless on that morning he was more or less free from pain. By his side walked his kinswoman the Duchesse de Mouchy (née Princesse Anna Murat), who had only arrived a few minutes previously and joined him thus informally at her own request, as she had an important communication to make. It was to the following effect: That same morning, M. Thiers, through the intermediary of the Marquis Philippe de Massa, had requested an interview with her. She, the Duchesse, was to prevail upon the Emperor to grant Thiers a private audience. 'What can M. Thiers want with the Emperor?' the Duchesse had exclaimed in a tone of surprise. The surprise was not unjustified, considering that M. Thiers at that time was not only the avowed enemy of the Empire, but of the Emperor himself. She was less surprised at Thiers's selection of an ambassador in the shape of a captain of a crack regiment of dragoons, and personally attached to the Emperor. The second husband of the marquis's mother was Comte Roger (du Nord), a consistent Republican and an intimate friend of Thiers, at whose house the Comtesse spent many evenings, and whither her son accompanied her now and then. The Emperor could be vindictive enough, but his vindictiveness was, at the best, sporadic, and he often swallowed a camel in the shape of an offence while straining at a gnat. He never forgave Lady Jersey for having pooh-poohed his request for the hand of her daughter; he sent

David d'Angers into exile for having refused to finish the tomb of Queen Hortense ; while he condoned, as I will show in the course of these pages, much graver injuries against himself. Adam Smith has said somewhere that people will sooner tolerate the enemies of their friends than the friends of their enemies. Louis Napoleon was the exception ; he showed no resentment against the friends of his enemies, but he would scarcely have tolerated the enemies of his friends. Thiers, on the other hand, knew no such generosity ; he tolerated the enemies of his friends—if he could get something by it—while it is doubtful whether he would have welcomed the friend of an enemy. In this instance, Napoleon III. did not object to his young ordnance officer visiting the house of Thiers ; Thiers, on the other hand, would not have admitted him for a moment, but for his constant hope of worming some more or less important secret out of a charming and accomplished dragoon who had virtually the run of the Tuileries. It could scarcely be otherwise with one bearing the name of Régnier. In view of all this, the Duchesse de Mouchy, though surprised at Thiers's request, was not surprised at his choice of the ambassador.

"In reply to the Duchesse's question, M. de Massa gave some additional information. 'M. Thiers,' he said, 'wishes you to tell the Emperor that a near, nay, impending, war between France and Prussia is unavoidable; that, to carry on this war successfully the Emperor will require men of tried knowledge and experience instead of the incapable ones of which the Ollivier Cabinet is composed; that the Emperor will require, above all, popular men who have the ear and confidence of the nation, and that, under the circumstances, he is ready and willing to form a ministry under his own leadership.'

"The Duchesse pondered for a moment. 'You are right,' she remarked at last; 'the news is indeed very important and serious, but before I can communicate it to the Emperor, I must have M. Thiers's personal permission.' M. de Massa at once saw the force of the remark. He went away immediately and in less than half an hour returned, accompanied by Thiers, who not only repeated what M. de Massa had said, but pointed out to the Duchesse the necessity of her seeing the Emperor at once. So anxious, in fact, was Thiers to set the matter going that he offered to stay at the Duchesse's while she proceeded to St. Cloud. Here again we have particulars which will remove the faintest doubt as to the absolute truth of the whole affair. Among other precious autographs she had a collection of letters from Fénelon to her husband's kinswoman (the Vicomtesse de Noailles), during the great controversy between the famous Archbishop of Cambray and Bossuet. Thiers asked permission to examine them while awaiting her return.

"The Emperor had listened to the Duchesse without interrupting her by as much as a word; he had only smiled, with one of those ineffable smiles which, to his friends, needed no interpretation, which all the misinterpretation of his enemies failed to rob of its charm. When she had quite finished, he led the way to his room, still in silence. 'My dear Anna,' he said, when they were seated; 'this is not the first nor the second time M. Thiers has made similar overtures to me under one pretext or another. But very recently, Madame Colonna[1] came to offer me his co-operation to found the parliamentary *régime*. I may frankly tell you that I have not much faith in, nor much sympathy with, this very meddlesome, arbitrary, and irrepressible personage. I have a distinct recollection of his tactics in the early days of the Presidency. He positively pervaded the Elysée. Each morning he came, as it were, to settle with me—in reality for me—my programme for the day; he brought me my speeches, practically his speeches, ready written out; in short, he endeavoured to interfere in everything. He had to have a finger in every pie; no question was to be discussed or decided without

---

[1] Adèle, Princesse Colonna di Castiglioni, *née* d'Affry, better known to the world at large under her artistic pseudonym of "Marcello" the sculptor.

him. More than twenty years have passed since the ceremony of inauguration of the chief magistracy, but I remember very vividly his look of stupefaction and anger, when on the morning of that day I gave him back the manuscript of a speech he had composed for me, telling him at the same time that, though deeply grateful for his counsels and his arduous interest in me, I intended henceforth to manage my own affairs. Our estrangement and his frenzied opposition date from that morning. I have been told that journeymen bakers suffer excruciating pains in their muscles, when an accident compels them to leave off kneading the dough. M. Thiers suffers similarly from being bereft of power, from being no longer the arbiter of the Government. His restless opposition is in reality the acute St. Vitus's dance of inactivity. But for this St. Vitus's dance he would be dead. Nevertheless, in view of the grave events with which we may be confronted at

[1] "And in fact, up till 1830, when he was nearly forty-four, he (Guizot) had never seen the sea. 'And if it had not been for an electoral journey to Normandy, I might not have seen it then': he said. I pointed out to him that M. Thiers had never had a country house; that he did not seem to care for nature, for birds, or for flowers. 'Ah, that's different,' he smiled. 'I did not care for the country, because I had never seen it. Thiers does not like it, because the birds, the flowers, the trees, live and grow without his interference, and he does not care that anything on earth should happen without his having a hand in it.'"—*An Englishman in Paris*, vol. ii. ch. 2.

any moment, I would recall him to power, if I thought he could be useful. I do not say that such a step would afford me pleasure, for I do not like the man and have no reason to like him; but it would give me no pain. Unfortunately, I am no longer the master in this respect. I have taken in earnest to my part of a constitutional ruler, and will not depart from it. The actual Ministry commands a considerable majority in both Chambers; to dismiss this Ministry abruptly and without a valid motive, would be an act of personal interference which I must no longer commit. If, at some future period, near or distant, the Chamber should overthrow M. Ollivier's Cabinet on an interpellation of M. Thiers or on an important question, I might entrust M. Thiers with the task of constituting a Ministry; but at present I am bound to attempt nothing against a Minister who appears to enjoy the confidence of Parliament. Pray thank M. Thiers for me, and tell him that, while deeply obliged for his warning and trouble, I cannot, at any rate for the present, accept his proposal. He is an old and experienced parliamentarian, and will no doubt understand and appreciate the motives that prompt my conduct.'

" Whether Thiers understood the motives of the Emperor's refusal of his services or not, it is certain that he failed to appreciate them; for when the Duchesse de Mouchy, on her return to

her house in the Parc Monceau gave him the
Emperor's answer — toned down, we may be sure,
and shorn of the sovereign's prefatorial remarks
as to Thiers' character—Thiers flew into a tower-
ing rage, stamped his feet and bounced out of
the room, exclaiming in that shrill treble of his,
' Is that it ? He does not want me. He'll find
to his cost that he does want me. And then I'll
not want him.' "

CONCLUSION

I REACHED Paris on Saturday night, 16th July, 1870, hence, four-and-twenty hours after the virtual though not the official declaration of war between France and Prussia. I had no longer a home in the French capital, for both my relatives were gone. In spite of all that I had heard and seen for fourteen years, during which I had been an attentive listener and, considering my age, a careful observer, I felt almost certain that France would hold her own in the forthcoming struggle, but I did not imagine for a single instant that she would inflict so crushing a defeat on her adversary as her adversary eventually inflicted on her.

Before I went to bed that night my opinions had undergone a considerable change—I will not say a radical one. I did not like the tone of the prologue. I had seen the preliminaries to the war with Austria in '59, and although I was too young then to judge discriminately, they began to recur to me as I made my way slowly through the dense crowd lining the Boulevards from the Faubourg Poissonnière, where I had taken up my quarters, to the Café de la Paix, whither I was bound.

Against my will, as it were, a comparison between the scenes of eleven years before with those I was beholding at that moment gradually forced itself upon me. Worse than all, my recollections, having got loose from their moorings, drifted to Berlin, during the latter end of June, 1866, at the outbreak of the war between Prussia and her then formidable rival Austria. I am no physiognomist, but I candidly own that I have more faith in the man who at the hour of supreme danger sets his teeth tightly and stares as if his eyes would come out of their sockets than in the man who grins open-mouthed and yells and rolls his eyes in fine frenzy. With the exception of the one shout that greeted Bismarck's appearance on his balcony on that Friday night of which I have spoken in a previous chapter, I heard no howling, no imprecations against the Austrians in the Prussian capital. Nor did the Berliners sing. There were tightly wedged masses *unter den Linden* from the Brandenburg Gate to the Palace of the King, but they were earnest and subdued, and under the broiling, almost tropical sun they waited patiently for a sight of the sovereign to whom were confided their destinies as a nation.

I cannot speak from personal experience of the attitude and demeanour of the Berlin people in July, 1870, but there is, perhaps, more valuable evidence than mine could be. It is that of a representative Frenchman in the highest sense of the term.[1] " At seven o'clock in the evening of the 19th (July), the Secretary of the Senate handed me my passports. I was ready to start, and I left Hamburg immediately. Behind me lay Germany, uprisen from one end to the other and rushing to arms, grave, solemn, full of hatred, conscious that she was engaging in a mortal struggle, ready for every sacrifice. In Paris I only beheld people yielding to violent excitement, tumultuous scenes, bands of drunken men, indulging in patriotic saturnalias. The contrast was heartrending."

What was heartrending to the truly patriotic Frenchman became well-nigh disgusting to the alien with less fiercely pulsing blood in his veins, but who, alien though he was, had learned to love France during and for the many happy years he had spent within her borders. I was almost sorry I had come to Paris; the confidence of the previous four-and-twenty hours in France's ability to confront the imminent danger with something like moderate results received a shock there and then. I had not been taught to regard the Bible

[1] M. G. Rothan, Minister-Plenipotentiary to the Hanseatic Free Towns.

as an absolutely divinely inspired book, but my teachers had always insisted that it was the most marvellous, the most complete manual for the guidance of humanity under all circumstances. My thoughts involuntarily went out to this septuagenarian monarch in his modest palace in Berlin, between whom and King Ahab of Israel I began to trace some resemblance. Wilhelm had also complied with the first—and the just—demands of his would-be conqueror, and he also, hearing of the brawling and bragging and bellowing of the French, of their cries of "A Berlin, A Berlin!" might say—" Let not him that girdeth on his harness boast himself as he that putteth it off."

It took me nearly an hour to get to the Café de la Paix, where I knew I should find the only man in Paris whom I could frankly ask for information without exposing myself to the risk of a rebuff and worse perhaps. Joseph Ferrari was my uncles' old friend, and knew their nephew well enough not to suspect him of being a spy in the pay of Bismarck. Even at that early stage of the proceedings I did not feel quite certain in this particular respect with regard to my relatives' French friends, for it must not be supposed that the spy-mania sprang full-armed from the French brain at the outbreak of the Franco-German War. The first symptoms of the disease had shown themselves soon after Sadowa. I remember perfectly well that shortly after my return from Germany at that time I gave some of our familiars a description—as far as I was able—of the regiments I had seen, and in the course of the conversation I happened to quote the remark of a Prussian officer to whom I had been introduced, about Baron Talleyrand-Perigord, Benedetti's predecessor. The words had scarcely left my lips when I felt rather than saw that I had made a mistake. My uncles, who were kindness personified, looked uncomfortable, but they did not comment upon my want of reticence that night. Next day Joseph Ferrari called earlier than was his wont. "My dear boy," he said in his fatherly way, "you allowed your tongue to run away with you. You will probably spend a great deal of your time in France when both your uncles and I will be gone. You are not French, and if you were to live a hundred years among them they would never consider you nor call you such. The extent of their graciousness would be to call you a real Parisian, a doubtful compliment to my mind. But even that doubtful compliment would have to be gained by the thorough suppression of your own individuality and your absolute abstention from enlightening them on any and every thing that implied a doubt of their superiority as a nation. Last night when we left here, two of your uncles' constant visitors and oldest acquaintances wished to know why you went to Germany, and asked me seriously whether

I thought you were in communication with Bismarck. Of course, in plain, unvarnished language it meant: Did I think you a spy? I know who you are, and what you are, but I considered it wise to give you a timely hint."

I need not say that, ever after that day, I had not the slightest hesitation in asking my uncles' friend for information on any situation whatsoever. I did this all the more readily in this instance, knowing that diplomatically he was not only the best-informed man in France, but the man who had probably thoroughly sifted whatever information he had got and subjected the residuum to the most critical, not to say microscopically, mental analysis.

Ferrari was seated outside the café amidst a group of seven or eight, Imperialists to a man. I knew most of them by sight, but no more. There were a couple of erstwhile prefects, and as many editors, and, if my memory serves me aright, for I did not take down their names in the note I wrote next morning, MM. Charles Abatucci, the son of the former Keeper of the Seals, and Jolibois, the eminent barrister who subsequently was counsel for the defence in that terrible lawsuit of Jules Favre against his friend Laluyé, who had accused him of having falsified the civil registers, during which lawsuit the family affairs of the plaintiff were mercilessly laid bare by M. Jolibois.

Ferrari shook hands with me very cordially, but

did not even ask me when I had arrived. It was the
first time we had met since, a twelvemonth earlier,
we had parted on the platform of the Northern
Railway Station, whither he had accompanied the
remains of my younger uncle on their way to
their last resting-place in a little cemetery near
Amsterdam, where the yellow waters of the Y
splash in low, plaintive ripples against the shore.

I took the hint, ordered some coffee, and sat
silently by his side for nearly three hours, at the
end of which I had arrived, at any rate, at one
conclusion, viz., if Bismarck, as was alleged at
the time, spent a great deal of money in maintaining a staff of spies in France, he was absolutely
flinging these sums out of the window. There
was no need to go hunting for secret information;
everything worth knowing seemed to be known
to at least half-a-dozen persons nearest to the
Emperor, and they in their turn made no scruple
about telling their friends. A decently-bred and
well-dressed man, provided with a few letters of
introduction to some of the best-known deputies
and officials, or to a couple of members of the
court circle, would simply have to listen. In less
than an hour, for instance, I felt perfectly certain
with regard to two or three main points. There
was neither a fixed plan of mobilisation nor a plan
of campaign. With regard to the alliances France
might possibly have contracted, all Ferrari's interlocutors agreed that various attempts had been

made to secure them; but while one section stoutly maintained that the treaties relating to them were lying sealed and signed in the archives at the Quai d'Orsay, the other was equally positive that the negotiations had altogether fallen through. And yet all these men surrounding Ferrari, and intelligent to a degree—though, of course, intellectually, not to be compared with him—would have gasped at the bare suggestion that their country might be crushed in the coming struggle. These men had many admirable qualities and not a few virtues; their great defect, vanity—for their national pride was only collective vanity—rendered all these virtues practically useless. "Vanity," said la Rochefoucauld, "if it does not overthrow all the virtues of a man, at any rate shakes them in their foundations." "Vanity," wrote Florian, "makes us as much dupes as fools." These men, I doubt not, had all read their "Maximes" and their "Fables," and yet two of the most valuable lessons they contain had been lost upon them.

"Now, you have heard the bells ring, but you do not know who pulls the ropes," said Ferrari to me that night as I left him at his door. "I fancy I can show you not only the bell-ringers themselves, but enlighten you as to the strength of the ropes they are pulling." And from that hour until a few days after Woerth, when I left Paris temporarily, he indicated to me the "undercurrents" that had been and were still at work. The information gathered from him piecemeal, as well as what I saw personally during those three weeks, is embodied in the following pages. I have, moreover, read and heard a good deal since, which, for convenience's sake, I will incorporate here instead of making separate footnotes.

"You heard the whole of them last night," Ferrari said next morning; "you heard the whole of them talking last night about France's alliances. There is not a word of truth in the statements of either of the parties. There is not a single treaty to that effect deposited in the archives of the Ministère des Affaires Etrangères, nor have any negotiations fallen through. Both Austria and Italy—Napoleon's main dependence—are playing a waiting game; if you want it more plainly, both Nigra and Metternich are leading the Emperor and Gramont by the nose. It would not be very difficult to do this in the case of the latter under any circumstances; it would be more difficult with the Emperor, but for his excruciating disease, which leaves him rest neither night nor day except under the influence of morphia, and I defy the most clear-headed intellect to work out a problem or to pursue even its own thoughts under such conditions. Except Conneau and a few doctors, no one suspects how ill he really is, for your Napoleon, whom I like nearly as much as your uncles did, is a real man of courage. If he were not as ill as he is, he might become alive to the fact that just now those Rhine provinces which are fundamentally the sole cause of the mischief, are unattainable, or at any rate not attainable by the means he proposes to employ, namely, by attacking Prussia and by inviting Austria and Italy to help him.

"To begin with, Austria and Italy will not, cannot, and dare not help France. Let me explain to you why.

"I will leave Italy aside for a moment. In the first place because such aid as she may be able to afford France will be almost worthless without the equally active co-operation of Austria. In order to be of any use at all, Italy would have to call out at least 100,000 troops, and in her present state of military organisation it would take her at least six or seven weeks to do this. That is, if the two burning questions, those of the temporal sovereignty of the Papacy and the occupation of Rome, had been satisfactorily settled to the advantage of Italy beforehand. Without that, I tell you, there is not the remotest chance of Italy stirring a finger. I know my country better than the Emperor, and feel positive that, if Victor Emmanuel attempted to mobilise his army without that stipulation—and mind, a public not a secret stipulation—his army, much as it loves him, would refuse to move at his bidding, supposing it did not stir against him. Our statesmen at the risk of being taxed with ingratitude say to themselves, 'Italy's position with regard to her unification—read with regard to the possession of Rome—would not be improved by the victory of France over Prussia; it would be materially improved by a defeat of France, or even by a *drawn* campaign, which would necessarily lead to a Congress.' This, I own, is black ingratitude, but I am not responsible for it, and if I were, I would follow the tactics of Lanza or of whomsoever stood in his place.

"Granted, however, that all these difficulties were satisfactorily removed offhand, I repeat, it would take, then, six weeks to mobilise 100,000 troops, which, if Austria still held aloof by that time, would have to be directed on to Lyons and have to cross a great part of France by rail. By then, take my word for it, the issue of the struggle would have been virtually decided. If France be able to hold her own single-handed for six or seven weeks after the real outbreak of the war, she will be able to do so afterwards, and will need no help from any one—provided she interprets the words 'holding her own' in their most literal sense. If she attempts territorial aggrandisement—the territorial aggrandisement Napoleon has been dreaming of for years—

under no matter what specious title, she will practically make a scourge for her own back, for in spite of Napoleon's hare-brained theories on the subject, the South German States want none of his protection against Prussia; and if they do not rally around her now, they would rally round her then, and what is more, Austria, who is wavering now, and who, like Italy, is waiting to see how the cat jumps, would waver no longer. Austria's love, like Juliet's, would spring from her only hate. She would scarcely care to see Würtemberg and Bavaria under French protection or allied to France, for in such conditions Baden would scarcely prove an obstacle to an otherwise unhindered march of the French into Bohemia. Austria has had enough of that kind of thing under Napoleon's uncle."

"Then why those drafts of projected treaties at the existence of which you yourself hinted?" I asked.

"Did not I tell you that both Austria and Italy are waiting to see how the cat jumps? If those drafts exist, and I feel certain of the existence of one, and nearly certain of the existence of the other, then final execution, I mean the signing of them by the three contracting parties, would still be dependent on so many conditions that at the last moment one or both of France's contemplated allies might find a pretext

for retreat. Do not lose sight of the following
facts, Austria will not act without Italy. That
is no surmise on my part, but an ascertained
fact. Austria is, moreover, a Catholic power,
and as such determined to maintain the temporal sovereignty of the Papacy which Italy
is equally determined to destroy. If you had
been here during the last six months instead
of in England, you would have noticed a gradual
change of Emile Ollivier's attitude with regard to
Rome. The Premier, who is also Minister of
Justice and Public Worship, conveniently forgot
in this instance that Emile Ollivier as a member of the Opposition quintet of the Empire
constantly claimed Rome for the Romans, that is,
for Italy. This alone would prove to me beyond
a doubt that Ollivier is a better statesman
than his present colleague Gramont, or than the
Minister for Foreign Affairs with whom Ollivier
inaugurated his ministerial career. That poor
Count Napoleon Daru. He was as fit to take
the head of Foreign Affairs, even if it had been
all smooth sailing, as the captain of one of your
saloon steamers on the Thames is fit to take the
command of the Channel Fleet. I do not know,
though, which of the two is worse ; he, Daru, who
would have let the vessel of the State drift on the
rocks, signalling for help all the while ; or Gramont, who does not know whence the wind blows
and steers the ship right on a sandbank, confident

all the while of help to take him off, which help will never come.

"Added to this; notwithstanding the pacific sentiments with which Ollivier is credited, he co-operated knowingly in the acceleration of this war—which *du reste* was inevitable at some future period remote or near, as long as Napoleon would not give up his senseless pretensions to those Rhenish provinces.[1] But," and here he took out his watch, "I have outstayed my time; I shall see you again by and bye, and will tell you more."

With which he left me to my own devices and reflections. The former were few, the latter many. Under different circumstances, I should have looked-up my French acquaintances. After an absence of more than a twelvemonth, I should have had a friendly welcome, albeit that during that twelvemonth not one had probably given a thought to me. The Parisian character is essen-

---

[1] How absolutely correct Ferrari's views were in this respect is proved by an extract from a letter of M. Georges Le Sourd, the French Chargé d'Affaires in the absence of Count Benedetti, just before the outbreak of the War. "13th July. The news that the candidature was withdrawn, spread here at ten o'clock last night. Bismarck arrived from Varzin at six; he intends to start for Ems this morning. He has communicated the withdrawal to the Italian Minister; he will return to Varzin to-morrow. There is an end of the incident then, but security is by no means restored, and the game has probably only been deferred. One feels almost disposed to regret a solution which adjourns a war in which we should have now engaged under excellent conditions, *always provided that we are ready.*" The Italics are not mine.

tially constituted in this way. " Out of sight, out of mind." But I felt uncertain of my reception in the present state of affairs, so I made up my mind to have luncheon by myself, and to wander about the streets in the afternoon. Half an hour later, I felt glad at my decision. My uncles and I had frequently dined at the Faisan Doré in the Rue des Martyrs on our way to the Rue de la Tour d'Auvergne, where there was a curious little playhouse managed by M. Charles Boudeville, of whom I have spoken in a former book. As I grew up, I lunched there now and again when the state of my purse would run to it, and when the fare of the Brasserie des Martyrs next door, or Dinochaux's hard by in the Rue Bréda was not to my taste. Consequently, I was not altogether a stranger there. I might have been for all the notice I got on my entering the establishment, from the principal down to the cashier and the waiters, *all of whom* had seen me but a twelve-month before. On the 13th or 14th July, I should probably have had a sign of recognition and a smile from every one ; on the 16th I had become an alien and an enemy to France, perhaps a spy. I have never set foot in the Faisan Doré since, though for five years I had to pass its doors twice a day to go and eat elsewhere.

I ate my meal in silence, notwithstanding the familiar faces of several of the customers, for the *clientèle* of the Maison Doré was chiefly made up of *habitués*. I went out, and at the corner of the Faubourg Montmartre ran against my friend Korner.[1] "I am glad I have met you before I go," he said, holding out his hand; "let us have the stirrup cup, if it be only the stirrup cup of coffee," he laughed, no doubt in allusion to my frugal habits in the way of liquor.

"But I thought that in virtue of certain laws you were exempt from military service," I remarked when we were seated.

"So I am," he answered.

"Then you are going to join as a volunteer?"

He looked amazed. "I am not going as a volunteer at all. I was born in Paris, that's true, but I am too German to fight on the side of the French, and too conscientious to fight against them. So I am going to Brussels." Then he stopped, but in another moment he went on. "Practically, this is the doing of the French themselves, who maintain that men of German blood, even if born in France, can never become Frenchmen. They are right; nevertheless, I should have stayed here to await events if the manager of the bank had not dismissed me yesterday morning without rhyme or reason apparently. 'You had better be gone, monsieur,' he said. 'I cannot have you here. Your

---

[1] See *My Paris Note-book*, ch. iv., p. 115 of the English Edition.

fellow-clerks would make life intolerable to you.' With this he handed me a voucher for a month's salary. I went home somewhat crestfallen, I own. On the doorstep I was met by my concierge. 'Monsieur,' she whispered, 'the proprietor has asked me to tell you to remove your furniture as soon as possible, and yourself with it. He will make you a present of the quarter's rent that has begun. It is not his fault, perhaps. This morning, after you were gone, the tenants came down in a body, and swore that, if you were not out of the house in forty-eight hours, they would be, and the proprietor might fish for his rent.' 'But, madame,' I remonstrated, 'I was born and bred in this house; my mother, father, and grandfather died here. Where am I to go?' 'Ah, ça,' she replied, shrugging her shoulders as only a Frenchwoman can, "ça ne me regarde pas.' And she went on with her sweeping; which indifference did not prevent her from accepting fifty francs this morning under the following circumstances. As you know, my grandfather died in January, and I felt very lonely in this large flat by myself. I thought of giving it up, and, in fact, gave notice to that effect at the end of the March quarter. About six weeks ago I became engaged, and the flat not being let, I decided to keep it on. You know that I am not altogether dependent on my salary at the bank. If all had gone well, I should have been married by the end of the month. I went straight to my intended's parents to tell them what had happened ; before I could open my lips, my fiancée's father informed me that my engagement was broken off. There was a lot of high falutin' about the enemies to his country. I did not take the trouble to answer him, and turned on my heel. But there I was with a houseful of furniture on my hands, and nowhere to put it, for I knew that if I did not shift it within forty-eight hours it would be flung into the street, and I knew, equally, that it would be of no use to appeal to the law at this moment. Three people to whom I successively applied to move and store it refused. They virtually gave me the same answer. They were not going to help a German to get his chattels away, and as for storing it, they would not be defiled by the furniture's contact. I went to a fourth to try and sell it. The answer was the same. The concierge has sold it for me ; she said it was left for rent. At a rough guess it is worth about 4,000 frs., for it was all very good and solid. I got 900 frs. for it, out of which I gave the concierge 50 frs."

In the evening I told Ferrari the story. "That's just it," he laughed. "Napoleon, with his ridiculous theory of nationalities, pretends that the mere fact of annexing them would convert those Germans on the left bank of the Rhine into Frenchmen when two centuries of French rule, and by no means stringent rule has failed to do so in the case of the Alsatians. Look at the Irish in America and the French in Canada, they have remained Irish and French in spite of everything. There is a French colony in Berlin which dates from the revocation of the Edict of Nantes. Well, in spite of their identity of religion, the descendants of those Frenchmen have remained French. The messages of their Consistory are still drawn up in French, their food is French, the houses built by the administration of the colony have French inscriptions—"Fondation de l'Eglise du Refuge." What about Nice and Savoy? The inhabitants of these countries have, roughly speaking, a common origin with the French of these parts. That is why they have amalgamated without great difficulty. But all this is of a piece with Napoleon's dream of turning Austria, the persistent enemy of France, into her friend. Henri IV. and Richelieu, who were as good politicians as the son of Hortense, looked at Austria in that light. But Austria is clever, and hating France, as she does and always did, does not mind making a cat's-paw of her. Marie Thérèse sends Kaunitz to the Pompadour, and the latter inveigles Louis XV. into the Seven Years' War. It is the Pompadour's revenge on the great Frederick, who had called her uncomplimentary names. Francis Joseph sends M. and Mdme. de Metternich to Eugénie, who worries her husband into a war with Prussia which she calls "ma guère, à moi," for Napoleon, in spite of those confounded Rhine provinces, would probably have continued to trust to his sinuous policy to get them. Why the Emperor should persist in regarding Austria as a friend beats my comprehension, and why he should imagine that Austria looks upon France in a friendly light is still more puzzling to me. Marie Louise, the consort of the greatest man that ever lived, shakes the dust of France from off her feet the moment she can; she leaves her son to the tender mercies of her father and old Metternich; on the evening of the day she learns the news of Napoleon the Great's death she goes to the theatre as if nothing had happened. Automarchi, who comes to tell her of the hero's death, is not even received by her. The Duc de Reichstadt is practically sequestrated, and his grandfather sanctions all the questionable proceedings of his mother with regard to him. Now look at the other side. Marie Antoinette is murdered in France, the first Napoleon simply treads Austria under foot, and when he marries one of her daughters still conspires against her (against Austria); Napoleon's nephew despoils Austria in Italy. In the day of Austria's trouble with Prussia, he leaves Austria to face that trouble by herself, although his policy dictates to him a different course; the death of Maximilian, the madness of Maximilian's wife are virtually Louis Napoleon's doings. Notwithstanding all this he is befooled by Francis Joseph and Metternich *fils*, on the strength of a few sheets of paper which are not even signed, for these sheets of paper do exist, although in due time, if it suits her, Austria will deny this.[1] But even if they were signed they would be no good, as Andrassy warned the Emperor as early as three years ago. 'Permit me to observe to your Majesty,' he said at Salzburg, 'that a treaty only counts in proportion to its possibility of execution; and I can guarantee your Majesty that Hungary will never allow Austria to make war upon Prussia.' I can only ascribe Napoleon's blindness to the desperate state of his health; for as far as I can see, unless a miracle save both, he is leading France and himself to headlong destruction.

"That he is very ill there is not the least doubt. In a consultation held a fortnight ago between six of the most eminent medical men of France, it was considered necessary to proceed immediately to an operation. But Nélaton shirked the responsibility, owing to his want of success with Niel last year. And now it is too late."

These are but a few of Ferrari's prognosti-

[1] Ferrari spoke prophetically. Austria did deny the existence of those draft treaties a few years later on, and when the Empress wished to refute the falsehood by producing the documents, they had disappeared from Chislehurst.

cations. Yet, in spite of these, the terribly crushing defeats of Reichshofen, Woerth, Beaumont and Sedan were surprising to me, but when I landed again in Paris on the afternoon of the 3rd September, I was fully prepared for the overthrow of the Empire.

As I have already said, I learnt a good deal during the three weeks that went by between the declaration of the war and the battle of Woerth; I learnt still more after this disastrous engagement, and until the final collapse of the French army on the banks of the Meuse. The whole of this information and observation led to one and only one conclusion in my mind; namely, that the Empire could and probably would have been saved by Napoleon III.'s presence in Paris. *Hence, I distinctly charge those who prevented his return thither with the whole responsibility of the fall of the dynasty.* The motives for keeping the Emperor away from the capital have been set forth elsewhere;[1] I may be obliged to re-enumerate them here. I shall be told that, ill as he was, Napoleon III. could not have lifted a finger to avert the revolution of the 4th September, 1870. My answer is simply this. If Napoleon III. was too ill to direct affairs from the Tuileries, he was certainly too ill to assume the command of the army at the outset of the campaign, and to drag

[1] *An Englishman in Paris*, vol. ii., chs. 9 & 10. London: Chapman and Hall. 1892.

at the heels of the army in no capacity whatever
after Woerth. If a rejoinder be forthcoming at
all, which is extremely doubtful, it will probably
be couched as follows : " Had the Empress been
aware of her husband's critical state of health, she
would not have allowed him to go, least of all
incited him to go." Granted, however, that the
Empress was ignorant of the consultation held on
the 1st July, 1870, between six of the greatest
medical authorities in France — and to dispute
this ignorance would be practically framing an
indictment against her, the seriousness of which
would appal even me[1]—she could not have
remained ignorant of the Emperor's condition
after his departure for the seat of war on the 28th
July, assuming that she was blind to it on that
day. For even the least observant were struck
by his haggard appearance as he walked between
his wife and son along the platform of the private
station in the park of Saint-Cloud to take his seat
in the train. Dr. Germain Sée, the only doctor
who signed the report of the consultation referred
to, stated after 1870 that at his urgent request a
young but exceedingly skilful surgeon accompanied the Emperor, and that this young prac-
titioner was provided with all the appliances to
perform an immediate operation should still
graver symptoms than those which had prompted

---

[1] M. Jules Richard, one of the staunchest Imperialists, and an exceedingly talented writer, has done this.

the consultation render such an operation necessary. The presence of this stranger among them must have given rise to questions on the part of some of the *entourage* of the Emperor. The spy-scare, though affecting the educated less violently than the masses, was doing its work among the former then. Did these questions remain unanswered? If so, Dr. Sée's *locum tenens* would have been arrested there and then, and taken back to Paris under a strong escort.

For the sake of argument we will admit that in the bustle and intense excitement of that moment, his presence was overlooked, or if not overlooked, not commented upon then. Could this have been the case while the Imperial train was rolling towards Metz? And what about the fact that the Emperor had to be lifted bodily out of his saddle, after Saarbruck, viz., on the 2nd August? Are we to believe that Lebœuf and Lebrun, who performed the painful task, also said nothing of this to any one. It would be taxing one's credulity too much. More than twenty-six years have passed since that day, and notwithstanding all the documents that have come to light, it is very difficult to minimise the blame attached to Lebœuf's name in connection with the initial phases of the Franco-German war; yet, it is certain that he did not overrate the importance from a French point of view of the piece of theatrical display, known to the world at large as " the fire-baptism of the

Prince Imperial." It is equally certain that whatever the mistakes committed by Lebœuf at the outset, he was thoroughly alive to the demoralising effects of the presence of a mentally unhinged and physically unfit chief upon an army like the French one. There is proof that between the 2nd and 6th August, he gave unmistakable hints to the Emperor himself of this danger. Whether Napoleon had made up his mind not to return to Paris until after a more signal victory than Saarbruck, or whether the Empress, afraid of such a return, had virtually nipped the idea of it in the bud will, perhaps, never be accurately known; the presumption, though, is in favour of the latter theory. But after Forbach, and especially after Woerth, the Emperor distinctly declined to follow the openly expressed advice of Lebœuf. While acknowledging that his state of health did not allow of his placing himself at the head of his troops, he said that he could not relinquish the command with the humiliation of two defeats fresh upon him.

Curiously enough, this one remark of the Emperor is repeated almost word for word in a telegram from the Empress to him on the 7th August; on which day M. Francheschini Piétri, the Emperor's private secretary, took or appeared to take a personal initiative, and in a confidential despatch informed the Empress of Lebœuf's views as to the expedience of the Emperor's return to the capital. " In the event of another reverse (*inverses*) the Emperor would, at any rate, not have the responsibility of it. This is also the opinion of the true friends of the Emperor"; he wired. To which message the Empress replied, " I have received Piétri's despatch. Have you considered all the consequences of your return to Paris *with the blow of two reverses fresh upon you?*" (The italics are mine.) " As for me," the message went on to say, " I dare not take the responsibility of advising you. But if you make up your mind to the step, it should, at any rate be represented to the country as provisional. The Emperor must come back to Paris to reorganise the Second Army, transferring the chief command of the Army of the Rhine, meanwhile, and only for the time being, to Bazaine."

The likeness between the main sentence of the Emperor's answer to Lebœuf and that of the Empress' telegram seems almost too great to be the result of pure accident or even of the predominance of the self-same thought in two minds. One cannot help suspecting that the one sentence is the echo of the other. And if we admit this, there can be no doubt as to which was the voice and which the echo. The Emperor suggesting either personally or vicariously his return to Paris would not have courted a lukewarm assent to, and least of all a categorical disapproval of, the proposed step by a galling reference to the moral effects of two fresh defeats. We may, therefore, take it that when he made use of these words, he was repeating those of his consort, with the sentiment of which he, perhaps, agreed in the main. This, again, would lead one to conclude that the Emperor's return to Paris was the subject of more than one conversation on that memorable 7th August, viz., the day after the terrible reverses at Woerth and the almost entire annihilation of the six regiments of cuirassiers at Morsbronn and Reichshofen. It is not difficult to surmise what happened between the Emperor and Lebœuf on the morning after MacMahon's dearly bought retreat on Froeschwiller. The marshal's hints of the last four days as to the advisability of the Emperor relinquishing the command and returning to Paris became more pressing, and probably took the shape of a frankly though respectfully expressed request. There is no reason to think that the Emperor's inherently vacillating disposition, which had increased of late years in consequence of his excruciating pains, had suddenly changed into firmness of purpose amidst the anxiety and consternation of the critical events fast succeeding each other; and the presumption is that while agreeing partly or *in toto* with Lebœuf, he felt unable to arrive at a decision. "It is certain my belief increases infinitely the moment I can convince another mind thereof," remarks Novalis (Hardenberg). At this moment the Emperor was casting about for some one to fortify his scarcely self-acknowledged desire to return to the Tuileries. But this "some one" had to be the elect of his heart rather than the elect of his brain, for, as I have endeavoured to show once or twice, Napoleon III. more often allowed himself to be guided in his judgments by those whom he loved than by those whom he esteemed, and of the former there was no one near him but his son and his cousin, the one a mere lad, the other an unquestionably safe adviser in politically critical circumstances where his personal interest was not directly at stake, and therefore a presumably sincere one at this particular juncture. Unfortunately for the Emperor, Prince Napoleon was known to be as bitterly opposed to the interference of the Empress in public affairs as Persigny, who was then in disgrace for having too frankly expressed his views on the subject some time before, in a memoir which caused much heartburning and animosity. The Empress had not been slow to embitter the situation, and she, it must be borne in mind, was at this instant virtually the ruler of France. Besides, albeit that the Emperor loved his cousin and Persigny not less, he certainly loved the Empress more. Those who have not taken sufficient cognisance of this fact throughout the pages of this book will have absolutely read it in vain. During the whole of the reign there were only two men whose influence over the Emperor did not give umbrage to the Empress, and whose, perhaps, equally great though not quite so visible influence over the Empress did not irritate the Emperor. These two men were Mocquard and Fleury. The one was dead, the other too far away to be available for instantaneous counsel.

The first conversation with Lebœuf in the early part of the morning produced no result then, as far as the relinquishing of the Emperor's command and his return to Paris were concerned. But though not productive of a result, it produced a germ which might have developed into a result, if Fleury had been at the Emperor's elbow to take up Lebœuf's argument, to the effect that there were still twenty divisions left intact with which Frossard, in spite of his defeat, might attack the scarcely-formed armies of Steinmetz and the Red Prince and prevent their junction. I say Fleury, because I know of no one else who could have performed the task; and lest my estimate of the man's powers should seem exaggerated, I would refer the reader to the frequent testimonies given by Alexander II. with regard to the confidence and affection with which Fleury inspired every one around him. The Martyr-Tzar did not hesitate to say subsequently that if Fleury's high sense of a soldier's duty had not prompted him to leave St. Petersburg, the sequel to Sedan, in spite of the Tzar's relationship to and veneration for the conqueror might have been different to what it was.

In default of this much-needed presence, the Emperor relapsed immediately after Lebœuf's departure into his by this time chronic state of vacillation, aggravated no doubt by his acute sufferings. There is every reason to believe that M. Francheschini Piétri was as loyal and devoted a servant as any; that he failed to command the Emperor's entire confidence at this particular moment was not his fault, but the fault of his master's peculiar temperament. It boots little to inquire whether he sent the telegram *solely* on his own responsibility or was guided in its despatch by a mere remark from the Emperor or even a mere sign in the generally impenetrable face. In either case, the Empress' answer to it would have been the same. *She did not want the Emperor in Paris* (the italics are mine), because his being there would have prevented the overthrow of M. Emile Ollivier, upon which she had set her heart. Lest this should be disputed by those who are so fond of taking me to task, I beg to quote the unguarded confession of no less a personage than the late Jules Simon. "We succeeded without difficulty in overthrowing the Government, because all the different parties, *even the Court party*, were our auxiliaries."

The why and wherefore of this dislike of Emile Ollivier on the part of the Empress need not be repeated here. If it be argued that in such a supreme crisis a woman imbued with the slightest knowledge of the magnitude of the interests that were at stake would have forgone her private resentment or would, at any rate, have temporarily stifled its promptings, I can only answer that at no time during her husband's reign or afterwards did the Empress grasp the full or even the partial significance of the political part she aspired to play; at no time did she forgo the gratification of a private resentment. If proofs are asked for, I will give them, but in my own way—*i.e.*, forward them to any newspaper in the kingdom that will consent to print them. These very small documents will be forthcoming by the dozen, and be authenticated in every instance by names the bearers of which were and are famed for their loyalty to the fallen dynasty.

Nor will it be difficult to prove by somewhat more ample evidence, which on that account cannot find a place at the end of a book, that the gratification of private resentment was, at that moment, only a secondary motive for the desired overthrow of M. Ollivier. But the Empress and her "party"—the clique had grown into a party, or at all events fancied itself to be such—were thoroughly aware that the Emperor would not lend himself to such proceedings, that, in fact, he had had to a certain extent a foreboding of these machinations and endeavoured to guard against them in the "letters patent" which conferred upon

the Empress the regency she had coveted for so
many years, by withholding from her the power to
summon parliament. She summoned the parliament in spite of this, and the Emperor, notwithstanding his exceedingly great love for her, never forgave her.[1]

This is why the Emperor had to be and was kept out of Paris by shifts, prevarications and direct falsehoods, imposing upon the majority of the nation to a much greater degree than upon him, albeit that he himself did not seriously suspect, if he ever conceived at all, the final result aimed at in this ostracism, namely, his abdication in favour of his son with the Empress as regent for at least the next three years—which step would have been cavalierly proposed to, nay, perhaps brutally forced upon him in the event of one single French victory,[2] in the

---

[1] For the better understanding of all this, I must refer the reader to *An Englishman in Paris*, vol. ii., chs. 9 and 10.

[2] I am writing this practically from memory, the printers are waiting for copy, and my notes on this particular month are inaccessible from where I write. I am, however, absolutely certain that the statement referring to the abdication emanated from M. Rouher, not in the form, perhaps, in which I have set it down, for he was too guarded to have been so thoroughly outspoken, but both in substance and spirit. The reason why I have printed it is that it "tones down" to a certain extent a much graver charge against the Empress' party preferred in *An Englishman in Paris*, although it does not altogether disprove it. I am quite willing to believe that the *coterie* would have been content with abdication, but they would have preferred the stray bullet for which some openly wished to end the difficulty. But I cannot give many footnotes; firstly, for the reason just mentioned; secondly because the requisite number would swell the volume to an inordinate size.

possibility of which the Empress still believed. This belief of the Empress was, however, not founded on more or less encouraging reports or hopeful messages from the seat of war, but on signs, tokens, prognostications, warnings, miraculous apparitions, cock and bull stories told to her by her *entourage*, and similar childish and senseless methods for blinking the truth. Charles X. going to Rambouillet to shoot in the latter days of July, 1830, on the strength of a vision which had told him that everything would come right, was not more blind than she. In fact, both minds belong to the same category. I repeat, I have not my notes at hand; if I had, I could not avail myself of them in every small instance, but I remember perfectly well one of my relatives coming home one day and telling us that the Empress had fainted on the previous night in her husband's arms, because that charlatan Home had predicted from the stars that the Prince Imperial would not sit on the throne of his father. Among the papers found at the Tuileries after the 4th September, there was the rough copy of a telegram the Empress had addressed to the Prince Imperial on the 31st July (three days after his departure) to the effect that the little girl of the Duchesse de Malakoff had found another couple of four-leaved shamrocks which she, the Empress, would send to him. In 1873, after the Emperor's death, when the restoration of the Comte de Chambord was in the wind, the patience of M. Rouher—the then acknowledged leader of the Imperialist party—was often put to a severe test by the tendency of the ex-Empress to give partial or entire credence to the most absurd fabrications of some of her former courtiers. They regretted the loaves and fishes of the Empire much more than the Empire itself, and accused M. Rouher of lukewarmness, dilatoriness, and especially want of courage in not cutting the grass from under the feet of the Duchesse de Berri's son. In one instance they announced to the Empress that they had found a *soi-disant* military chief who had been at work among the Paris and Versailles garrisons, which were ready to besiege the Government in the latter place. In another instance, in order to justify their contemplated desertion of the Imperial cause, should the Monarchical one prove successful, they invented (absolutely invented) an influential member of the Society of Jesus, who offered the Empress the mediation of Pius IX. with the future Henri V. to make the latter adopt the Prince Imperial as his heir.

I am not prepared to say that the Empress was entirely taken in by these so-called projects, but she was unquestionably fascinated by them, and M. Rouher had to stand the brunt of their discussion till he was positively weary.

If such was the credulity of the Empress in

1873, amidst the comparative calm after a three years' old and either apparently final or possibly retrievable defeat, I need not waste the reader's time and mine by a description of her state of mind during the whole of August, 1870, with her *entourage* giving its advice whether asked or not, but all or nearly all insisting that the Emperor's return to Paris as the living, breathing image of France's military reverses must be prevented at all costs. And lest there should perchance arise among the people a feeling of pity for the sovereign and the man to whom, after all, the nation owed eighteen years of unparalleled prosperity, the excruciating condition of this man's health was either carefully concealed from the public at large, or when this was impossible represented as calling for no immediate anxiety. There was, however, one Minister who in spite of his culpable weakness at the outset of the Hohenzollern imbroglio, or perhaps because of his knowledge of this weakness, refused to have the nation hoodwinked in this way. This was M. Emile Ollivier. It would not do, perhaps, to dissociate his political from his personal motives, or to analyse either *au fond;* but by now, one thing is indisputably certain. M. Ollivier perceived plainly that the absence of the Emperor constituted a greater danger to his dynasty than his presence. And I am not far wrong in saying that of all those whom the Emperor had lifted from deserved or undeserved obscurity he was, perhaps, the only one who was moved to sincere and deep compassion at the cruel fate of the sovereign to whom most of the others as late as three months before that date had proffered lip-service in profusion; that he was, perhaps, the only one who refused to avail himself of the convenient and comforting formula that "the sovereign who allows himself to be ousted from his throne *fails in all the oaths of allegiance that have been sworn to him.* This formula, paraphrased from *Rivarol's* "You did not wish to be my king, I refuse to be your subject," was not likely to appeal to M. Ollivier, for misguided in many things though he may have been, he was and is of an essentially loyal and sympathetic nature. The wish to remain in power in order to repair, if possible, the mistakes of the beginning, for which, after all is said and done, he was only partially responsible, inasmuch as neither the army nor the generals who conducted or misconducted its operations, were of his choosing, still less of his making, this wish to retrieve the fortunes of the liberal and constitutional Empire may have had something to do with his determination to have the Emperor back; but there is ample evidence from the man's private character, that the bodily and mental sufferings of the monarch, exiled by those who reigned in his name and in virtue of the powers conferred by him, influenced his Minister's attitude to an equal extent.

To this determination and attitude the Empress and her clique felt in a measure bound to oppose something less arbitrary than a merely obstinate and logically indefensible *non-possumus;* but their combined ingenuity went no further than the adoption of a device which, though it fairly surprised M. Ollivier by its brazenness, was simplicity itself. Almost immediately after the receipt of Piétri's telegram and the Empress' reply to it, M. Maurice Richard, the head of the Arts Department at the Ministry of Public Education, was despatched to Metz. To what end? Ostensibly, to satisfy the Prime Minister's apprehensions, *i.e.*, to inquire into the state of health of the Emperor and to ascertain the degree of confidence with which he inspired the troops, just as if both these points were not by then as clear as the sun at noon on a summer's day. But although there was little capacity among the *entourage* of the Empress, there was a good deal of cunning, and their main object was to show that the Minister's wishes had been complied with, that his fall, which they were preparing, was not due to them but to a want of confidence of the Chamber. In reality, M. Richard was despatched to deny by implication all the rumours that had been circulated. He justified the confidence placed in him, for when at the Cabinet Council held on the early morning of the 9th August, M. Ollivier brought the question of the Emperor's return before his colleagues, and appealed to M. Richard, who had come back late on the previous day, to support his views, the latter remained obstinately and ominously silent, although it was well known that in a conversation with the Empress, an hour or so before the meeting of the Cabinet, he had fully made her aware of her husband's condition.

Enough. The fiat went forth dooming the unhappy and broken-down monarch henceforth to wander aimlessly in the wake of his already discouraged legions—a commander destitute of command, a moral burden to his generals, a sovereign deprived of a sovereign's will, a human creature wracked with physical agony to whom the hardest worked house-surgeon of the most crowded hospital in the lowliest neighbourhood would have spared a couch to rest his weary body.

This fiat Napoleon III. attempted to upset only once, viz., eight days later, on the 17th August, when, towards midnight, Trochu returned to Paris with a proclamation in his pocket appointing him Governor of Paris, and beginning with the words "I precede the Emperor only by a few hours." It is but fair to say that the proposed return lacked the indispensable element of dignity, and that the Empress was justified in her opposition to an Emperor's slinking back to the Tuileries in the dark like a pursued criminal. It would have been well for her own share in the history of the Second Empire had she remembered the necessity for a display of dignity in her exit from the Tuileries on the 4th September. The daughter of Victor Emmanuel did remember it at her departure from the Palais Royal.

It should also be said that the Emperor's proposal was prompted by his generals. He himself was too ill, too crushed to take the initiative in anything; fatalist though he was, he knew that Fate had forsaken him, wearied by his repeated indecision to take the cues given to him. If on the 8th August he had boldly announced his determination to M. Richard to return to Paris be the consequences what they might, of two things one would have assuredly happened, in spite of his illness. If he could keep on his legs at the headquarters of the army, he could have kept on his legs in Paris; but even in a contrary case, his mere presence in the capital would have put an end to the Regency if he had so willed it. And with the end of the Regency, the meeting of the Chambers, which was originally fixed for the 11th, not the 9th, August, could have been avoided, for throughout we must not lose sight of the fact that the most illegal act of the Regency was this summons of the Chambers. By the terms of the Constitution the right to summon the Chamber belonged exclusively to the Emperor. In reality, the Empress, notwithstanding her private dislike of M. Ollivier, would have never resorted to this step but for her irresistible wish to overthrow him after she became aware that on two points he would not give way to her, namely, the return of the Emperor and that of the Prince Imperial. I am not speaking without authority, for it is well known that at the beginning, that is, after the declaration of the war, the Empress was as firmly opposed to the continued sittings of the Chambers as were the Emperor and M. Ollivier, and that she approved of the latter's instigation of their somewhat abrupt prorogation. If, on the other hand, the Emperor, seeing what had happened, had allowed the Chambers to meet, rather than break the promise contained in a communication to the Senate and the Corps Législatif to the effect that the Empress would summon them in case of need—though only on the authority of his signature—he would have once more prorogued them within four and twenty hours of their meeting, namely, after their having voted the troops and money required. This could and would have been done by a simple "order" in the *Journal Officiel;* which order would have prevented all further debates and possible recriminations in the Chamber. The Corps Législatif might have accepted the order

THE SECOND EMPIRE

submissively or not, the whole of its Republican members would have been arrested the next day, and afterwards have found themselves on a warship at Cherbourg closely guarded and without the means of escape. This, by his own subsequent confession, was M. Ollivier's plan, and there is not the least o ubt that the Emperor would have sanctioned it—unless he had a better one instead.

Would the plan have succeeded? In spite of everything that has been said to the contrary, I am inclined to think it would. I am not libelling the memory of Thiers, Favre, Gambetta, Arago and the rest of the Republican ringleaders in denying them an extraordinary amount of physical courage, and I feel pretty certain that the generals then in Paris would have followed the lead of the Emperor, discredited though he was, rather than that of *un tas de pékins*. They would have certainly not refused to act at the call of the Emperor, but they would have refused to act at the sole bidding of Ollivier to repress a revolution, if one had broken out in consequence of the imprisonment of the deputies, just as they would have refused to be instigated by Favre and Gambetta into fomenting one. French military leaders have an invincible objection to take their orders from, or even operate in concert with, civilians, an objection of which Prince Louis Napoleon was thoroughly aware when he sent Fleury to Algeria to enlist his military co-operators for the *Coup d'État,* but Napoleon III., after eighteen years' reign, was no longer a civilian.

I am all the more confirmed in my opinion that not one of the generals would have acted at Ollivier's request, and that the Emperor's presence was therefore necessary, by what I saw and heard on the 4th September, and by what I have gathered since.

During the twenty-six years that have gone by, there has practically not been a week which has not added some important item to my large collection of notes on this subject. And all these, without exception, prove to me, beyond the shadow of a doubt, two things.   1st. That a single resolute general not only could have prevented the invasion of the Palais Bourbon by the mob, but have driven them thence if they had effected an entrance, and have secured the so-called founders of the Third Republic almost without bloodshed. I say almost ; compared with the blood that was shed by the fancy strategy and tactics of Gambetta and his coadjutors it would have been as the Serpentine to the Atlantic.   2nd. That the resolute general's success would not have been of the slightest use unless the Emperor had been at hand to follow it up by an immediate appearance in the streets and among the people.   His doing so might have meant sudden death to him.   I do not think it would ; the *fait accompli* would have produced its effect. I repeat, in the absence of the Emperor the success would have been of no use, for the general would have either had to eat it raw, like "the cat ate the steak" in Heine's adage, or have had to hand it to the Republicans to cook. With this difference, that there was not a single general whose mental and political digestion was equal to the sudden swallowing of such a raw dictatorship. Maria Theresa or Catherine II. would have faced the storm, the former did on one occasion with good results; Catherine I., nay, Elizabeth of Russia, or Marie Antoinette might have faced it; the Duchesse d'Orléans (the grandmother of the present Duke) attempted the thing in vain. But it would, at any rate, have been worth trying. The Empress, who for many years had endeavoured to personate several of these women in turns, left at the first rumblings of the storm, hence there was no one to enact the sequel to its weathering, except MM. Favre and Gambetta, whose policy, it need scarcely be said, was to let the storm spend itself, taking care meanwhile to secure the valuable cargo in the shape of ministries and so forth.

Lest all this should read like so much unfounded assertion on my part, I produce the note of a conversation with an eye-witness of, and actor in the events of the day, whose sincerity is unimpeachable,[1] and who, I believe, subsequently amplified

[1] M. Louis Charles Estancelin, one of the most faithful followers

his statement in print; but of this I am not certain.

Twice, according to my informant, did the troops emerge from the Rue de Burgoyne, twice did they draw up in line of battle at the foot of the Pont de la Concorde, twice were their rifles levelled at the rabble on the bridge, twice were their rifles lowered because the order to "fire" did not come. In each case they returned silently whence they had come. Who had countermanded the defence of the Palais Bourbon? My informant was unable to tell me. He only knew that "a resolute man with a few hundred troops at his back could have made a clean sweep of the rabble even after it had invaded the House itself, and, moreover, have arrested Favre, Gambetta and Co. there and then without the least trouble"; for he tried and succeeded partially, but Favre and the rest were gone. Morny would have done it in time had he been in the presidential seat, but his successor M. Schneider was not Morny. M. Schneider with or against his will also had a share in the overthrow of the Empire by his timidity to enact

of the fortunes of the d'Orléans family, and a member of the Corps Législatif on the 4th September. The conversation alluded to took place on the day of the late Comte de Paris' silver wedding. It was begun at Kingston station, after the religious ceremony at the Kingston-on-Thames Catholic Chapel, and continued in the afternoon during the reception at Sheen House. The note was handy, in consequence of its having appeared in *The Fortnightly Review* in one of my articles; so I took it away with me.

his part, even before the 4th September, at which period he worried the Empress with his apprehensions of what the opposition might do if Ollivier continued in power against their will.

That the Chamber would be invaded in a few minutes, my informant did not doubt for a single instant, and invaded it was almost immediately after he had returned to his seat. Thereupon he went down to the court-yard at the back of the Palais Bourbon and borrowed a hundred and fifty men of the National Guard of their commander. Preceded by four drummers—whose instruments were unfortunately not sufficiently tightened to sound the charge at once, and whose delay in doing this made him miss the ringleaders, he gained an entrance into the House by the mere discharge of his pistol and the co-operation of the quickest of the four drummers. In five minutes the place was clear. But just as he entered by one door, he saw Favre disappear by the opposite one.

The inside of the building being safe, my informant began to think about preserving it from an attack on the outside. Hailing an empty cab, he drove *unmolested* to the headquarters of General Trochu at the Louvre, where he met the general just coming out of his private apartments on his way to the drawing-room where the officers on duty spent their intervals of leisure. Trochu was not even in uniform. M. Estancelin exposed the situation in a few words. "Too late, my dear sir," replied Trochu quietly. "I myself wanted to go to the Chamber, but the crowd was so dense on two of the bridges, that I was compelled to turn back. Besides," he added, when his interlocutor pointed out to him that he had come in a cab, "besides, on my way back, I met a good many of your colleagues, who told me that it was all over. Too late, my dear sir, too late!"

"Practically," remarked M. Estancelin, "Trochu was right. When I passed alongside the gardens of the Tuileries once more, I learnt that the Empress was gone, and on my return to the Chamber I naturally went straight into the House itself, thinking that the deputies, after the departure of Favre and Gambetta, followed by the mob, would have resumed their sitting. With the exception of a few minor officials, there was not a soul there. I was told that the deputies were assembled in the picture gallery of the President's private residence. They might as well have gone home for the good they did. Although they were not aware as yet of the Empress' flight, they had already decided to send a deputation to the Hôtel-de-Ville to put themselves in communication with the provisional Government; which decision was tantamount to an acknowldgement of and adhesion to this Government. The latter wanted neither acknowledgment nor adhesion. Supported by the mob, they had taken possession of the reins of power, and if that quasi-acknowledgment and adhesion had been withheld they could and would have said, 'Then, come and dislodge us.' It was too late to do that; 'Too late, my dear sir,' as Trochu said to me. In order to prove to you that the mob-elected, or rather the self-elected and mob-confirmed Government of the National Defence wanted none of the deputies' acknowledgment or adhesion, I may tell you this. A little while after my return to the Chamber, Thiers came back also, and notwithstanding Buffet's efforts to the contrary, prevailed upon the deputies to retire altogether, and to leave the Government of the Republic—one should mark the distinction—the charge and responsibility of the new situation events had created. Translated into pertinent language, the advice came to this: 'Your active help we do not require for the moment, inasmuch as it would interfere with our personal ambition and the fat posts we have secured for ourselves; and we do not even think you sufficiently powerful to lock you up in the event of your opposition, as Louis Napoleon did on the 2nd December '51.'"

MM. Victorien Sardou, Armand Gouzien, who died lately, and Ferdinand de Lesseps absolutely saved the Tuileries from being pillaged by a signal and spontaneous display of tact, and with even less recourse to armed force than M. Estancelin.

Am I not justified, then, in surmising that the Emperor, had he been in Paris, would have averted the fall of his dynasty by a similar display or by a repetition of the 2nd December, 1851, and that those who prevented his return thither, are responsible for this fall? Am I not justified in thinking that, ill though he was, both his blood and his pride would have rebelled at the thought that those whom he had swept from his path eighteen years ago like so much refuse, should beard him in what was still nominally his own house; that he would have risen to the occasion in spite of his cruel sufferings, and that the Franco-German War would have probably terminated at Sedan? For it is not the least reproach to the Empress and her party that they did not send negotiators to King Wilhelm's headquarters the moment the news of the Emperor's surrender reached them, which was on Friday, the 2nd September, between 6 and 9 p.m.

※   ※   ※   ※   ※   ※

Placing myself for a moment in the reader's position, I perceive one flaw in my argument which, if not removed, would probably damage the whole. The man who had not sufficient firmness of mind and purpose to override his wife's decision on the 7th August, and who on the 17th August allowed her once more to dictate to him, would have proved equally irresolute on the 3rd–4th September face to face with an insurrectionary movement on the part of his enemies, the Republicans. This, I expect, will be the conclusion of three-fourths, perhaps of nine-tenths, of those who have followed me to the end.

I will deal in their natural order with the two first-named dates, which, in my opinion, settled the fate of the Second Empire more irrevocably than the two battles that preceded them or the one that came afterwards.

There is not the least doubt that on the day after Woerth, Napoleon III. showed himself miserably weak in submitting to the Empress' veto. If there were no previous evidence whatever that the son of Hortense belonged to the category of husbands graphically characterised as "henpecked," this one instance of tame submission would be conclusive. But we have yet to learn that the henpecked husband is necessarily a physical coward in the hour of danger; remembering as we do the story of the Herculean liontamer who repaired to the cage of the forest-king to sleep off his night's potations rather than join the nuptial couch, partly occupied by a very small but shrewish wife, who, nevertheless, when she found him next morning branded him as a poltroon. We also remember a Thane of Cawdor who was as wax in the hands of a scheming spouse and who obtained his kingdom by means

more violent than those of Napoleon III., but
who in spite of all this held it bravely to the last,
who not only had the lawlessness but the daring
of the usurper. We should at all times be reluctant to believe Shakespeare at fault in his psycho-
logy, even if Macbeth were only the creature of
his imagination. We know that he was not;
Hollinshed's *Chronicles* are there to prove his
existence ; Wyntown's *Cronykill of Scotland*
proves the battles between Macbeth and Macduff.
But we need not go to fiction, based upon imper-
fectly-recorded history, for our examples. Assuredly, none would deny the courage of Henri IV.,
Peter the Great or Victor Emmanuel. I am
selecting the first three out of a score that recur
to me at once. Well, the Bearnais who wore a
plume of white feathers so that he might be more
easily distinguished in the fray, who in the thick
of it shouted to his captains " Ecartez-vous,
messieurs, je veux paraitre," showed the white
feather on more than one occasion in his domestic
wrangles with Marie de Medici when she aspired
to have a voice in the foreign policy of the
country.

The founder of the Russian Empire as we know
it, a strong man physically, morally, though not
moral in the conventional sense, and mentally, if
ever there was one, whose daring and endurance
have become proverbial, the conquerer of Charles
XII. at Pultawa, and the giant who bearded the

Strelitz and broke their power, allowed the creature
—a kitchen-wench or tavern-strumpet—I leave the
choice to the reader—whom he had raised from
the gutter to the throne to turn and rend him.
By the uplifting of a finger he might have flung
her back into the social sewer whence she sprang,
or he might have quasi-legally made an end of her
just as he did of his son and heir—far less guilty
than she—yet he refrained. Those who would
still doubt Napoleon's resolution had he been in
Paris face to face with the Republicans, and base
their doubt on the want of firmness displayed in
his dealings with his wife, had better ponder
the following. The Empress, in spite of all her
faults, must not for one moment be compared
with the second consort of the Great Peter ; but
this makes the argument all the stronger, for on
the other hand the Strelitz were assuredly more
formidable foes than either Thiers, Favre, Gambetta and the mob that made the latter two
dictators under the occult influence of the first-
named of the three. Nevertheless, the erstwhile
kitchen-wench, illiterate, uncouth and ugly, in
spite of the assertions to the contrary of Court
historians, poets and novelists, got the whip hand
of the man who in ages to come will stand forth
as the "Culturheros" of Russia ; the pigmy—for
Catherine was short and stumpy—defied the giant.
She not only did not wince at his threats, but
argued their futility. One day Peter led her into

a room with a magnificent Venetian mirror in it. "Look," he said, significantly; "this thing is made of vile stuff; it has passed through the fire which has ennobled it as it were, so that it has virtually become an ornament to a palace; but one blow from my hand can reduce it to its original insignificance." And, suiting the action to the word, he shattered the mirror into a hundred fragments. She, however, did not budge, not a muscle of her face moved; she simply said, "Was such destruction worthy of you, and do you think your palace has become more beautiful in consequence?" And he at whose frown an empire trembled kept silent.

After this any picture of the "henpecked hero," with or without a crown, would be stale, flat and unprofitable. If he is crownless the hen pecks at his head, in the other case she pecks at his crown. And as there are few heroes, whether crowned or uncrowned, who have the courage to interrupt curtain lectures by that clever sentence of the Regent, Philippe d'Orléans—"I do not discuss business on a pillow"—the crowned one in virtue of the great hospitality offered him elsewhere indulges in frequent absences from the nuptial chamber, although he nearly always fares worse by going farther. Or else he resists the perfidious love-calls of his mate in the manner of Bonaparte who, when Josephine happened to knock at his door while he was at work, answered without opening, "Il faut ajourner l'amour après la victoire."

Of course, the temperament of the hero himself will to a great extent influence his view of, and action in, such conjugal amenities. Victor Emmanuel, with his first wife's sympathies practically with the power against which his every effort is directed, remains cheerful throughout; with her successor, of whom he is considerably more afraid, his conduct becomes now and again absolutely farcical, but, farcical or not, the hero of Novara—a hero in spite of defeat—submits to be henpecked and dictated to by the daughter of the erstwhile trooper in the Bodyguard, just as the hero of Pultawa refrained in the end from all opposition to the plotting of the kitchen-wench. That Rosina Vercellana's opinions or want of opinions did not materially affect the course of events which culminated in a free and united Italy was simply Victor Emmanuel's good fortune; that Empress Eugénie's so-called opinions, to use the mildest term, contributed to the downfall of her husband's throne was his misfortune, but we feel practically certain that had Napoleon III.'s case been Victor Emmanuel's, the results would have been equally disastrous. They who would contend that all this is so much irresponsible and fanciful deduction on my part, who would maintain that to judge by precedents is a dangerous thing, have assuredly no safer basis for their arguments than I have. One of the most important facts of modern history was the direct outcome of the action of a bigoted and shrewish woman on a man with a bad digestion who suffered in consequence. I am alluding to the Revocation of the Edict of Nantes. Louis XIV. was only forty-seven when he signed that memorable document; he had been married to Mme. de Maintenon only for a twelvemonth and his state of health, though not good, was flourishing compared with that of Napoleon III. who was fifteen years older and who had been married nearly seventeen years to a woman who at any time during that period could and did twist him round her finger. One more remark before I close this apparently useless, but nevertheless necessary, digression. One day while Italy was preparing to cast off Austria's yoke, Victor Emmanuel was presiding at an important Ministerial Council at Turin, which is only about four miles distant from la Mandria which he had built for Rosina Vercellana. Rosina, who was of an exceedingly jealous disposition, did not like him to be away for any length of time and she sent a mounted messenger asking the King to return immediately. Of course he could not leave at a moment's notice, and he sent an answer to this effect. In a little over an hour, the messenger returned with a second note which this time he showed to his Ministers, saying; "Rosina wants to see me. I must go, for she threatens to throw herself out of the window if I don't come. I know her and she would be as good as her word."

Thus far the wholesale submission of Napoleon III. to his wife up to the fall of the Ollivier Cabinet. I do not profess to know all the "undercurrents" of this particular period, but I know a great many and on no other theory than that of his abject moral fear of the Empress is Napoleon's submission and his acquiescence in Ollivier's removal explicable to me. We must, moreover, not lose sight for one moment of his state of health. Under such conditions a man may revolt for a single instant against his wife's tyranny, but not for longer than that.[1] This, Napoleon attempted to do on the morning of the 7th August and failed. His further submission is more intelligible, even if Rouher had

---

[1] A delightful instance of such a short-lasted revolt recurs to my memory as I write. The story may compensate for the somewhat serious manner of the whole of this conclusion, which manner I was advised to adopt much against my inclination. Truly, the story only relates to a publican, but a henpecked potentate differs very little from a henpecked publican. About the middle of the eighteenth century there was a well-known public-house in Russell Street, Covent Garden, the "Ben Jonson's Head," kept by Joe Weatherby. Weatherby was dangerously ill and was being attended by Dr. Barrowby, one of the foremost physicians of those days. A fierce election contest was raging at Westminster between Lord Trentham (afterwards Lord Gower, I believe) and Sir George Vandeput. Barrowby was one of the latter's partisans. Mrs.

not explained it afterwards. I am using his own words as nearly as I can remember them, but I am practically certain that my memory is not at fault. The fact of Rouher's enmity to Ollivier and his (Rouher's) almost unconditional adhesion to the programme, tactics, sparring for wind—call it what we will—of the Empress and her party need not invalidate this one particular statement. To a certain extent this enmity on the one side and blind obstinacy on the other are calculated to add weight to this explanation inasmuch as it came after the fall of the Empire when he, like a good many others, was probably sorry for what he had done.

According to Rouher, then, the Emperor, after the first fruitless attempt to return to Paris—*i.e.* that of the early part of the 7th August—only made the subsequent ones in a half-hearted way, in other words, for form's sake, " pour acquit de conscience," as the French themselves would say.

Weatherby one of the former's and both the *medicus* and the wife had tried to convert the patient; *platonically* as it were, for neither had the hope to see him leave his bed to go to the poll. In fact, Mrs. Weatherby deeply bewailed her husband's condition because it prevented his voting for Lord Trentham. On the occasion of one of Barrowby's visits he found the sick man up and almost dressed. " I am going to the poll, doctor," said Weatherby in explanation. " My wife is away for the morning and I thought I could get as far as Covent Garden Church (St. Paul's?) to vote for Sir George." This was unexpected news for Barrowby and he let Weatherby go. Two hours afterwards he died, scolded by his wife and her friends, adherents to the Court party.

The Emperor fully expected the opposition that was offered, but he was also aware that it wanted but a word from him, uttered decisively, to override this opposition. The powers conferred upon the Empress by him were subject to one condition, namely, that of his taking command of the army, and remained valid only during the time he exercised this command. Nominally this command ceased on the 12th August[1] when it was transferred to Bazaine. Hence from that moment the Regency had no *raison d'être*, it was no longer a legal power, and one word from the Emperor would have sufficed to put an end to it.

Why did not he utter it? Because, still according to Rouher, the Emperor was thoroughly cognisant of the critical situation when no government, whatever its nature, must be meddled with, however slightly, on the penalty of perishing altogether. And he knew that his return to Paris would shake this Government of the Empress to its foundations; he was, moreover, by no means certain that some of the Ministers, acting in concert with the Empress, would consent to act with him who was already designated as the living image of defeat.

[1] In reality it ceased four days before, viz., on the 8th August at the receipt of a letter written by the Empress on the 7th, and a rough copy of which was found at the Tuileries. I remember one sentence of it well. "Come to an understanding with Marshal Bazaine about all future operations." This was tantamount to depriving the Emperor of his command. Somewhat peremptory, is it not? I fancy my theory of the "henpecked" husband does not require much stronger proof.

And thus, weary in mind and body, he resigned himself to drift, praying that death would come, nay, absolutely courting it in several instances. Like those of Peter the Great, with whom I would not altogether compare him, Napoleon's physical sufferings, though excruciating indeed, were as nothing to his mental agony. Like Peter's, Napoleon's thoughts must have become bitter as gall. There is no Shakespeare to portray for us the appalling pessimism of Peter's mind while he was literally "dying by inches"; nevertheless, there was a great German poet who, among many gifts, had the Shakespearean sense of proportion wherewith to gauge the Russian Titan's disgust of the world and his revolt at the lingering torture. Karl Immermann makes him say :—

> Nicht sterben können ! Endige ! Schon klingt Geräusch
> Arbeitenden Verwesens. Bei dem Werke sind
> Geschäftig-laut die Würmer. Meine Zunge quält
> Ein salzig-faulischer Geschmack, als läge d'rauf
> Der Welt Gemeinheit.
>
> Would that I could but die, force the end ;
> Already hearing, as I do, corruption hard at work
> And worms busy at their labours.
> A salt and sickening taste torments my tongue,
> As though the world's baseness were lying there.)

It requires no great effort of the imagination to credit the war-tossed Emperor, wracked with disease, virtually disowned by almost every one, with similar thoughts. The "heavenly liberator" whom he invoked, refused, however, to come at his bidding, and released him only three years and five months afterwards. Both Fate and Death were less merciful to Napoleon III. than to Peter the Great. The latter did not have to drain the bitter cup of humiliation to the dregs, and, to judge from the death-bed scene as reproduced by those around him, Peter did no meet his partial disappointments with the fortitude and dignity displayed by Napoléon amidst the whole collapse of his fortunes. The Emperor's bitterest enemies cannot deny this dignity. The reflections of the half-tutored Russian savage and those of the over-civilised semi-Italian, semi-Frenchman—for he was only a Frenchman on the mother's side—may have been identical, as far as the world's ingratitude and baseness were concerned ; their manifestation was widely different Peter raved and stormed when the end was near, and brought unspeakable, though absolutely just, accusations against her whom he had raised to the throne. Napoleon III. did not utter a word of reproach against any one in the early morn of the 2nd September while preparing for his final exit from the stage on which he had reigned supreme for nearly eighteen years, on which he had enacted almost as marvellous a comedy as that enacted by his uncle, though with far smaller intellectual means, far weaker support and, above all, less loyalty from his caste than the former. No bitter word fell from his lips, and lest the features should tell their own tale he put on *rouge*, and put it on more artistically than he did on the morning of his escape from Ham, for he had learnt the trick meanwhile from Bouffé, the actor.

Why should he not have put on *rouge*? Any illusion he might have fostered during these eighteen years to the effect that his was not a comedy like the four preceding ones, in which his uncle, Louis XVIII., Charles X. and Louis Philippe had respectively played the principal parts, or that, if a comedy, it would hold a permanent place in the dynastic repertory of France, must have been dispelled by then. Had there been a doubt left, it would have vanished three or four hours later when, on leaving the weaver's cottage at Donchery, he gave Madame Fournaise five gold pieces. I believe they may be seen there to this day. Each of the five coins bore a different portrait. There was one of Napoleon I., one of Louis XVIII., one of Charles X., one of Louis Philippe and one of himself. A check-taker at an ordinary theatre seeing so many differently labelled passes would argue from it that the patrons of the establishment at which he officiated were fickle, too fond of novelty and, above all, too prone to worry the management. "*A bon entendeur, salut.*"

THE END.

www.ingramcontent.com/pod-product-compliance
Lightning Source LLC
Chambersburg PA
CBHW022149300426
44115CB00006B/409